PRAISE FOR *Fierce Convictions*

A book everyone should read, a life everyone should know, and one that many should emulate.

—ERIC METAXAS, BEST-SELLING AUTHOR OF
BONHOEFFER AND *SEVEN MEN*

I'm so glad I read this book. I knew nothing about Hannah More before being introduced to her by Karen Swallow Prior's wonderful biography. Hannah More—a marvelous writer and a courageous opponent of the slave trade—is now one of my special saints!

—DR. RICHARD MOUW, FORMER PRESIDENT
OF FULLER THEOLOGICAL SEMINARY

Karen Swallow Prior isn't satisfied with arresting the intellect. She goes after the imagination and the affections as well with truth, beauty, and wisdom. This book will grip you to the point that you will turn the last page asking, "How does this change the way I live from now on?

—RUSSELL D. MOORE, PRESIDENT - SOUTHERN BAPTIST
ETHICS & RELIGIOUS LIBERTY COMMISSION

Hannah More was an educational pioneer and a best-selling evangelical author of "cheap tracts" for England's poor in the tumultuous years of the American and French Revolutions. As educator, writer, reformer, and public Christian she was much lauded, but also much lampooned, during her own lifetime. With careful research, balanced judgments, accessible prose, and unusual insight, Karen Swallow Prior's biography shows clearly why Hannah More made such an important impact in her own age, and also why her life can speak in significant ways to readers today.

—MARK A. NOLL, AUTHOR OF *THE RISE OF
EVANGELICALISM: THE AGE OF EDWARDS, WHITEFIELD,
AND THE WESLEYS* AND FRANCIS A. MCANANEY
PROFESSOR OF HISTORY, UNIVERSITY OF NOTRE DAME

Karen Swallow Prior is an extraordinary thinker, writer, voice in the church today. Simply—I cannot miss anything she writes. This generation is in desperate need of lives like Hannah More's. I can't wait to see how her story changes the current landscape of the church and raises up many with fierce convictions in this generation

—ANN VOSKAMP, BEST-SELLING AUTHOR OF *ONE THOUSAND GIFTS*

Here is that rarity of a book: scholarship of impeccable rigor that's also a compulsive page-turner. Reading Karen Swallow Prior feels like a privilege.

—LEONARD SWEET, BEST-SELLING AUTHOR, PROFESSOR, DREW UNIVERSITY AND GEORGE FOX UNIVERSITY, AND CHIEF CONTRIBUTOR TO *SERMONS.COM*

Hannah More was an extraordinary woman with extraordinary convictions . . . much like Karen Swallow Prior. This book is a feat in and of itself and I'm excited that lives of brave women can be told by the next generation of brave, young women. As an abolitionist, I find strength in knowing there are many that have gone before and many who will come after.

—CHRISTINE CAINE, FOUNDER, THE A21 CAMPAIGN AND BEST-SELLING AUTHOR OF *UNDAUNTED*

Professor Prior's perspective, which combines literary and historical insights, gives a valuable window into the character of Hannah More, who is interesting, not just because she is so sparky but also because More's interests were so many and she is so full of contradictions. It does us local history people good to have the biographical links with More's writings pointed out and explained. I believe Professor Prior has made a valuable addition to the literature about More, and hope the book gets the success it deserves.

—WILLIAM EVANS, TREASURER AND TRUSTEE OF BRISTOL & GLOUCESTERSHIRE ARCHAEOLOGICAL SOCIETY, FORMER SOLICITOR TO THE UNIVERSITY OF THE WEST OF ENGLAND

Whether confronting the evils of slavery, pressing for change in the treatment of animals, urging prison reform, or championing a broader literacy, Hannah More was a clear and steady champion of a moral philanthropy grounded in faith. More deserves to be much better known, and Prior's fine treatment of her life ensures that she will be.

—WAYNE PACELLE, PRESIDENT AND CEO OF THE HUMANE SOCIETY OF THE UNITED STATES

Hannah More, famed as a gifted playwright, was a witty ornament of London parties in the later eighteenth century. Yet she was also a defender of the British constitution, an architect of Victorian family life and a resolute opponent of the slave trade. Karen Swallow Prior has given a rounded portrait of a woman who combined literary ability with Evangelical piety in a most attractive way.

—DAVID BEBBINGTON, PROFESSOR OF HISTORY,
UNIVERSITY OF STIRLING, SCOTLAND

Prior has crafted an absolutely absorbing and rigorously researched biography. The interweaving of Hannah More's own voice via letters and conversation reveals a witty, determined, and socially conscious woman bolstered by her radical faith. The result is a vibrant tale of perseverance under trial and enduring female fortitude in the face of societal challenges.

—NATASHA ALEKSIUK DUQUETTE, ASSOCIATE DEAN,
TYNDALE UNIVERSITY, TORONTO, CANADA, EDITOR
OF JANE AUSTEN AND THE ARTS: ELEGANCE, PROPRIETY,
HARMONY AND SUBLIMER ASPECTS, AND AUTHOR OF VEILED
INTENT: DISSENTING WOMEN'S THEOLOGICAL AESTHETICS

As the "heart and hands" behind Britain's movement to abolish slavery, Hannah More deserves long-overdue recognition as one of the great moral reformers of her time. Karen Swallow Prior's fascinating biography *Fierce Convictions* restores her to just that place, alongside John Newton and William Wilberforce. This compelling book is a must-read for anyone interested in how people of faith can make a real difference in their world.

—THOMAS S. KIDD, PROFESSOR OF HISTORY, BAYLOR UNIVERSITY

Hannah More was not without faults, or failings. These underscore her humanity, as author Karen Swallow Prior so rightly discerns in this finely balanced book. But then, there are also the seasons of life when we see someone like Hannah More come into her own, or sacrifice much to make a better world. For her abolitionist labors alone, she deserves a place alongside her great friend, William Wilberforce. But then, there are so many other fascinating aspects of Hannah More's life. Such the reader will find in the pages of this book. *Fierce Convictions* is narrative biography at its best: restoring a great soul to her rightful place in our living cultural memory.

—KEVIN BELMONTE, BIOGRAPHER, HISTORIAN, AND AUTHOR
OF WILLIAM WILBERFORCE: A HERO FOR HUMANITY

Many believe in the power of faith to effect social, as well as personal, transformation; but few of us have actually seen it in practice. To us, Karen Swallow Prior offers the life and legacy of Hannah More, a woman of piety and grace, intelligence and passion—a woman whose evangelical convictions and literary wit turned her world upside down. As we fight for justice, pursue peace, and work toward a better future, *Fierce Convictions* reminds us that the way forward also includes learning from the past.

—HANNAH ANDERSON, AUTHOR OF *MADE FOR MORE: AN INVITATION TO LIVE IN GOD'S IMAGE*

Karen Swallow Prior introduces us to a woman we should have met long before now. In this inspiring new biography, Prior captures the remarkable life of one of the most influential women of her day. Prior's portrait of Hannah More is an engaging and fascinating read that shows the power of words to change the world.

—JOHN RINEHART, AUTHOR OF *GOSPEL PATRONS*

In the pages of this vibrant biography, Karen Swallow Prior paints a living picture of Hannah More: a modest and imaginative woman with the courage to cultivate biblical femininity and the wisdom to avoid the snares of early feminism. Her story must be retold in every generation. Ours is now covered.

—TONY REINKE, AUTHOR OF *NEWTON ON THE CHRISTIAN LIFE: TO LIVE IS CHRIST*

Karen Swallow Prior's research and ability to capture the narrative of More's life will keep you turning the pages.

—TRILLIA NEWBELL, AUTHOR OF *UNITED: CAPTURED BY GOD'S VISION FOR DIVERSITY* AND *FEAR AND FAITH*

When faced with the overwhelming needs of our world today, I now find myself asking, "What would Hannah More do?" And the answer is simple . . . More would do something. It was that resilient willingness to use her words for good when others were comfortable keeping quiet that allowed her to literally move the world.

—NOEL BREWER YEATTS, AUTHOR OF *AWAKE: DOING A WORLD OF GOOD ONE PERSON AT A TIME* AND VICE PRESIDENT OF WORLD HELP

FIERCE
CONVICTIONS

FIERCE CONVICTIONS

The Extraordinary Life of Hannah More—
Poet, Reformer, Abolitionist

KAREN SWALLOW PRIOR

An Imprint of Thomas Nelson

Published in Nashville, Tennessee, by Nelson Books, an imprint of Thomas Nelson. Nelson Books and Thomas Nelson are registered trademarks of HarperCollins Christian Publishing, Inc.

Published in association with the literary agency of MacGregor Literary, Inc., P.O. Box 1316, Manzanita, Oregon 97130.

Interior designed by James A. Phinney.

Thomas Nelson, Inc., titles may be purchased in bulk for educational, business, fund-raising, or sales promotional use. For information, please e-mail SpecialMarkets@ThomasNelson.com.

978-0-7180-2191-7 (IE)

Library of Congress Cataloging-in-Publication Data

Prior, Karen Swallow.
  Fierce convictions : the extraordinary life of Hannah More : poet, reformer, abolitionist / Karen Swallow Prior.
     pages cm
  Includes bibliographical references.
  ISBN 978-1-4002-0625-4 (hardback)
  1. More, Hannah, 1745-1833. 2. Authors, English--18th century--Biography.
  3. Authors, English--19th century--Biography. 4. Educators--Great Britain--Biography. I. Title.
  PR3605.M6Z83 2014
  828'.609--dc23
  [B]

                                2014010985

                    Printed in the United States of America

                    14 15 16 17 18 RRD 6 5 4 3 2 1

In memory of
Peter H. Hare, PhD,
who first imagined this book,
and Belle,
who was my constant companion until she was no more

Contents

Contents

FOREWORD

THAT MY FRIEND KAREN SWALLOW PRIOR HATH WRITTEN THIS biography of Hannah More maketh me to wish to sing a paean of praise. (Are there any other kinds of paeans?) In lieu of that, I am writing this foreword.

Until 2006, I had never heard of Hannah More. It was only in that happy year, in the course of writing my book about William Wilberforce (*Amazing Grace: William Wilberforce and the Heroic Campaign to End Slavery*) that I stumbled across her. But it was hardly the kind of stumbling that suggests a person stubbing his toe on a half-buried log in the woods and much more the kind of stumbling that suggests coming across a gurgling Bernini fountain in the midst of a desert. It was not merely surprising; it was staggering: a revelation. *How did this get here, and am I the only person who knows it's here, and what shall I do about it?*

It was at first simply difficult to believe that this charming and witty and superlatively talented woman really had existed. What was probably the most troubling part of it all was that not only was

I ignorant of her existence, but everyone I knew was ignorant of her existence. It was as though she had noiselessly tip-toed out of the pages of history and been removed to page-less oblivion. So when I came to discover her and fathom who she was and the role she played in the history of Abolition and the so-called Reformation of Manners, I became positively disturbed at the outrageousness of the ellipsis. To remedy it in the tiniest way, I crammed all I could about her into my Wilberforce book in a few breathless pages—without putting in so much that it would betray that my affection for her had temporarily eclipsed that of my affection for Wilberforce himself (my affection for them is now equal, but different), and I almost violently hoped that someone might write a full popular biography of her as soon as possible, prating of it to anyone who would listen.

So when in visiting Liberty University some years ago to talk about my *Amazing Grace* book, I found myself in conversation with the person who had invited me—and in that conversation learned that she had written her dissertation on More and had hoped to one day write a biography of More, I was beside myself. Not literally, but close enough. I prated afresh and later learned that my wild-eyedly enthusiastic response to her declaration had not merely startled her, but had also somehow prompted her to revisit the idea and then to write the book proposal, I had involuntarily shouted that she must write as soon as possible because I knew of an editor and so on and so on. That I might in the smallest way have helped midwife the birth of this volume made me wish to trill the *nunc dimittis* and skip away into the next world. But then I wouldn't have been able to read the book. It is a book everyone should read; it is a life everyone should know, and one that many should emulate.

One part of the tremendous importance of Karen Swallow

Prior's resurrecting the great life of Hannah More into the popular consciousness is as a corrective to the idea that the only way to effect change in the world is via political action. Many have put all of their eggs in legislative baskets and the current awful state of things makes plain the mistake of that thinking. Although I tried to make it abundantly clear in my own book that Wilberforce and his co-laborers in Abolition—and in the many other reforms of that period—knew that cultural pressure and influence was as important as political pressure and influence, many who read my book nonetheless came away with the idea that what our broken culture needed was another Wilberforce. It is true that we can always use another Wilberforce (or three), but what we need far more is another Hannah More—and if we could get more than one More, all the better. More's role as a cultural figure and as a woman of letters is precisely what we need as a model for those interested in bringing about social and cultural change. It was in her relationships with members of London's cultural elites—actors such as David Garrick, and writers such as Dr. Johnson and Horace Walpole, and painters such as Joshua Reynolds, and ecclesiastical dignitaries such as Beilby Porteus, and society matrons such as Mrs. Elizabeth Montagu—that she made her value known. She swam in their circles and spoke their language and was able to do in high culture what Wilberforce could do in politics.

Just as More and the early advocates of Abolition knew that without a man in Parliament to champion their cause they were doomed to failure, so that man in Parliament knew that without Hannah More, he and their cause were doomed to failure. We should know it too, because it is true, and because we are failing. If our generation could deliver one or more More's, we might see our own Reformation of Manners and much else besides. So if you want to know how you might change the world to God's glory, read this book and learn the ways of the singular life within its pages. Then go and do likewise. *Selah.*

Eric Metaxas
Montauk, New York
June 2014

PREFACE

Buoyed by empty streets, the shouts of Bristol's town crier echoed into the city churches and down the aisles, startling the worshippers assembled as usual one midsummer Sunday morning. The crier announced a reward of one guinea to anyone who would bring forward a runaway African girl who'd fled into hiding. The girl's master had threatened, for some unknown reason, to ship her to a slave-trading island to be sold, and she'd disappeared. Although slavery had been illegal within the borders of England and Wales since 1772, a "domestic servant" from Africa, such as this girl, was common even if possessed of ambiguous legal status. The reward offered for the girl's return, one guinea, was the British coin minted by Bristol's Royal African Company as currency for trade in western Africa. In its original language, *guinea* meant "black person."[1] The morning's worship was being interrupted by the offer of a guinea for a Guinea. Twenty shillings for a few stone of flesh.

Sometime after the solemnity of the city's worship had been

broken by the town crier, the girl was found, and the "trembling wretch was dragged out from a hole in the top of a house, where she had hid herself, and forced on board ship." The account is recorded by Hannah More, who was living in the countryside outside Bristol at the time. "Alas!" More wrote in a letter to a friend, "I did not know it till too late, or I would have run the risk of buying her, and made you and the rest of my humane, I had almost said *human*, friends, help me out, if the cost had been considerable."[2]

When she wrote this letter in 1790, More had been actively immersed in the fight against the slave trade for a long time. In contrast, the friend she addressed in her letter—whom, we see, she indirectly chided for being not quite "human"—did not support abolition, nor did most of More's fellow countrymen and country-women. But with this letter, along with many other words from her pen, More painted a picture she hoped might move her friend's imagination. Perhaps then his heart, mind, and actions would follow.

She wrote again to the same friend, Horace Walpole, when she learned what happened to the runaway girl. After being placed on the ship, the "poor creature" escaped some twenty miles up the river and walked barefoot all the way back to Bristol. Then in "defiance of all human flesh merchants," More reported, a group of Quakers took the girl in and took out a warrant to keep her in protective custody.[3] Her fate after this attempted rescue is not known.

We do know, however, what More accomplished. Expanding the moral imagination through her words was her life's work. Those words fill volumes with plays, poems, essays, and stories. The traces of her pen offer glimpses into the revolutionary questions of her age. The force of her convictions leaves traces in our own.

Chapter 1

A Bright Imagination[1]

"Come! Let us ride to London to see bishops and booksellers!" The invitation comes from a small girl standing atop a wooden chair. Her bright eyes sparkle. The chair she commands is one in a small train of chairs, arranged front to back, inside a school-house nestled among rolling hills in the English countryside near Bristol. It is a late afternoon around the year 1750; the students and their schoolmaster, the girl's father, have left for the day, leaving the child and her four sisters free to transform the room of the charity school into their own private playground.[2] The chairs have become a carriage, and the girl, Hannah More, is about to embark on an imaginary ride from this little village all the way to the bustling metropolis of London to see the men whose words she knows, even at this young age, have the power to shape the world: the bishops and the booksellers.

Little did the plucky child know that someday her words would help shape the world. But great adventures must begin some-where, and here is as likely a starting point as any: this room, this schoolhouse, this lively imagination that even in its earliest years loved wisdom and words.

According to More's first biographer, William Roberts, whose *Memoirs of the Life and Correspondence of Mrs. Hannah More* was published the year following More's death, she was known from a very early age for her remarkable memory, quick wit, sharp tongue, and "thirst after knowledge."[3] But in the middle of the eighteenth century, women's education—when it was attained—was generally limited to the alluring and useful arts: dancing, painting, and speaking French to lure prospective husbands; embroidering, cooking, and sewing to employ once a husband was caught. The idea of teaching young ladies the "masculine" subjects such as mathematics and classical languages was seldom entertained—and frowned upon when it was.

Hannah's mother, on the other hand, recognized her daughter's intellectual promise and longed to see it fulfilled. So when Hannah was just three or four, Mary More set about teaching her daughter to read, only to discover that Hannah, who had been listening in on the reading lessons her mother had been giving her older sisters, had already begun to read on her own. Family lore offers other early evidence of Hannah's intelligence. Before her fourth birthday, Hannah impressed the parish minister by repeating her catechism at church and received sixpence as a reward.[4] The minister likely would have been less taken with Hannah's pastime of delivering sermons to her family from a play pulpit.[5] Quakers of the eighteenth century might have allowed women to preach, but good Anglicans did not. And a good Anglican Hannah remained for her entire life. One of Hannah's early biographers, writing in 1838, explained that along with restrictions on girls' education, "spiritual acquirements were regarded too exclusively the heritage of man to be invaded by the feebler sex. A practical

Mohammedanism prevailed; women were educated as destitute of minds and souls."[6]

Unlike Hannah's mother, Jacob More, Hannah's father and the schoolmaster, espoused the prevailing attitude toward female education. He felt alarm at how quickly Hannah picked up the rudimentary lessons in Latin and Greco-Roman history that the teacher in him couldn't resist imparting even though they were improper subjects for girls. Hannah also showed an affinity for mathematics, another unfeminine subject. Her father quickly abandoned these lessons, although the Latin was allowed to continue. Not surprisingly, Hannah wrestled with the internal tension reflected in her father's conflicted attitude toward female education and ambition for the rest of her life.

French was a more socially acceptable language for cultured young ladies to learn, and Hannah's first French lessons were brought from her eldest sister, who attended a French school in Bristol during the week and returned home each weekend. England warred with France throughout the eighteenth century, and many French prisoners of war were held in various locales throughout England. Even though the prison in Fishponds for French prisoners wasn't built until Hannah was much older, it was common in the mid-eighteenth century when she was a girl for French prisoners of war to be paroled locally, providing opportunities for her to speak the language.[7] Hannah became easily conversant in the language of her country's longtime enemy. The family's eventual plan was for the girls—Mary, Sarah (Sally), Elizabeth (Betty), Hannah, and Martha (Patty)—to open a school of their own. Teaching was the only profession acceptable for women of neither the laboring nor the aristocratic class, and this was the end toward which Jacob More educated his daughters. Despite his traditional views about female education, he displayed a liberality at odds with the age and more in tune with his daughters' abilities, particularly those of Hannah. He had lost a son, his namesake, born after Hannah and dead before the boy's second birthday.[8] In the qualities she possessed and the treatment she received, Hannah occupied, in some ways, the place that would have belonged to that lost son.

All the More sisters were known for having strong, ambitious, and distinctive personalities, but the records of their lives and their correspondence confirm that the whole family doted on Hannah to a remarkable degree. Certainly, some of this treatment had to do with the fragile health that haunted Hannah her entire life. As in most debates over nature versus nurture, one cannot tell whether Hannah's nature of being "high-strung, easily stimulated, affectionate, and oversensitive to criticism" was the cause or effect of this attention.[9] But even among a large family of keenly intelligent members, Hannah's intellect garnered notice within the family and without.

From early on, Hannah's love of learning and words seemed insatiable. Her childhood nurse had also cared for the son of John Dryden, England's poet laureate in the previous century. Hannah was known for begging the woman again and again for stories of the famous poet, playwright, and critic. She composed her first complete poem when she was only four.[10] Following are two surviving lines of the poem—a satire on Bristol, where the road running alongside the More home led:

> *This road leads to a great city,*
> *Which is more populous than witty.*[11]

Here Hannah's love of language, her quick wit, and her keen observation of humanity are on full and early display. A writer had been born. Hannah's request on every gift-giving occasion never deviated: paper, which was a commodity far more precious then than today. She filled every scrap she could find with poems and essays, many pointing toward a moral lesson of some kind.[12] As with her affinity for words and knowledge, this moral bent formed as much of Hannah's makeup as did her delicate health, flowing hair, impish smile, and sparkling eyes.

Like the majority of his countrymen, Jacob More was a member of the established Church of England and aligned with the more Catholic-leaning, high-church tradition. According to family lore, however, he had some Presbyterian and even Puritan ancestors. Two great-uncles are said to have served as captains in Oliver Cromwell's Puritan army during the English Civil Wars. This background of diverse, yet passionate, denominational affiliations yielded a distinctive religious tolerance in Jacob More, one that his daughter made her own. Jacob's mother regaled the family with accounts from the war between the Established Church and the renegade Puritans, and how her father had guarded with brandished sword clandestine worship services held in their home. The elder Mrs. More chastised the younger generations for undervaluing the gospel message she and her elders had risked so much to follow.[13] Young Hannah took these admonitions—and bold examples—to heart. Eventually, she would move from mere piety to an authentic faith, the kind her age would come to call the "religion of the heart."

This religion of the heart grew throughout England as a result of a spiritual revival in the late eighteenth century. In 1742, a few years before Hannah's birth, John Wesley, the founder of Methodism, preached a sermon that fueled a new religious fervor within the Church of England. In it Wesley proclaimed that the source of true religion lay not in "right opinions" but in "the understanding." Although someone "may be orthodox in every point" and may defend correct doctrine like a zealot, Wesley preached, one may yet be a "stranger" to "the religion of the heart."[14] The revival spawned by John Wesley and his hymn-writing brother, Charles, along with George Whitefield, helped birth the evangelical movement in which Hannah would participate.

Although there is no record of their ever meeting in person, Wesley's ministry radically shaped Hannah's life. Wesley built the first chapel for his newly formed Methodist Society in Bristol, just a few miles from the Mores' home, in 1739. It took some years for Hannah's natural piety to translate fully, in Wesley's words, from "understanding" to "the heart," but that process began at the family hearth.

The idealized version of the More family handed down by Hannah's first biographies is likely just that—idealized. Much of what is known about More's father and mother comes via oral tradition. The story handed down for two centuries is that Jacob More was born to a Norfolk family of some means and with "expectations of high respectability."[15] It was common for young men of such families to pursue a career in the church, and accordingly, More went to the Norwich grammar school—in those days, grammar schools were so named for offering a curriculum focused primarily on Greek and Latin grammar—where he excelled as a student. However, after he lost his inheritance through a family lawsuit, More had to find work to support himself. In a class-based society in which wealth was tied to land ownership, such a loss was no minor alteration; it was a demotion to the working class, for working one's way back to the class of landed gentry was not possible. Jacob More met a certain Mary Grace, recorded only as being the daughter of a "humble but most respectable and religious farmer"[16] and possessing a "vigorous intellect,"[17] and they married. Of politics, Jacob More was said to be a Tory, and of religion, a high churchman. In

1743, through the influence of Norborne Berkeley—a baron, Tory, and the future Lord Botetourt and royal governor of Virginia—More was appointed master of the Free School at Fishponds. There, in a building that housed both the schoolroom and the More family's quarters, Hannah was born.

There is only one problem with this story: it appears to be untrue.

Private and published accounts contain little about Jacob and Mary More, but sufficient public records exist to tell a different story. Through meticulous tracking of public records, meeting minutes, parish registers, and newspapers, William Evans of the University of the West of England has in recent years traced a more accurate story of Jacob and Mary More than those provided by Hannah's first biographers and retold thereafter in countless subsequent biographies, books, and articles.[18]

Evans found no trace of a Jacob More matching Hannah's recollections of his origins. A Jacob More born in Norwich in 1699 appears to have been Hannah's father. Although no Jacob More born at the time ever attended the grammar school in Norwich, Hannah's father somehow acquired enough education to find employment as a bailiff, draftsman, appraiser, and surveyor before being appointed as schoolmaster of the school in Fishponds. No record of the estate that Jacob More is said to have lost through a family feud can be found. Nor can early biographers' claims that Jacob More was a supervisor of excise in Bristol be substantiated, although he may have held a lesser post in Bristol's customs office.

Furthermore, no trace of a Mary Grace, the maiden name attributed to Hannah More's mother in every biography, exists in public accounts. Instead, on July 2, 1735, in Saint Werburgh's parish in Bristol, Jacob More married a woman named Mary Lynch, aged sixteen. The marriage was by license, faster and more discreet than the more customary public announcement of the banns. Mary Lynch did not come from a family of farmers; rather, the only existing written records of the family indicate they were masons and therefore beneath farmers on the social and economic ladders. This places More's maternal lineage lower in the social hierarchy than had been traditionally portrayed. Accounts of More's mother gave her status as an intellectual woman, but nothing is really known about her education. The tie to the Grace family seems to have come through Mary Lynch's youngest sister, Susannah. This aunt, mentioned affectionately in Hannah's will, married a carpenter named John Grace after the death of her first husband.

Jacob More, rather than Mary Lynch, appears to have descended from farmers. From 1733 to 1735, the year of his marriage, More worked as a farm bailiff for John Symes Berkeley of Stapleton, the father of More's later patron, Lord Botetourt. It's likely that Mary Lynch served in the Berkeley household as a servant girl and that was how the two met. According to the farm's account books, shortly before Jacob More's marriage to Mary, More was given eighteen guineas, his wages in full, suggesting dismissal from service. Because no record is found of More working elsewhere for some years afterward, this departure was almost certainly not by choice. Berkeley most likely disapproved of the marriage of his reasonably educated, respectably paid bailiff to a poor servant girl. The age difference between the thirty-five-year-old More and the sixteen-year-old bride likely deepened his employer's disapproval. With the emergence of this new research, locals today wonder whether a shotgun wedding resulted from Jacob More's taking advantage of a young innocent.[19] At any rate, no historical records of the newly married Mores appear until More was appointed to the Fishponds school in 1743, two years before Hannah entered the world.

The meagerness of Jacob More's salary as the schoolmaster required him to supplement his income with additional work surveying and assessing land. Despite financial limitations, his learning and profession allowed him to provide his daughters with an education beyond the standards of the time for girls, leaving them far richer than wealth alone could have.

As was customary, the school continued to pay him a salary after he retired from teaching. At some point in the later years of More's service, the trustees of the private charity funding the school discovered monies entrusted to him were unaccounted for. The matter was clouded in discrepancies and miscommunications and may have been the result of confusion and misunderstanding on the part of More or the trustees. Nevertheless, the shadow surrounding More's departure from Berkeley's employ so many years ago descended again and did not dissipate, despite efforts by his widow and eldest daughter to defend More to the trustees.[20]

The picture painted by this new and thorough research portrays a mother and father of less fortitude and character than Hannah surely would have wished for, especially later in life when she was surrounded by respectable members of fashionable society and counted members of royalty among her friends. Jacob More appears to have been a man of some questionable scruples scrambling to make his way haltingly through life. If this—or worse—was the case, once grown, his pious and proper daughter likely struggled to reconcile the person she had become with the people from whom she came.

Both Jacob and Mary More were buried at Stoke-Gifford in unmarked graves. Most of the details about them handed down through history came after Hannah's death. Honest human error and inevitable but unrecognized human bias likely played at least a part in the false narrative of More's parents that has been passed down all these years. The sister of William Roberts, More's first biographer, was More's friend and the executrix of her papers, making Roberts as knowledgeable as anyone might have been about More's history. Even so, memories were still the main reservoirs of family histories, making it easy to get much wrong without corroboration from written records. More was never precise about names and dates in her family history as her letters show. She seemed not to have cared much about her ancestors at all, a common sentiment for those from social classes in which genealogy mattered little. In addition, More's memory failed significantly over the course of her last years, making her recollections even less reliable. Furthermore, Roberts acknowledged having edited and altered her correspondence with an eye toward conforming her to his religious conservatism, a problem raised in one of the first published reviews of the work.[21] The hagiography that Roberts produced of More played no small part in bringing her into disfavor among subsequent generations less sympathetic to sanctimonious saints. The second biography, published in 1838 by Henry Thompson, did not differ substantially from the first (Roberts's 1834 biography) in this regard, even though Thompson collected much of More's history from her in person during her later years. By the time of these two works, the narrative had been spun and is only now coming into question. It's an interesting and instructive question too.

The notion that More might have felt an increasing sense of shame at her parents' humble lives as she rose in social status might offer an explanation for any part she played in cultivating the myth around her origins. Either intentionally or subconsciously, More—along with her friends and biographers, in turn—may have softened the edges of her parents' possibly less-than-decorous pasts. Rags-to-riches stories were not seen as quite so romantic then as now.

Indeed, such tales were scarcely imaginable; even in fairy tales the frog was truly a prince. And it is undeniable that More tended, as we shall see, to be obsequious and insecure once she began to rub shoulders with her social betters; certainly, she exhibited all the anxieties of the nouveau riche—a category practically nonexistent in her time and thus, in her defense, a role for which she had no model to follow.

The facts of More's parents are important to modern criticism of her works too. Many critics and biographers, particularly feminist critics, have characterized More as being "her father's daughter."[22] This description can be affirmed in many senses of the phrase. Her scholarly aptitude and didactic nature reflect her father's character. Moreover, several of her earlier dramatic works feature a sometimes conflicted, but always dutiful, father-daughter relationship. Some modern scholars complain of More's compliance as a daughter, too similar to her father and not independent enough as a woman. Such critics claim that More's conservative views were geared toward winning the approval of men, starting with her father—as though that was the only source of conservative views. But More was definitely her father's daughter in one respect: almost nothing certain is known about her mother.

Despite being an affectionate family and despite Hannah's unassailable dutifulness as a daughter, she seemed in her adult years to be fond of her parents, yet emotionally distant from them. If Jacob More had been as personally and emotionally involved in his daughter's early education as the first biographers indicated, it seems likely that there would have been more communication between the two of them about her later successes. She did not return to Bristol from London when her father died in 1783, even though she called him then "the dearest and best of Fathers." During what would prove to be the final weeks of Jacob More's life, his daughter seemed unable to face the fact of his impending death, wrestling with guilt afterward over not going to see him during those last days of his life. Her close friend remarked that Jacob More's death had made Hannah "serious but not sad."[23] In a letter from 1785, More reported that her mother was ill, but when Mary More died in May 1786, Hannah again remained in London. Later, it was her friend Sir James Stonhouse, not either of her parents, whom Hannah described as the "counsellor, physician, and divine; who first awakened me to some sense of serious things."[24]

With the help of this father figure, her awakening to serious things was genuine and all-encompassing, generous enough to provide at the end of More's life a loving view of her father because of the Father. As she wrote in one of her last works, *The Spirit of Prayer*, "Of all compellations by which the Supreme Being is designated in his holy word, there is not one so soothing, so attractive, so interesting, as that of Father; it includes the idea of reconcilement, pardon, acceptance, love." She called this picture of God the "most endearing image the Psalmist could select," one that conveys "the kindest sentiment of God's pity towards them that fear Him . . . the pity of a 'father for his own children.'"[25] One biography considered this late passage a sign of More's affection for her earthly father as well as her heavenly one.[26] It certainly could not have been penned by one who harbored ill will to the man who, with her mother, brought her into the world, no matter how low the conditions of their union may have been.

Her affections for her parents might be seen as arising more from filial duty and respect. If so, then such a relationship and explanation would reflect contemporary attitudes well. The extreme lifelong intimacy of the More sisters is far more remarkable than its absence between her and her parents. Existing records offer no explanation for this distance, although Roberts stated that he did not include intimate family letters in his biography. Yet a full picture of her and her sisters' mutual affection and reliance exists in the letters he did draw upon. The self-made success of the More sisters was likely more their own doing than has been represented by most accounts.

The little girl born of that union, a girl whose imagination took root in a charity school in Fishponds, would emerge as one of the most fascinating women of her time. Real stories, such as the story of More's parents, may be at variance with our wishes and hers. Yet More's life shows that the facts and our wishes can produce great stories when serving things much grander than ourselves, and that the stories we tell ourselves and others matter. This is the power of the moral imagination, the kind that Hannah possessed and used to move the world. By the power of her pen, she would journey to London for real—not only in her childhood imagination—where she would see bishops and booksellers, and more, much, much more.

CHAPTER 2

A SCHOOL OF SISTERS

LIKE MOST OF ENGLAND'S NEWLY INDUSTRIALIZED URBAN CENTERS, Bristol was bustling. The proliferation of religious denominations since the English Reformation played a part in the flourishing British economy as religious independence helped yield economic independence. Disenfranchised Nonconformists of the Church of England had to make their way in the margins of English society without the resources possessed by the landholding, politically empowered class. As such striving became more widespread, social mobility—the movement from one economic class to another, unimaginable just a century ago—became possible.

Another factor contributed to the economic growth in Bristol. The burgeoning Atlantic trade system had swelled the port city's population such that it was now the second largest city in England. Commerce in sugar, tobacco, rum, and cocoa, along with industries producing sugar, chocolate, and tobacco—in addition to another form of trade, as we shall see—had created expansive wealth in the city. The growth of wealth meant it spread, too, as the economy shifted from one based primarily on land, a finite resource, to one based on sea, increasing Bristol's connection to goods, capital, labor, and trade, which resulted in the expansion of the middle class. Increased capital brought investments in local industries such as glass and textile manufacturing, foundries, and shipping ventures. Although tea was replacing coffee as the favored drink of the nation, coffeehouses—the "penny universities"—still served as the place where traders, merchants, and sea captains gathered to read newspapers, smoke tobacco, and debate the topics published in the newspapers and periodicals that circulated there.

In one of those publications, the *Bristol Journal,* an ad appeared several times during March and April 1758: "On Monday after Easter will be opened a School for Young Ladies by Mary More and Sisters, where will be carefully taught French, Reading, Writing, Arithmetic, and Needlework. . . . A Dancing Master will properly attend."[1]

Some men in the coffeehouse likely went home at the end of the workday with an idea brewing. They might never acquire the manners of the aristocracy, but they could see them imparted to their children. All it took was a fine education.

The five More girls were widely known for their piety, intelligence, and high moral character. Twelve years spread between the eldest and the youngest. Mary, the eldest, exhibited the traits typically associated with a firstborn: she was responsible, mannerly, and had a take-charge attitude. Later in the sisters' lives, she would be called "the man of the house." Just twenty years old when the school opened, Mary was headmistress. Two years younger, Betty—who later acted as the "wife" of the family of five sisters—was sweet and warm. Sally, fifteen, was the sassy sister, witty, funny, and talkative. She even wrote at least one novel, which has since been lost. Next came Hannah. Thirteen years old when the school opened, she started out as a pupil before joining her older sisters as a teacher by the time she was sixteen. The youngest, Martha (or Patty), born five years after Hannah, was not only Hannah's baby sister but also her closest companion and partner in many of her endeavors. Patty is said to have acted alternately as Hannah's "slave" and her "tyrant," but she dedicated no less than her life to her.[2] The five women were, and remained for the duration of their lives, a sisterhood.

For centuries, formal education had been solely the privilege of the upper class and then only the male children. The grammar schools that had been established in England as far back as the Middle Ages had served only boys. The most prominent of these institutions were generally boarding schools that served the sons of aristocrats and squires. As education gradually broadened across England, more opportunities were offered to the male members of the rising middle class, and by the seventeenth century, some commercial schools had been established throughout the country. The eighteenth century saw such tremendous growth in these schools that education in Great Britain completely transformed.[3] Schools modernized, expanding their offerings from the ancient classical curriculum and including the modern disciplines such as mathematics, geography, and the natural and physical sciences. Universities, which had existed for centuries solely for educating men for holy orders, were now teaching young men in lay vocations too. Eventually, many of the larger cities also offered grammar school education to boys from the growing population of merchants and tradesmen. Increasing numbers of England's boys were gaining access to education from outside the home.

But what to do with the girls?

A handful of schools for girls had cropped up during the seventeenth century, but by no means was there agreement about how widely or what kind of formal education should be given to girls. Female education was a topic on the tip of every tongue and pen. Opinions abounded. Samuel Johnson remarked that he "well remembered when a woman who could spell a common letter was regarded as all accomplished; but now could vie with the men in everything."[4] Few, if any, believed that girls should be schooled in the same subjects or according to the same methods as boys. The objections to too much or certain kinds of female education had various bases: practical, traditional, social, and pseudoscientific.

Jean-Jacques Rousseau's influential educational treatise, *Emile*, published just a few years after the opening of the More sisters' school, struck a sexist pose: "Men's morals, their passions, their tastes, their pleasures, their very happiness also depend on women. Thus, the whole education of women ought to relate to men. To please men, to be useful to them, to make herself loved and honored by them, to raise them when young, to care for them when grown, to counsel them, to console them, to make their lives agreeable and sweet—these are the duties of women at all times, and they ought to be taught them from childhood."[5] Rousseau's views on female education mirrored the prevailing attitudes of the time. Jacob More had only reluctantly offered Hannah as much schooling as he did, and many women—even learned women—had reservations about a girl becoming too educated. In 1774, the poet Anna Letitia Barbauld expressed concern about a friend's proposal to begin a girls' academy. "Young ladies," she said, "ought only to have a general tincture of knowledge as to make them agreeable companions to a man of sense, and to enable them to find rational entertainment for a solitary hour." Furthermore, even these limited accomplishments should be obtained, Barbauld cautioned, "in a quiet and unobserved manner" for the display of knowledge by a woman is "punished with disgrace."[6] Besides, the *Monthly Review* complained in a 1763 review, "intense thought spoils a lady's features."[7] Even a century later, an American doctor published research claiming women could not be educated in the same manner as men without causing significant harm to their reproductive organs and their nervous systems.[8] The voices against women's education were as varied as they were damning.

Fortunately, for the More sisters and the rest of womanhood, other views about female education were percolating. Protestantism's emphasis on the need for individuals to read the Bible for themselves rather than having scriptures mediated through a priest meant that women as well as men should be provided enough education to be literate. Of course, basic literacy was far from the classical training provided to aristocratic men, or even the more modern education increasingly available to the male children of upwardly mobile merchants and tradesmen. As early as 1694, Mary Astell published *A Serious Proposal to the Ladies for the Advancement of their True and Greatest Interest*, a call for the establishment of a religious community where women could live and learn together. Although Astell was a member of the Established Church, her proposal sounded too much like the monasteries and nunneries of England's pre-Reformation past for English leaders to take seriously, and Jonathan Swift and Richard Steele satirized the notion in their popular literary journal, *The Tatler*.[9] Nevertheless, Astell's proposal helped advance the idea that women's education, rightly done, would enable women to better serve God and their families. Her idea never came to be, but Astell established a charity school for girls in partnership with the Society for the Propagation of Christian Knowledge, the first missions outreach of the Church of England.[10] Progress for women was being made.

There were practical as well as theological reasons for expanding women's education. With the growth of wealth came the commodification of education, making it more accessible to more people than ever before. The first private schools for girls were established in London in the early seventeenth century, and by the mid-eighteenth century, rural areas boasted schools too.[11] Earlier in the eighteenth century, when new trades and related businesses began to flourish, wives often partnered with their husbands in their entrepreneurial efforts.[12] As the income in such households increased, tradesmen with an eye toward upward mobility strove to imitate their social superiors by turning their wives and daughters into leisured ladies. Leisured ladies didn't work; they were educated. A ready market was in place for a school such as that of the More sisters.

However, a genteel education did not a gentlewoman make. Increasing numbers of middle-class girls were being educated in subjects that would never do them any good; no matter how much profit their fathers' businesses made, these girls would never achieve the inherited status of aristocrats. Thus, the impracticality of such an education became increasingly clear. University education would be denied to women in England until the nineteenth century when London University began to enroll women, followed by the establishment of women's colleges at Cambridge and then at Oxford University.[13] Not until the twentieth century, however, did either Oxford or Cambridge allow women to take degrees. Some decried this new trend of the upward mobility of educating daughters beyond their stations. For example, an article published in 1739 in the widely circulated *Gentleman's Magazine* offered "A New Method for Making Women as Useful and as Capable of Maintaining Themselves as the Men Are, and Consequently Preventing Their Becoming Old Maids or Taking Ill Courses."[14]

In her *Strictures on the Modern System of Female Education with a View of the Principles and Conduct Prevalent among Women of*

Rank and Fortune, More expanded on some of the tensions defining the female education debate. Although she published this work
in 1799, well after her years teaching in her sisters' school, it accu-
rately reflected the ongoing state of women's education throughout
the century as well as the development of More's ideas on the issue.
The fashion in female education resulted merely, More stated, in
"swarms of youthful females, issuing from our boarding schools,
as well as emerging from the more private scenes of domestic education, who are introduced into the world, under the broad and
universal title of 'accomplished young ladies,' of all of whom it
cannot very truly and correctly be pronounced, that they illustrate
the definition."[15]

Indeed, the typical education for middle- and upper-class
women offered mere snippets of modern languages, music, drawing and painting, embroidery, and manners; Latin, mathematics,
and natural history were considered unsuitable for girls. More
attributed this "superficial nature" of much of women's education to a "false and low standard of intellectual excellence," and
she blamed not truly learned women, but those she termed "smat-
terers" for discrediting women and advancing the powers against
female education.[16] Frivolous education created shallow women,
she argued. "The impatience, levity, and fickleness of which women
have been somewhat too generally accused, are perhaps in no small
degree aggravated by the littleness and frivolousness of female pursuits."[17] In her 1777 *Essays on Various Subjects,* she observed, "One
would be led to imagine, by the common mode of female education, that life consisted of one universal holiday, and that the only
contest was, who should be best enabled to excel in the sports and
games that were to be celebrated on it."[18] Such "ornamental accomplishments," she wrote, "will but indifferently qualify a woman to
perform the duties of life, though it is highly proper she should

possess them, in order to furnish the amusements of it."[19] Eighty years later, the radical, libertine novelist George Eliot (Mary Ann Evans) would echo More's thoughts in her essay "Silly Novels by Lady Novelists."

The courses of study that tended to this stunting of women's abilities included drawing, acting, speaking foreign languages, and playing music, subjects that women were often encouraged to dabble in merely for the purpose of ornamentation rather than understanding. But for More, the purpose of learning a foreign language was actually to converse in it, and she lamented that a "frenzy of accomplishments" boasted by the female gentility "rages downward" such that the middle orders, too, "have caught the contagion."[20] In her *Essays on Various Subjects*, she pointed out that one reason for the popularity of certain subjects—such as music, dancing, and languages—was that progress in them could be easily measured. In contrast, an education in intellectual, spiritual, and moral formation develops over time; its progress cannot be so definitively marked. There are, More wrote in the *Essays*, "more who can see and hear, than there are who can judge and reflect."[21]

Rather than fluff and frivolity, More recommended that "scrupulous exactness" be required of female students, encouraging them to "maintain the most critical accuracy in facts, in dates, in numbering, in describing, in short, in whatever pertains, either directly or indirectly, closely or remotely, to the great fundamental principle, TRUTH." In so doing, she hoped to help counteract a tendency toward the dramatic, which the natural "liveliness" of youth, she said, makes difficult to restrain.[22] She particularly recommended such exactness in the study and use of words: "It is therefore no worthless part of education, even in a religious view, to study the precise meaning of words, and the appropriate signification of language."[23]

Even in their reading, More charged, too many women were prone to superficiality. In search of a passing knowledge of books and authors, many read anthologies of excerpted works that selected the brightest passages but left out deeper contexts— eighteenth-century versions of *Reader's Digest* were quite popular. More cautioned against a habit she viewed as cultivating a taste only for "delicious morsels," one that spits out "every thing which is plain." Good books, in contrast, require good readers: "In all well-written books, there is much that is good which is not dazzling; and these shallow critics should be taught, that it is for the embellishment of the more tame and uninteresting parts of his work, that the judicious poet commonly reserves those flowers, whose beauty is defaced when they are plucked from the garland into which he had so skillfully woven them."[24]

Among the writers More recommended for female students was the philosopher John Locke. She agreed with the "just remark of Swift" that "after all her boasted acquirements, a woman will, generally speaking, be found to possess less of what is called learning than a common school boy."[25] Both Swift and More believed women's minds were capable of much more than was being demanded. Thus, she advocated an education that would harden soft female minds: "Perhaps there is some analogy between the mental and bodily conformation of women. The instructor therefore should imitate the physician. If the latter prescribe bracing medicines for a body of which delicacy is the disease, the former would do well to prohibit relaxing reading for a mind which is already of too soft a texture, and should strengthen its feeble tone by invigorating reading."[26]

Although she sought to cultivate deeper literacy skills in female readers, More emphasized that in encouraging deeper, more serious reading she was not doing so to turn them into writers—despite being one herself. "Let it be observed," she said, "I am by no means encouraging young ladies to turn authors, I am only reminding them, that Authors before they write should read; I am only putting them in mind, that to be ignorant is not to be original."[27]

The curriculum offered by the More sisters was fashionable enough to attract even the superficially minded—a dancing master was hired, after all—but progressive enough to conform to the principles More outlined. In her system of education, More adhered to the prevailing view that "each sex has some kind of natural bias" and sought to preserve the "distinction of character" between men and women.[28] She sought to advance female education in order to fulfill women as women, not to make them like men. "On the whole," she posed in her 1777 treatise *Essays on Various Subjects, Principally Designed for Young Ladies*, "is it not better to succeed as women, than to fail as men? . . . to be good originals, rather than bad imitators?"[29]

The growth of schools for girls expanded opportunities not only for the pupils but also for the teachers, for whom vocational opportunities outside the home were extremely limited. Teaching brought respectability to a woman of the middle class even though the aristocracy thought it vulgar for a lady to work. Women of the working class who lacked the financial support of a father or husband had few career options that were not considered "indelicate."[30] Although women teachers received substantially less pay for the same work done by their male counterparts, girls' schools provided an acceptable and respectable career for unmarried women.[31] Thus, when the elder More sisters, Mary, Elizabeth, and Sarah—joined in a few years by the youngest two—opened a new school at 6 Trinity Street, College Green, Bristol, it seemed a natural, logical, and prudent course, one likely to succeed.

And it did.

While the school's start-up funds came from subscriptions, loans, or gifts, it wasn't long before the venture turned a profit. Within a few years, the Mores had to relocate to larger accommodations at another Park Street location, and the school eventually became renowned throughout the country. Sixty students at a time were enrolled in the new location, and many others waited for openings.[32] Throughout their administration, the More sisters were lauded for their financial management, high principles, and general benevolence in running the school.[33] It was profitable enough for the sisters to retire in 1789 after thirty years of operation. One of their former pupils, Selina Mills, took over the school, and it operated at least through 1808.[34] In comparison, schools later begun by more famous sisters—the Brontës, for one, and another by the Wollstonecrafts—were unsuccessful.[35] By all accounts, the More sisters' accomplishment owed greatly to their remarkable social skills, respectability, and ability to attract affluent students and patrons.

Among the school's students were many with ties to Bristol's new Theatre Royal. One was the daughter of the theater's manager, the celebrated London actor William Powell, and naturally, making regular outings to the stage performances was part of the school's appeal.[36] Opened in 1766, the Theatre Royal is the oldest continuously operating theater in England, where modern-day actors Daniel Day-Lewis and the late Peter O'Toole began their stage careers. Despite many renovations and changes over the centuries, the building retains the original look and feel of the eighteenth-century original with more than five hundred seats divided among the floor level and the three baroque balconies that circle halfway around a proscenium stage. It is easy upon entering the Theatre Royal today to imagine the More sisters seated there with their young charges.[37]

The connection of the theater with the school led More to write the prologue to a spoken performance of *Hamlet* delivered by Powell in Hotwells, Bristol, during the 1765 season. More's friendship with Powell only deepened after he became manager of the Theatre Royal in Bristol. Powell died just three years after accepting the job as manager, becoming ill after throwing himself into the wet grass following a strenuous tennis game. In an even stranger turn of events, he died in the arms of More, who had come to sit at his bedside so that his wife could have a short reprieve.[38]

A tuition bill for Miss Martha Lintorn from 1776 written by Hannah reveals something about the day-to-day functioning of the school. The bill was for half a year's board along with extra charges for dancing and music lessons. In line with the ever-practical More family, these were clearly extras, not part of the tuition included with the board. Numerous items related to dress—muslin, hairpins, and shoemaker's fees, for example—indicate the breadth of the school's oversight for its pupils' needs. In addition, the bill included charges for a volume of poetry and two tickets to the theater.[39]

More had an engaging and warm teaching style. She emphasized the imagination, frequently incorporating into the lessons various kinds of stories, whether from the Bible, fairy tales, or nursery rhymes, in such a way, one firsthand witness recalled, that one "fancied [More] must have lived among them herself."[40] Some people considered such teaching methods to be irregular, as a controversy over staging some of her plays revealed. She wrote several plays based on biblical stories that were later published as *Sacred Dramas* in 1782. When an attempt was made to put some of these plays on the stage in Hull in 1793, the effort was prevented by religious conservatives, who deemed it profane to enact biblical stories on the secular stage.[41]

More's methods as a teacher accord exactly with the advice she gave later in the *Strictures* for teachers to avoid "mere verbal rituals and dry systems" and to communicate lessons "in a way which shall interest their feelings, by lively images, and by a warm practical application of what they read to their own hearts and circumstances." "Even religion must not be dry and uninviting," she advised: "Do not fancy that a thing is good merely because it is dull." Rather, the effective teacher should "enliven these less engaging parts of your discourse with some incidental imagery which will captivate the fancy; with some affecting story, with which it shall be associated in the memory."[42] Her goal when she taught Bible stories was for her students to see Christ walking on the waters of the river Thames.[43]

Perhaps her personal and intellectual weaknesses helped More develop this engaging teaching style. Despite her natural intelligence and wit, she was neither a disciplined student nor writer. She worked quickly and impatiently, relying on innate ability more than endurance and effort.[44]

But her lively approach to teaching was not to be confused with frivolity. An incident detailed in a letter from a student in the school illustrates that practicality was the foremost priority for More:

A young lady was placed with the Misses More for education. Her eldest sister (who gave the relation herself) was invited to spend some time with them as a visitor. She had attained to considerable excellence in drawing, and as often as her drawings were exhibited, they drew forth much admiration. One person there always was present, who observed a strict silence, much to the mortification of the young artist; and that person was Hannah More. One morning this young lady made her appearance rather late at the breakfast-table. Her apology was this, that she had been occupied in putting a new binding on her petticoat. Mrs. Hannah More,* fixing her brilliant eyes upon her with an expression of entire approbation, said, "Now, my dear, I find you can employ yourself usefully, I will no longer forbear to express my admiration of your drawings."[45]

It is certainly owing to the More sisters' education, talents, and likability that their school succeeded. Even today they are credited with pioneering an unusual spirit of entrepreneurship.[46] Another factor in their success, as we have seen, was Bristol's thriving economy. This in turn was determined by one enterprise above all: the slave trade.

From the Middle Ages through the mid-eighteenth century, sea trade of various kinds generated Bristol's primary income. With the end in 1698 of the Crown (government) monopoly that had belonged to the Royal Africa Company, new opportunities for private industry in slave trading opened up, and merchants in Bristol and other port cities took full advantage of the new free market. By 1730, Great Britain led all other countries in the slave trade. From 1690 to the end of Britain's slave trade in 1807, at least 2.8 million African slaves were carried aboard British ships,[47] 500,000 of them on Bristol's vessels.[48] By 1737, Bristol had become England's busiest slave port. From 1698 to 1807, more than two thousand slave ships set out from Bristol, accounting for one-fifth of Britain's slave trade.[49]

During the eighteenth century, more and more sugar and tobacco from the slave plantations in the Caribbean came to Bristol, increasing employment opportunities in the city's sugar and tobacco industries. Approximately twenty sugarhouses in Bristol transformed the dark brown sugar imported from the plantations

---

* It was customary at the time to use the title "Mrs." for mature women regardless of marital status.

into fine white granules. Cotton produced by slave labor was also imported to the city, where it was spun and woven into usable cloth. Tobacco workers processed the leaf tobacco imported from slave plantations. Local industries in iron and brassware also provided goods sent out on the slave ships and traded for human cargo destined for slave-holding colonies in the West Indies. From there the ships were stocked with sugar, tobacco, cocoa, and rum that was eagerly awaited by British buyers back home.

This thriving industry doubled Bristol's population in the first half of the eighteenth century, from about 25,000 to 50,000, increasing to 68,000 by 1801.[50] By the Victorian era, the wealth of one in six of the city's richest citizens had some connection to the slave trade.[51] The city's booming population and economy made it a regular destination for the cultural elite, and the city hosted some of the age's most renowned speakers, actors, and actresses, as well as members of the nobility. Bristol boasted not only booming businesses but also a thriving intellectual and cultural life, including a new theater and sufficient wealth for many of the city's daughters to receive a fine education from the reputable and able More sisters.

Hannah More's blossoming took root in the soil of slavery.

CHAPTER 3

THE ROAD TO SINGLEDOM

"A WOMAN MUST HAVE MONEY AND A ROOM OF HER OWN IF SHE IS to write," Virginia Woolf famously declared in *A Room of One's Own*.[1] A century and a half after More, how true these words were. In a world of vast inequality between men and women, women lacked the space and support necessary to write. They lacked the essential freedom. As the eighteenth-century legal scholar Sir William Blackstone observed, the "very being or legal existence of the woman is suspended during the marriage, or at least is incorporated or consolidated into that of the husband: under whose wing, protection and *cover*, she performs every thing."[2] More escaped that fate, not according to plan, however, and at great personal and emotional cost. Were it not for a broken engagement with a country gentleman by the name of William Turner—whose name "is preserved from oblivion," said one of More's biographers, "solely because he jilted Hannah More"—we might not remember the name Hannah More either.[3]

William Turner was the cousin of two students at the Mores'

school, and he had a considerable fortune. Several miles from Bristol, his estate, Belmont, boasted horses, carriages, gardens, and a gorgeous panoramic setting. By all accounts, Turner was an exemplary gentleman: he exhibited all the graces of good character and good education. He was noted for his honor, integrity, propriety, and intellect, as well as his good taste in poetry and landscape, areas of intense interest in eighteenth-century British culture— and of interest to a certain young schoolteacher too.

Turner's two young cousins often spent holidays at Belmont, and the two youngest Mores, Hannah and Patty, sometimes accompanied them. Although Hannah was twenty years younger than Turner, she was old enough for the age disparity to be less glaring than it had been in the case of her mother and father when they married. Besides, Hannah was an old soul in many respects, and she and Turner shared numerous common interests and tastes, including gardening and poetry.

During their courtship, Turner provided More with a "room of her own" in which to write in the form of a cottage named after her.[4] He further supported her writing by posting some of More's poems engraved onto wooden plaques placed around the grounds of his estate.[5]

Their courtship was no fleeting whimsy, to be sure. The days More spent at Turner's estate grew into veritable dress rehearsals for a future as the mistress of the fine estate. Indeed, Turner treated More much as a respectful husband would a wife, seeking her taste and judgment as he adorned his grounds. Here she cultivated the gardening skills for which she would gain renown later in life.[6] Gardening was a passion in eighteenth-century Britain, the locus for the exercise, display, and judgment of taste; some would even have said character. The most favored gardens during this latter half of the century struck a balance between the highly cultivated and artificial, neoclassical gardens of France and the wild, untamed look that would characterize the romantic age to come.

More's aesthetic taste bridged those two worlds. She continued the neoclassical impulse she had shown in her early dramas and verses. For example, in an imitation of Hesiod she wrote, "Inscription on a Cenotaph in a Garden." Turner later had the poem inscribed on a monument set on the summit of a wooded path on the estate. Yet Belmont and its owner cultivated a youthful and feminine romanticism in More too. More's romantic flair is seen in a maudlin poem set in Belmont, *The Bleeding Rock*, a verse tale featuring a landmark stone on the estate. Made in part of red sandstone, the rock appeared to bleed on rainy days. With her imagination unleashed by her pen, More turned a merely geological phenomenon into a magical tale of wounded love. The poem's opening lines describe Turner's estate, setting the tale, "Where beauteous Belmont rears her modest brow / To view Sabrina's silver waves below." By the poem's end, she has transformed Failand, the hamlet that neighbored the estate, into "Fairy Land," displaying both a delicate taste in flora and a dreamy tendency that dissipated in later years:

> Around no noxious plant or flow'ret grows,
> But the first daffodil, and earliest rose:
> The snow-drop spreads its whitest bosom here,
> And golden cowslips grace the vernal year:
> Here the pale primrose takes a fairer hue,
> And ev'ry violet boasts a brighter blue.
> Here builds the wood-lark, here the faithful dove
> Laments his lost, or woos his living love.
> Secure from harm is ev'ry hallow'd nest,
> The spot is sacred where true lovers rest.

To guard the Rock from each malignant sprite,
A troop of guardian spirits watch by night;
Aloft in air each takes his little stand,
The neighb'ring hill is hence call'd Fairy Land.[7]

More received more than a poem, a love of gardening, and disappointment in love from Turner. She gained a living and a literary life.

She readily accepted Turner's initial offer of marriage, likely made in 1767, although no exact date is recorded.[8] It appeared to be a divine match. It certainly offered a significant step up economically for a poor schoolmaster's daughter, yet it was also a marriage of equals in mind and spirit. The newly affianced woman proceeded according to form. She withdrew from her sisters' school and invested, at some considerable expense, in the clothing and personal items befitting the wife of a wealthy man.[9]

The period of engagement lasted about six years. A wedding date was set, only to have the groom-to-be back out, not once, not twice, but three times.[10] Even after this third postponement, Turner begged for one more chance, offering to appear at the altar on any date she named. More refused. Her sisters and friends, too, "persevered in keeping up her determination not to renew the engagement."[11]

The reasons for Turner's ambivalence remain unknown. Likely, More's fiercely loyal friends and family kept quiet to minimize additional humiliation from gossiping tongues. Their efforts were so successful that most from the story has been withheld from posterity. But the existing accounts largely agree on the few known details. The most authoritative record was provided by Frances Lintorn, one of Turner's cousins and a lifelong friend of More. After More's death, Lintorn reported that her cousin seemed not to have the "cheerful and composed temper" required for marriage. Lintorn alluded to "other objections" to the marriage, unspecified, "on which it is unimportant to dwell."[12] One wonders whether the euphemistic term *confirmed bachelor* applies in Turner's situation. Rumors circulate to this day among some residents of the county of Somerset that Turner had a homosexual inclination. This would explain his wavering about marriage to a woman with whom he was otherwise so compatible. It may also further explain what More's early biographer Charlotte Yonge described as a case of "an elderly man growing shy."[13] More's later relationship with the flamboyant and eccentric Horace Walpole, widely believed to have had homosexual tendencies, indicates her affinity with such men. The historical record allowed only speculation on the reason for Turner's backing out, although the results were certain.

The ordeal took a dreadful toll on Hannah's health, always prone to setbacks under severe distress. Fresh air was common medicine in those days, so she headed to the seaside resort of Weston-super-Mare, eighteen miles or so southwest of Bristol, to recover from what doctors identified as ague. There she met Dr. James Langhorne, then vicar of Blagdon, but best known for translating *Plutarch's Lives* with his brother. Langhorne was also a poetry reviewer for the well-respected *Monthly Review* and a poet in his own right. He had married twice, losing both wives in childbirth. With a reputation for gallantry and a penchant for expending his charms on witty women, he was a balm for More's wounded spirit.[14]

Both More and Langhorne were in the habit of exercising their leisure hours on horseback upon the sands of Weston-super-Mare. Often they rode together, Hannah settled atop her horse on the pillion seat behind her servant. When they took separate jaunts, they left notes for each other in the crevice of a post set near the shore. One day, however, while riding together, the chivalrous Langhorne decided to make the sand his canvas and scratched a few verses to her there:

> *Along the shore*
> *Walk'd Hannah More;*
> *Waves! let this record last:*
> *Sooner shall ye,*
> *Proud earth and sea,*
> *Than what she writes, be past.*
>
> JOHN LANGHORNE[15]

More, not to be outdone, responded in kind, writing with her riding whip below Langhorne's verses:

> *Some firmer basis, polish'd Langhorne, choose,*
> *To write the dictates of thy charming muse;*
> *Thy strains in solid characters rehearse,*
> *And be thy tablet lasting as thy verse.*
>
> HANNAH MORE[16]

Soon, Langhorne proposed marriage.[17] But whether it was a case of once jilted, twice shy or simply that spinsterhood offered more freedom than domesticity, More rebuffed the overture. Despite turning down Langhorne's marriage offer, More, winsome even in her refusals, maintained a lifelong friendship and correspondence with her erstwhile suitor.

When Hannah returned to Bristol in the fall of 1773, she turned down Turner's entreaties for one more chance at the altar. Finally, Turner offered her an annuity, which she also rejected. At that point, family friend Dr. Stonhouse intervened. He met with Turner, who again offered an annuity as well as a promise to marry Hannah if she would agree to set a date one more time. On More's behalf, Stonhouse accepted the annuity rather than the promise. At Turner's insistence, the annuity was to be sufficient to allow More to pursue a literary vocation as compensation for the time she devoted to him.[18] The amount settled upon was two hundred pounds per annum, which was enough for a living and for more than a room of her own. Her sisters approved the deal, and Hannah, with some pressure, reluctantly accepted. Such settlements were common, and as one of her biographers explained, "The More sisters were neither wholly saintly nor wholly worldly, but practical."[19] Following the conclusion of these arrangements, the less-than-genteel Patty remarked cheekily to the sisters' friend Ann Gwatkin of Hannah's new status, ". . . why this Poet of ours is taken care of and may sit down on her large behind and read, no, devour, as many books as she pleases without molestation."[20]

The reasons More never married have been the subject of much speculation amid little concrete substantiation. A twentieth-century biographer wondered whether Hannah's lifelong state of singlehood might have been owing to her possession of an "extreme reserve, a marked distaste for the caresses of an intimate relationship."[21] Notably, none of the More sisters married, leaving ample room for speculation about family dynamics. Perhaps the closeness of the sisters would not admit an outsider into the tight circle. Certainly, the suspension of a woman's legal status resulting from marriage would not appeal to such strong and talented women. Some women of this era adopted lifelong celibacy as an expression of belief in women's innate moral superiority to men, leveraging their moral authority in order to exert cultural influence at a time when most other avenues of power were closed to them.[22] Perhaps More's experience with Turner discouraged all the sisters from risking such rejection. Or maybe the household they eventually established, each sister with her own familial role, functioned so smoothly that additions would have been extraneous. The sisters even objected strongly and dramatically, but ultimately unsuccessfully, to the marriage of Selina Mills, the protégée to whom they eventually turned over their school, to the abolitionist Zachary Macaulay.[23]

Turner never got over Hannah. It is said that he toasted her with his first glass of wine every day. He consoled himself for his loss of her by asserting that "Providence had overruled his wish to be her husband in order to preserve her for higher things,"[24] and he spoke highly of her for the rest of his life.[25] Twenty years after their courtship ended, when More had made her country home at Cowslip Green—with the room of her own—a gentleman arrived there, drawn, he said, by the beauty of the landscape and the gardens. Welcomed to come in, the gentleman asked whose home it was, only to be informed that it belonged to Hannah More. The gentleman then revealed that he was William Turner. The friendship was rekindled. Turner became an occasional dinner guest at Cowslip Green, and Hannah gave him a copy of every work she published. Upon his death, Turner's bequest included one thousand pounds for the almost–Mrs. Turner, the final seal of his continued love and respect for the woman who would not be his or any man's but would be bestowed to the world.[26]

Chapter 4

The Making of a Female Pen

The work of artists often arises from suffering. More's love of writing stemmed, perhaps, from two sources of suffering: her own battles with numerous illnesses over the course of her life and the suffering around her that she sought to alleviate.[1]

Her love for words offered release. She was so moved when she first read Shakespeare as a girl that she couldn't sleep.[2] During one of many illnesses that kept her bedridden, the doctor came, and she engaged him in such a lively fashion on the topic of literature that both forgot her bodily complaint. The doctor was on his way out before he remembered the purpose of his visit and had to call from halfway down the stairs, "How are you to-day, my poor child?"[3]

Her suffering seemed to be constitutional. More contended all her life against bouts of illness: headaches, colds, numbness, nausea, vertigo, sharp pains, and "rheumatism in the face."[4] Many of her illnesses resemble what today would be identified as migraines; some of her bouts suggest even the possibility of clinical depression. Her bedridden bouts were often triggered by times of stress, such as her broken engagement with Turner and her yearly trips to London. Even as her illnesses increased with age, More's wit, will, and words provided her best medicine. And when she was well, which was most of the time, she demonstrated extraordinary fortitude.

From a young age, More had immersed herself in the world of words. Her teen years were a time of intellectual and social flourishing. Thirteen years old when her sisters' school opened, Hannah joined their effort first as a pupil, studying Spanish, Italian, and French. By age thirteen, she could converse fluently in French.[5] She continued her study of Latin with James Newton of Bristol Baptist Academy, who said that Hannah progressed more in her studies than any of his other pupils.[6] She translated a Spanish poem and attended lectures and the theater. Like most learned men of her day, she read the influential periodical *The Spectator*[7] and developed a writing style that the Victorian literary critic (and father of Virginia Woolf) Leslie Stephen later said exhibited "the old-fashioned flavour of the eighteenth century."[8] What her first biographer described as "her increasing acquaintance with books and men" helped More fulfill the expectations created by her early promise.[9] Indeed, the romantic poet Samuel T. Coleridge later described her as "undisputedly the first literary female I have ever met with."[10]

Over the previous century, writing had begun opening up as a profession for women. It was the only profession (besides the world's oldest) available to women outside the church or home. A century later, Virginia Woolf observed in *A Room of One's Own* of this time that "a change came about which, if I were rewriting history, I should describe more fully and think of greater importance than the Crusades or the Wars of the Roses. . . . The middle-class woman began to write."[11] Several features of the early modern age made this possible.

First, the old patronage system in which members of the court and nobility had financially supported artists and writers was on the decline. But with the invention of the printing press, production of literature became easier. The proliferation of printed reading material created a greater appetite for reading while expanding literacy created more readers. Into that market stepped a new class of entrepreneurial booksellers, eager to make a living by printing the works bought from authors and collecting tidy profits from the sales. The increasing number of texts generated more readers and a need for more authors—even women writers who had not received the classical education typical of the male authors of previous centuries.

But underlying these changes was a development of greater import and influence. Throughout the seventeenth century, Puritanism wielded tremendous sway in English culture. One Puritan belief was an increased emphasis on the authority of individual experience in spiritual formation. This belief would have revolutionary consequences. The emphasis on the individual soul and its importance helped to move men and women toward greater spiritual equality. And such spiritual equality naturally had implications for other spheres; spiritual equality expanded into personal, political, and social equality.

Furthermore, once personal experience—rather than church authority or tradition—became an accepted means of knowing God and one's own spiritual state, personal experience became an increasingly acceptable source of all kinds of knowledge. No longer were elite, classically or church-educated men the only ones who knew anything worth knowing—or the only ones capable of transmitting knowledge. Lesser men—and women too—could be purveyors of knowledge now that knowledge could be derived from experience as well as ancient books. New books, written by various kinds of individuals, could now be seen as legitimate sources of truth.

Of course, these ideas spread beyond and had sources apart from Puritan belief. England's first professional woman writer was a royalist firmly in the faction opposing Puritanism: the libertine playwright and poet, Aphra Behn. Other female writers were often far from puritanical, mainly writing tantalizing tales of amorous intrigue. Such works were widely read but given little serious attention by the learned world and viewed as scandalous by most standards. The proliferation of these works by women writers lowered even further the disdain generally felt for the *female pen*.

The implication of this derogatory term's phallic symbolism was that for a woman to write in such a serious, independent way was unnatural, perverse even, an act that went against her sex, and thus, her very nature. Virginia Woolf described the general view of the times as one in which "no woman of sense and modesty could write books."[12] Professional women writers were often judged as though they were participating in that only other profession available to them: prostitution. Indeed, women writers were sometimes accused of "unchastity" merely by writing.[13] Of course, the fact that some of the earliest successful women writers not only wrote scintillating works but also led lives surrounded by sexual scandal added to accumulating anxieties about women writers.

Women writers often defended their craft, and More was no exception. For example, More's contemporary, the novelist Maria Edgeworth, wrote a witty but pointed defense of women writers in her 1795 *Letters for Literary Ladies*: "Considering that the pen was to women a new instrument, I think they have made at least as good a use of it as learned men did of the needle some centuries ago, when they set themselves to determine how many spirits could stand upon its point, and were ready to tear one another to pieces in the discussion of this sublime question. Let the sexes mutually forgive each other their follies; or what is much better, let them combine their talents for their general advantage."[14]

More described the obstacles feared by women writers in her early verse drama *The Search After Happiness*:

> Tho' should we still the rhyming trade pursue,
> The men will shun us,—and the women, too;
> The men, poor souls! of scholars are afraid,
> We shou'd not, did they govern, learn to read,
> At least, in no abstruser volume look,
> Than the learn'd records—of a Cookery book;
> The ladies, too, their well-meant censure give,
> "What!—does she write? a slattern, as I live—
> "I wish she'd leave her books, and mend her cloaths,
> "I thank my stars I know not verse from prose."[15]

She noted elsewhere that the woman writer "will have to encounter the mortifying circumstances of having her sex always taken into account; and her highest exertions will probably be received with the qualified approbation, that it is really extraordinary for a woman."[16] But More's special savvy was in turning obstacle into opportunity. If esteem were necessary to succeed as a woman writer, she would gain that esteem. At times, perhaps, she valued that esteem too much. Her greatest illnesses occurred following attacks on her work.

More had natural talent for writing, but even natural talent needs support to find success. This was even truer for a woman writer. We might think of social networks as an invention of our age, but long before worldwide digital social connections existed, Hannah developed consummate skills in the art. Her early writing talents were cultivated by a community of patrons, friends, and admirers, many of whom possessed the authority and means with which to promote the fruit of her toils. From the little metropolis of Bristol, More took every advantage offered by a city that attracted the best minds of the age. As a result she gained widespread admiration even as a young woman for her powers of conversation, her demonstrated wisdom and modesty, and her rich imagination.

When James Ferguson, an eighteenth-century Renaissance man—a painter, astronomer, experimental philosopher, and globe maker—arrived in Bristol to deliver a series of lectures, More attended. Ever the networker even at the age of fifteen or sixteen, she managed to arrange an introduction to the famous man. Ferguson was so impressed with the young woman that he brought her under his tutelage, imparting to her some of his scientific expertise—topics out of reach for most students of the day, let alone a mere girl. In return, it was believed that he came to rely on her stylistic assistance in crafting his subsequent compositions.[17]

More's most public debut occurred later in 1763 when the famous Irish actor and orator Thomas Sheridan arrived in Bristol to deliver a series of lectures. The topic was eloquence, something Christians had been conflicted about since the first-century church when Paul wrote that in bringing the gospel, he did not come with "eloquence."[18] A few centuries later, Saint Augustine wrestled with the value of eloquence, associating it with his pagan background and training in Greek rhetoric while simultaneously employing it winsomely in his Christian writings.[19] Such suspicion of beauty and form, whether in art, literature, speech, or human flesh, has shadowed Christian thought throughout the history of the church; sadly so, considering God is the author of all beauty. More's eloquence was crucial to her success in influencing her culture, yet later in life as her religious convictions grew and she became less enamored with literary success, she would become more conflicted about it, much as Augustine had centuries earlier.

But such ambivalence came later. After Sheridan's lecture, she applied the speaker's ideas by writing a poem lauding him. The opening passage gives a sense of the girl's way with words as well as her way with famous men:

> If musick's charms can "soothe the savage breast,"
> And lull the busy cares of grief to rest;
> If magick numbers, if the Muse's art
> Can please the raptur'd sense, and reach the heart,—
> What nobler charms in eloquence are found,
> Where wit with musick, sense unites with sound!
> Oh could my unfledg'd muse the theme define,
> The well-earn'd praise, O Sheridan, were thine![20]

A mutual friend presented the poem to Sheridan, who "eagerly sought" the acquaintance of the writer of the verses, and More thus made one of the first in her circle of lifelong literary friends and supporters.[21]

Another early influence on More's development as a writer was John Peach, a man now relegated to obscurity. Peach was a friend and editor of the philosopher David Hume, who lived in Bristol for a short time in 1734 and who sent his *History of England* to Peach for correction. Peach is described as "a man of extensive reading and correct taste," and he instructed More in the same.[22] Although Hume's philosophy proved to be an anathema to the conservative Christian beliefs that More would come to hold later in life, Hume's friend Peach was a close friend to More and instructed her in literary criticism.[23]

In 1774, Edmund Burke, author of the important philosophical and aesthetic treatise *A Philosophical Enquiry into the Origin of Our Ideas of the Sublime and Beautiful*, came to Bristol while campaigning for Parliament. There he gave a speech just before the election results came in. More had written verses in support of Burke, and when his win was announced, the election party assembled outside the More sisters' school on Park Street where the sisters presented him with a rosette for his hat and a laurel wreath that they had made.[24] The excited townspeople cheered, too, for Hannah as the unofficial poet of the campaign.

Other notable friendships that More developed in Bristol during these formative years included those with Josiah Tucker, dean of Gloucester, and Elizabeth Somerset, fifth duchess of Beaufort and sister of Norborne Berkeley, trustee of the Fishponds charity school where More's father taught. But no relationship was more influential than the one with Mrs. Ann Lovell Gwatkin, the wife of a Bristol merchant whose daughter was a student at the school.[25] Mrs. Gwatkin was an early and significant supporter of the school, and to her Hannah dedicated her first published work, *The Search After Happiness*.

Written in 1763 when she was eighteen, the play was intended for use by the students at the school. It had only female roles and avoided the questionable material typically found in the popular dramas acted out in schools and homes. In a preface written for a later edition to the play, More explained that she wrote the drama out of "an earnest wish to furnish a substitute for the improper custom, which then prevailed, of allowing plays, and those not always of the purest kind, to be acted by young ladies in boarding schools."[26] This popular pastime among young people of acting out plays in private performances was shrouded in moral ambiguity—as famously dramatized a few decades later in Jane Austen's novel *Mansfield Park*. Since the days of the Puritans, acting was considered a form of dissembling; furthermore, acting roles often involved morally questionable behavior. But in writing her drama, More answered the latter objection by writing suitable roles for young girls.

Not surprisingly, given the play's purpose, the work was more didactic than artistic; nevertheless, More's biographer Thompson enthused that "the literary merits of this trifle are astonishing."[27] Astonishing, yes, if archaic and quaint, even by contemporary standards. Like many writers' juvenilia, *The Search After Happiness* strains to be erudite and sage, proudly tossing off literary and poetic knowledge to a garish degree. Yet the work achieved its aim. More wrote a play that was both sophisticated and suitable for the students of her school. Furthermore, she noted with satisfaction in her later preface that "this little poem" had "very frequently been adopted, to supply the place of those more dangerous amusements" for young people.[28]

The theme of the play was captured entirely by its title. Each character in the play lamented her failed attempts to find happiness, one in courtly pleasures and vanities and another in an imagination led astray by the reading of novels. While the play affirmed the traditional female roles of wife and mother, it asserted that girls were capable and worthy of great learning.

The character Cleora seemed closest of all of them to Hannah. Cleora admitted to seeking happiness through fame. She wished for flattery, praise, and admiration. "Impell'd by vanity," she "long'd to burst these female bonds," aspiring to the heights achieved by many of the literary geniuses read and admired by More:

> *To boast each various faculty of mind,*
> *Thy graces, Pope! with Johnson's learning join'd;*
> *Like Swift, with strongly pointed ridicule,*

To brand the villain, and abash the fool;
To judge with taste, with spirit to compose,
Now mount in epic, now descend to prose;
To join like Burke, the Beauteous and Sublime,
Or build, with Milton's art, "the lofty rhyme."[29]

Although written solely for the students at the Mores' school, the play gained some acclaim around Bristol, and More had it published in 1773.[30] By the mid-1780s, it had sold ten thousand copies, and a twelfth edition was printed in 1800.[31] In addition to exhibiting and honing More's earliest literary skills, the play set forth her developing views on female roles and education as well as morality and religion, a view that would mature but change little over her life. Through the errors in thinking and values of the play's type characters, the work demonstrated the tremendous power that wrong approaches to education could hold over one's thinking, a recurring theme in More's work. Furthermore, More's attempt to accommodate prevailing literary tastes to her conservative piety exhibits the pattern set for most of her later literary career.

A good amount of More's literary education consisted of foreign-language study. In 1763, an anonymous English translation of French moral tales was published by Robert Raikes, who would later found the Sunday school movement. This work, *Select Moral Tales, translated from the French by a Lady*, is believed to be the work of Hannah More.[32] As part of her studies of Latin, Spanish, and Italian, More composed a number of translations and imitations. Among these were works by the famous librettist Metastasio, and only one of these did More preserve: a loose translation of the 1750 Italian opera *Attilio Regolo* composed by Metastasio.[33] The work was the heroic tragedy of the Roman general Marcus Atilius Regulus, a victorious general in the First Punic War tortured to death after negotiating a peace treaty and nobly returning to fulfill his parole with his Carthaginian captors. Because of his heroic patriotism, he became a symbol of civic virtue, an ideal of no little consequence in a time when England would soon face a rebellion by its American colonists across the ocean. More's play *The Inflexible Captive* was an adapted and expanded version of the opera. It was one of her first public works, performed in 1774 on the nearby stage of Bath's Theatre Royal (all theaters opened following the Restoration in 1660 operated with a patent issued by the throne and thus had the name "Theatre Royal" attached).

More's skills in writing and networking were making a way for her. Then came a strategic push from a longtime family friend, Sir James Stonhouse. An Oxford-educated clergyman and physician, Stonhouse had been a deist. Deism, a trendy if controversial belief system of the century, espoused belief in God but, in discounting mystery and the supernatural, rejected the core tenets of Christianity. At some point, however, Stonhouse had become an evangelical and would become one of the most important early influences in More's life.[34] Stonhouse lent her some of his Oxford education by guiding her study and readings in theology. It was Stonhouse, More later said, who awakened her religious sense.[35] Close enough was their relationship that More wrote his epitaph in 1792.

Stonhouse launched More's literary career. Not only did he arrange the annuity from William Turner that gave More independence but Stonhouse also sent her manuscript of *The Inflexible Captive* to an influential friend in London, the famous London actor and dramatist David Garrick. With this introduction made, the door to the literary capital of England was opened. The journey to London to see bishops and booksellers imagined by that precocious girl in the charity-school classroom was going to take place.

CHAPTER 5

LONDON AT LAST

THE ROAD BETWEEN LONDON AND BRISTOL WAS WELL TRAVELED and, except for some stretches, in good condition in the 1700s.[1] The best means from one city to the other in those days was the British Flying Machine, a coach that made the one-hundred-twenty-mile, two-day trip three times a week.[2] More would come to know this route in what would become annual visits to England's capital city. She was most excited on this first trip to attend London's Theatre Royal.

Located in Covent Garden along Drury Lane in the center of the bustling city of Westminster, the Theatre Royal was the cultural center of eighteenth-century England. The stage had first opened in 1663 with a charter issued by King Charles II following the end of the Puritan rule, which had closed down the theaters. The first building was destroyed by fire less than ten years later. When the new theater built to take its place opened in 1674, it became England's largest and grandest stage yet. David Garrick had been its manager since 1747.

The most famous and revered actor of the day, Garrick had modernized the ancient art of theater and the craft of acting. While members of the upper class had always been happy to frequent the theater, historically, they had turned up their noses at rubbing shoulders with those in the theater's employ. Not only were actors from the working class but their work had always been tinged with scandal. Garrick, however, with his consummate skill and professionalism, had elevated the status of actors and was one of the first actors deemed respectable enough to break into the circles of high society.[3] When More made her first journey to London in early 1774, the ostensible purpose was to meet with the publisher of her play. But what she really hoped was to meet the legendary Garrick face-to-face.

A week after she arrived, More wrote a letter to her beloved Bristol friend Ann Gwatkin. The letter reported enthusiastically on her theater-going activities. She had attended Richard Sheridan's new play *The Rivals*—a work that remains to this day an important play from the period. She was disappointed, however, in not yet meeting Garrick.

Her next letter to Gwatkin offered rapturous details about her visit to Hampton Court Palace, built by Cardinal Wolsey and taken over by King Henry VIII two centuries earlier. Hannah described to her friend seeing the "astonishingly beautiful" paintings by Italian masters on display, the furnishings, the richly ornamented staircase, the room hung with relics from the battles of Alexander the Great and Julius Caesar, and the fine tapestries. But even more enthralling than Hampton Court was Twickenham, home of the late poet Alexander Pope. "You know, my dear madam," she wrote, "what an enthusiastic ardour I have ever had to see this almost sacred spot." The reality did not live up to her expectations. She confessed that "there is very little merit either in the grotto, house, or gardens, but that they once belonged to one of the greatest poets on earth."[4]

This renowned poet, author of some of the best English poetry of the century, had been Catholic and therefore subject to oppressive laws denying rights to Catholics. For example, Catholics could not vote, hold political office, or own land within the city. Pope had been buried, according to his wishes, next to his mother in St. Mary's Church in Twickenham. Thus, the first line of the famous epitaph on his tombstone reads, "To one who would not be buried in Westminster Abbey." More was drawn to the resting place of the mighty wordsmith. She wrote to Gwatkin, "You will easily believe, madam, that I could not leave Twickenham without paying a visit to the hallowed tomb of my beloved bard. For this purpose I went to the church, and easily found the monument of one who would not be buried in Westminster Abbey. . . . Pope, I suppose, had rather be the first ghost at Twickenham than an inferior one at Westminster Abbey."[5]

She made a startling confession of a bit of mischief too. "I could not be honest for the life of me," she wrote, "from the grotto I stole two bits of stones, from the garden a sprig of laurel, and from one of the bed-chambers a pen."[6]

During this same outing, she stopped by the famous home of David Garrick but did not encounter him there. Still in a playful mood, she deigned to absorb his shadow in another way: "His house is repairing, and is not worth seeing; but the situation of his garden pleases me infinitely. It is on the banks of the Thames; the temple about thirty or forty yards from it. Here is the famous chair, curiously wrought out of a cherry-tree which really grew in the garden of Shakspeare [sic] at Stratford. I sat in it, but caught no ray of inspiration."

After sitting in the legendary chair, she noticed the famous likeness of the man nearby: "[A] most noble statue of this most original man, in an attitude strikingly pensive—his limbs strongly muscular, his countenance expressive of some vast conception, and his whole form seeming the bigger from some immense idea with which you suppose his great imagination pregnant. The statue cost five hundred pounds."[7] What a different world this was compared to the humble Fishponds hamlet of her birth.

More stayed in London about two months, accompanied most likely by two of her sisters, Sally and Patty. Her health through much of this visit was poor, and she returned to Bristol down but not defeated.[8] This journey to London turned out to be a kind of trial run, the first of many there over the ensuing years.

Her next visit brought the success that eluded her on the first trip in meeting Garrick. More and her sisters attended his performance at the Theatre Royal in the tragedy *Zara*. A few nights later, they had the chance to watch Garrick perform in one of his most famous roles, that of the title character in *King Lear*.[9] More wrote an effusive letter to her friend Dr. Stonhouse, extolling the actor's talents and describing her euphoria in witnessing his moving performance.[10] Stonhouse, a friend of Garrick, took the opportunity to forward her letter to Garrick himself, providing quite an introduction.[11] Garrick must have been pleased with the words of praise because an invitation to visit him in his home at the Adelphi quickly followed.

Of course, Garrick had already been aware of More and her work since Stonhouse had previously sent the actor the manuscript of More's play *The Inflexible Captive*, which Garrick had graciously read and commented on.[12] *The Inflexible Captive*'s Bristol performance had been well received. Hannah's sister Sally reported, "All the world of dukes, lords, and barons were there. I sat next to a duke and a lord. All expressed the highest approbation of the whole. Never was a piece represented there known to have received so much applause. A shout continued for some minutes after the curtain dropt."[13] A glowing review appeared in the *Monthly Review*. It included a few lines of verse that proclaimed More's place, along with several other contemporary female authors, as new, British versions of the classical Muses, goddesses of inspiration:

> *To Greece no more the tuneful maids belong,*
> *Nor the high honours of immortal song;*
> *To MORE, BROOKS, LENOX, AIKIN, CARTER due,*
> *To GREVILLE, GRIFFITH, WHATELEY, MONTAGU!*
> *Theirs the strong genius, theirs the voice divine;*
> *And favouring Phoebus owns the British NINE.*[14]

Although they had not yet met, Garrick was well aware of the rising star.

A few nights after Garrick received the letter More had written to Stonhouse, his coach arrived at the More sisters' lodgings nearby. They were on their way to meet the mighty man at his home.

Located in the Westminster section of London, the Adelphi was a fashionable, upscale development of neoclassical, terrace homes built between the river Thames and the Strand, the historical thoroughfare dating to the ancient Roman period. Garrick, a famous celebrity of the day, resided with his wife in a home designed specifically for them. Furnished by Chippendale, the home showcased refined taste inside and out.[15] Other famous residents of the Adelphi over the years include playwright George Bernard Shaw, novelist and poet Thomas Hardy, and Sir J. M. Barrie, author of *Peter Pan*. Many of the most celebrated citizens of London passed through Garrick's door at the Adelphi. More knew how lucky she was to be among them.

The feeling was clearly mutual. More delighted Garrick. He soon introduced her to many of the great talents within his circle.

Even the royal family inquired of Garrick after her.[16] Soon, More was hobnobbing with the painters Sir Joshua Reynolds and his sister Frances; Edmund Burke, the conservative parliamentarian and author of *A Philosophical Enquiry into the Origin of Our Ideas of the Sublime and Beautiful*; the inimitable Samuel Johnson; the Irish playwright, Richard Sheridan; Joseph Barreti, an Italian émigré, literary critic, and (like his friend Johnson) lexicographer; Mrs. Elizabeth Montagu, the learned, philanthropic, and celebrated intellectual; and Edward Gibbon, who was writing his famous work, *The History of the Decline and Fall of the Roman Empire*. Upon reading this work, More would later say of Gibbon that "he is an entertaining and philosophical historian, yet, as Ganganelli said to Count Algarotti, 'I wish these shining wits, in spite of all their philosophy, would manage matters so that one might hope to meet them in heaven; for one is very sorry to be deprived of such agreeable company to all eternity.'" It "requires," she added, "an infinite degree of credulity to be an infidel."[17]

During her six-week stay in London, she gained the friendships of the city's "greatest names in intellect and taste."[18] More's sister reported home that at one gathering where she was introduced to a number of literary people, More "received the most encouraging compliments."[19] In another letter, her sister wrote, "Hannah is certainly a great favourite."[20] Such an enthusiastic reception "far exceeded her modest expectations and more than gratified the thirst she had so early felt for intellectual society."[21]

This rustic but witty ingénue presented an interesting novelty for London's jaded elites. This "young provincial woman seemed to bring a touch of fresh air to the stuffy atmosphere of London life."[22] Never remarked on solely for beauty, she was winsome all the same. Her appearance had "something of the china shepherdess," and her person was "on the small side with just the right amount of plumpness," usually adorned with simple but colorful dress.[23] An "innocent naughtiness lit up her countenance, quiet fun twinkled in her large dark eyes and a slight quirk twisted the corners of her mouth."[24] In Hannah, charm, wit, and modesty met. How could the world help but notice?

Over the course of many winters spent in London, More's circle of friends and acquaintances came to include the musicologist Charles Burney, father of fellow novelist Fanny Burney; the artist and bluestocking Mary Delany; Oxford's Hebrew scholar, Dr. Benjamin Kennicott; the president of Oxford's Magdalen College, Dr. George Horne (who would later become bishop of Norwich); and Dr. Beilby Porteus, bishop, first of Chester, later of London. Every day brimmed with new friendships. "Our breakfasts are little literary societies," More enthused.[25] Her days and nights were filled with the things she was passionate about and on which she thrived: "poetry, theatre, and conversation."[26]

One afternoon, Garrick called upon the sisters at their London lodgings. During the course of the evening, he picked up a copy of Alexander Pope's *Essay on Man*. Then, Sally later wrote, "He read several lines we had been disputing about, with regard to emphasis, in many different ways, before he decided which was right. He sat with us from half-past twelve till three, reading and criticising."[27] Meeting Garrick had been More's first order of business; with this accomplished, the second was to meet Samuel Johnson.

For the literati, Dr. Johnson defined the age—quite literally. He was, after all, the author of the standard-setting English language dictionary, published in 1755. In addition to this pioneering work, Johnson wrote poetry, fiction, essays, biographies, and criticisms. Even now, literary scholars refer to the latter half of the eighteenth century as the age of Johnson.

More's introduction to the legendary man took place at the

home of the renowned painter Sir Joshua Reynolds. While leading More up the stairs to meet the revered man, Reynolds warned her that she might be greeted by "one of his moods of sadness and silence."[28] Like Hannah, Johnson had depressive periods. Indeed, Johnson was known almost as much for his morose, curmudgeonly temperament as he was for his voluminous literary output. He was otherwise a lively and engaging conversationalist, known for his quick witticisms and sharp tongue.

Thus prepared by Reynolds, More faced a double surprise in what happened next. Johnson entered the room in a jovial mood, and he was holding in his hand a brightly colored macaw. When he opened his mouth to speak, he greeted More by reciting a verse from one of her very own poems.

The two made an instant and vibrant connection. Although Johnson was well into his sixties, with numerous ailments, he and More developed an immediate and strong affection for each other. Johnson was impressed by More's passion and "genuine and unaffected" personality, rare among the urbane and jaded London elite.[29] And who didn't love the eminent Dr. Johnson?

Soon Hannah visited Johnson at his home at 7 Johnson Court. She traveled there with Sir Joshua Reynolds's sister, Frances, in the Reynoldses' coach, which was "attended by silver-liveried footmen."[30] Upon entering Johnson's parlor to await his arrival into the room, Hannah spotted an impressive chair. She presumed it was the throne of "Dictionary Johnson." She mischievously scampered over and seated herself in it, "hoping," Sally said, "to catch a little ray of his genius." When Johnson later heard about the caper, he had a good laugh. It was, he explained, a chair he never sat in. He then told her about the time that he and his friend and biographer James Boswell, happened upon the place where, supposedly, the Weird Sisters had appeared to Macbeth. They got so worked up that they couldn't sleep. They arose the next morning only to learn they were nowhere near the spot after all.[31]

These first seasons More spent in London were delightfully marked by the looming presence of that literary giant, Johnson. At one social gathering, More and Johnson were given seats next to each other, and they kept up the conversation the entire night. Her sister reported afterward, "They were both in remarkably high spirits; it was certainly her lucky night! I never heard her say so many good things. The old genius was extremely jocular, and the young one very pleasant. You would have imagined we had been at some comedy had you heard our peals of laughter."[32] During another soiree, the two of them had a spirited argument that ended with raucous laughter that drowned out all debate.[33] She complained one morning of having a headache, caused "by raking out so late with that gay libertine Johnson."[34] Imagine More's delight when, one day, Johnson invited himself over for tea specifically to read Hannah's poem *Sir Eldred of the Bower*. Afterward, she reported modestly, "I shall not tell you what he said of it, but to me the best part of his flattery was that he repeats all the best stanzas by heart."[35]

Johnson's age exceeded More's by more than thirty-five years. That didn't prevent the tongues from wagging, even in jest. One of More's sisters boldly declared in a letter home, "If a wedding should take place before our return, don't be surprised,—between the mother of Sir Eldred and the father of my much-loved Irene; nay, Mrs. Montagu says, if tender words are the precursors of connubial agreements, we may expect great things; for it is nothing but 'child,' 'little fool,' 'love,' and 'dearest.'"[36] One night, More had the pleasure of taking Johnson home from a party. Elizabeth Montagu playfully voiced her concern that the two might not be trusted together "with such a declared affection on both sides" and feared the trip home would result in an elopement.[37]

It's unlikely any of this teasing was in earnest. Johnson was not only so much More's elder, but he was a confirmed widower. His late wife, Elizabeth, who had died many years before, had been twenty years Johnson's senior. She had been widowed with three children when the two wed in 1735. They seem to have been happily married, but among the witticisms for which Johnson is known are choice quips about marriage. His most famous and characteristic of this curmudgeonly prose is his description of a second marriage as "the triumph of hope over experience."[38] In a more serious vein, however, when his biographer and constant companion James Boswell criticized an acquaintance for marrying a second time, saying that to do so showed disrespect for his first wife, Johnson corrected his friend, "Not at all, Sir," he told Boswell. "On the contrary, were he not to marry again, it might be concluded that his first wife had given him a disgust to marriage; but by taking a second wife he pays the highest compliment to the first, by showing that she made him so happy as a married man, that he wishes to be so a second time."[39] Of course, Johnson never paid that particular compliment to his late wife. His flirtations with Hannah proved no more than lighthearted fun.

Along with wit and coquetry, the two shared conservative political positions and strong views. More said of him, "In Dr. Johnson some contrarieties very harmoniously meet; if he has too little charity for the opinions of others, and too little patience with their faults, he has the greatest tenderness for their persons. He told me the other day he hated to hear people whine about metaphysical distresses, when there was so much want and hunger in the world."[40] Such pleasing contradictions attest to the complexity and fallibility of character both More and Johnson possessed.

One day in 1782, Johnson took More to Pembroke College at Oxford, the school he attended. During their visit, Johnson took

More into a common room and brought her before a portrait of him that had been hung just that day. To Hannah's surprise and delight, the words on the plaque under the painting were from her own poem: "And is not Johnson ours, himself a host. From Miss More's *Sensibility*."[41] It is easy to imagine how giddy both were at the double honor.

Johnson attended Oxford for one year before having to drop out because of a lack of funds. He was haunted his whole life by the poverty into which he was born and struggled against ever afterward. The title of *doctor* that is affixed to his name to this day was bestowed with the conferral of two honorary doctorates later in his life. Although he never completed a formal degree, few in history have proved themselves as worthy of such a title as he.

This humble background formed another source of mutual understanding between him and More. One of her sisters relayed a conversation with Johnson about their school. "I have heard that you are engaged in the useful and honorable employment of teaching young ladies," he inquired one day, early in his acquaintance with the sisters.[42] To be a schoolteacher was a humble position even in those days. It could be particularly humiliating to those who were exceptionally bright and talented like Johnson and More, and who could hold their own among their intellectual equals in the upper class who, supported by their inherited wealth, did not work. No one knew this shame better than Johnson, who had been employed as a teacher, too, after having to drop out of college in order to make a living. With his kind and sympathetic inquiry, the sisters found themselves opening up to the now distinguished man, telling him about their humble origins, parentage, and schooling: "how we were born with more desires than guineas; and how as years increased our appetites, the cupboard at home began to grow too small to gratify them; and how with a bottle of water, a bed, and a blanket, we set out to seek our fortunes.[43] The tale moved the old man. "I love you both," he exclaimed to the two sisters. "I love you all five—I never was at Bristol—I will come on purpose to see you—what!—five women live happily together! I will come and see you. . . . God for ever bless you, you live lives to shame duchesses." Upon departing from this visit, Johnson offered "so much warmth and tenderness," the letter home relates that "we were quite affected at his manner."[44]

Johnson made good on that promise to call on the sisters in Bristol and visited "the Sisterhood" on April 29, 1776.[45] He had come also to inquire into the life and work of the young, late Bristol poet Thomas Chatterton. One night at dinner, Johnson held More's hand and teased her by saying that she and Chatterton should have married so that "posterity might have a propagation of poets."[46]

During her many visits to London, More found amusement in the follies she observed taking place around her, even as she took delight in a bit of indulgence in them from time to time. One night, Johnson remarked of a woman that she "had a bottom of good sense." A guest present reported:

The word *bottom*, thus introduced, was so ludicrous when contrasted with his gravity, that most of us could not forbear tittering and laughing; though I recollect that the Bishop of Killaloe kept his countenance with perfect steadiness, while Miss Hannah More slyly hid her face behind a lady's back who sat on the same settee with her. His pride could not bear that any expression of his should excite ridicule, when he did not intend it; he therefore resolved to assume and exercise despotic power, glanced sternly around, and called out in a strong tone, "Where's the merriment?" Then collecting himself, and looking awful, to make us feel how he could impose restraint, and as it were searching his mind for a still more ludicrous word, he slowly pronounced, "I say the woman was fundamentally sensible;" as if he had said, hear this now, and laugh if you dare. We all sat composed as at a funeral.[47]

Despite the warm friendship of London's most revered public intellectual, as well as many others, More couldn't help marveling to find herself in his company and that of so many celebrated names. Although she was no shrinking wallflower, More did not suffer from overconfidence, particularly among the elite. In one early gathering where she was introduced to some of the leading names in London, More confessed, "I felt myself a worm, the more a worm for the consequence which was given me by mixing with such a society."[48] Even after the successful production in London of her play *Percy,* she told her friend Frances Boscawen, "I always think people will like me the less the more they see me."[49] It is difficult to discern, at times, whether social propriety or social vanity motivated More. Likely, it was both. Once, while she and Johnson were part of a small gathering, Johnson asked her opinion on a new tragedy appearing on the stage. Later in a letter home, she admitted, "I was afraid to speak before them all, as I knew a diversity of opinion prevailed among the company: however, as I thought it a less evil to dissent from the opinion of a fellow-creature than to tell a falsity, I ventured to give my sentiments; and was satisfied with Johnson's answering, 'You are right, madam.'"[50] During another soiree, someone brought up the subject of poetry. "Hush, hush," Johnson warned. "It is dangerous to say a word of poetry before her," meaning More. He continued, "It is talking of the art of war before Hannibal."[51]

It is tempting to ascribe More's lack of confidence to false modesty given such praise from such an esteemed praiser. But doing this would be misguided. For one thing, one suspects a bit of a patronizing tongue in cheek with much of Johnson's praise. But even more significantly, with much to learn about high society, More was a bit awkward around her social and economic superiors.

One day the wealthy socialite and patron of the arts Hester Thrale, on a lark, created a chart rating her friends on qualities such as knowledge, humor, and powers of conversation. On these points, she gave More low marks—giving her twenty out of twenty points, however, for "worth of heart"—but cattily offered her no points whatsoever for "person, mien, and manner."[52] Even more telling is an observation reportedly made by More's beloved Johnson. In a conversation with a mutual friend, Johnson compared More to her friend and fellow writer Fanny Burney. Johnson noted More's intelligence, but continued, "She has by no means the elegance of Miss Burney."[53] Johnson also delivered, at More's expense, one of the biting insults for which he was famous.

In his *Life of Samuel Johnson,* Boswell—whose lewd morals made him no fan of prim Hannah—included a story that some have used to mischaracterize the relationship between her and Johnson. As Boswell recorded it, Johnson

"once bade a very celebrated lady [Hannah More], who praised him with too much zeal perhaps, or perhaps too strong an emphasis (which always offended him), consider what her flattery was worth, before she choked him with it." Now let the genuine anecdote be contrasted with this. The person thus represented as being harshly treated, though a very celebrated lady, was then just come to London from an obscure situation in the country. At Sir Joshua Reynolds's, one evening, she met Dr. Johnson. She very soon began to pay her court to him in the most fulsome strain. "Spare me, I beseech you, dear Madam," was his reply. She still laid it on. "Pray, Madam, let us have no more of this," he rejoined. Not paying any attention to these warnings, she continued still her eulogy. At length, provoked by this indelicate and vain obtrusion of compliment, he exclaimed, "Dearest lady, consider with yourself what your flattery is worth, before you bestow it so freely."[54]

Throughout her life, More showed a smarmy side, the veneer of an underlying and understandable insecurity that accompanied the inherent tentativeness of social advancement in that age.

Despite whatever social stumbling she may have experienced, More sparkled under the brilliant lights of London. She had a sharp pen and a sharp tongue. Both were well practiced and well received amid the literati. For the most part, she seemed to thrive in these lively social scenes. During a visit with some of her father's relations in Norfolk, she wrote home about the festive atmosphere she found there: "The table and the guests groaned with the hospitality of the entertainers, and we had wines that would not have disgraced the table of a Bristol alderman." Remarking on the state of her daily life, she reported in the same letter, "I am very well. I eat brown bread and custards like a native; and we have a pretty, agreeable, laudable custom of getting tipsy twice a day upon Herefordshire cider."[55] While she would come to adopt a more serious and sober lifestyle in the coming years, such stories suggest a deliberate exercise of virtue rather than the accident of innocence. Even during those less sober years, we see More weighing and judging the excesses that surrounded her.

"I am going, to-day, to a great dinner," she wrote to her sister during the London visit of 1775. She continued, complaining that "nothing can be conceived so absurd, extravagant, and fantastical as the present mode of dressing the head." She lamented the lack of modesty and simplicity among the fashionable city dwellers. Even so, she recognized, on the other hand, that straying too far from London's fashions would be to err toward the "pride of singularity." So she complied reluctantly to some degree of fashion, only to lament, after being dressed, "I absolutely blush at myself, and turn to the glass [mirror] with as much caution as a vain beauty just risen from the small-pox; which cannot be a more disfiguring disease than the present mode of dressing."[56]

Although she scorned the excesses of city life, More benefited tremendously there, both personally and professionally. In this cosmopolitan setting her talent as a writer was recognized and cultivated. Yet even amid all the gaiety London offered, More spent hours each day on her first loves: reading and writing. "I read four or five hours every day, and wrote ten hours yesterday," she wrote home in 1776.[57] Two of More's ballads, *Sir Eldred and the Bower* and *The Ballad of Bleeding Rock*—which she had begun writing at Belmont during her betrothal to Turner and finished with the help of Johnson—were issued by London publisher Thomas Cadell in 1775.[58] She was paid well for them. It was a great compliment, too, that Cadell offered to pay her what Oliver Goldsmith had received for *The Deserted Village*. The vote of confidence was well deserved, however; Cadell's publishing company made a considerable profit in publishing this and all More's best-selling books.[59]

The publication of *Sir Eldred* in the *Monthly Review* produced a fond, if embarrassing, memory for More. During one of her regular dinners with some of the London circle, Garrick picked up his copy of the journal and gave an extemporaneous reading of the poem for the assembled company. He read, More reported, "with all his pathos and all his graces." And despite herself, confessing to never being so ashamed in all her life, she said afterward, "He read it so superlatively that I cried like a child. Only think what a scandalous thing, to cry at the reading of one's poetry!" Her embarrassment lessened some in being joined in her tears by Garrick's wife, who, More wrote, "made as many apologies for crying at her husband's reading, as I did for crying at my own verses."[60]

Garrick's wife, the Austrian-born Eva Maria Veigel, had been a famous dancer and was known across Europe for her stunning beauty. She was a Roman Catholic, and her marriage to the Protestant, if nominally Christian, Garrick required two separate ceremonies, one Anglican and one Roman Catholic, performed on the same day. Theirs was one of the great celebrity matches of the age, particularly since a marriage to a mere actor, even one as famed as Garrick, was seen as beneath a woman who had danced in Europe's royal courts. Garrick abandoned his previous lifestyle as a philanderer and enjoyed an affectionate and loving marriage with Eva until his death. The affectionate couple was captured in a portrait by the famous painter William Hogarth.

One of the most important firsthand accounts of a performance by Garrick came from More in a letter describing him in his most acclaimed role of Hamlet. She recognized her good fortune that night in not only attending the theater with the "best company"—the Burkes and Sheridan—but also having one of the best seats in the house where she had an excellent view. "In every part he filled the whole soul of the spectator, and transcended the most finished idea of the poet," she wrote, calling his performance "a fiction as delightful as fancy, and as touching as truth."[61]

She was a true fan and admitted to seeing Garrick perform twenty-seven times in one season.[62] Upon his later retirement from the stage following his last performance, Garrick bestowed on Hannah the shoe buckles he wore in the role of Hamlet, a gift that More treasured.[63] Another gift from Garrick, one More loved to show visitors to her home even in her old age, was an inkstand made from the wood of a mulberry tree that belonged to Shakespeare.[64]

Garrick was the magnet who pulled her back to London each year. What started as a teacher-pupil relationship grew into something near familial between her and both Garricks, the childless couple treating the spinster woman as kin and friend.

In 1777, More's tragic play *Percy* was accepted and produced by the Covent Garden Theater, and More returned to London from Bristol to attend the opening. Garrick had written the play's prologue and epilogue, a boost More recognized for the honor it was. The play told the tragic story of Elwina, in love with Earl Percy, being cruelly forced to marry Percy's enemy after Percy had insulted Elwina's father. By play's end, all were dead except Elwina's father, who was left alone to repent of his stubbornness. This theme of forced marriages had been getting increased attention during the latter half of the century as the rise of the modern individual brought with it questioning of the age-old approach to marriage as being arranged by families rather than based on the love and compatibility of the young couple. More picked the theme again with more realistic treatment in her novel *Coelebs in Search of a Wife*.

Naturally, the Garricks accompanied More to *Percy*'s opening night. The three sat hidden away in a "snug, dark corner" of a theater box where they could watch the performance unseen by the audience. When it was over, the play was offered "bursts of applause," More wrote the next morning, "as much beyond my expectation as my deserts!"[65] The second night, which More also attended, received even more enthusiastic response than the first. The praises and accolades flowed in.[66] The play was performed for twenty-two nights, a remarkable run for the time.

One poet was inspired to pen an enthusiastic verse, "Impromptu on Seeing Miss More's Tragedy of Percy," in praise of the author after seeing the play performed. The poem ended with these lines:

> *Each auditor with loud applause,*
> *Confessed the fair had won the cause,*
> *And cried MORE? MORE, yes MORE.*[67]

The play was soon produced at theaters across England and in France and Austria. In two weeks, four thousand copies of the printed version had been sold. *Percy* was later performed in Bath as well as upon the very stage where More had first fallen in love with the theater: Bristol's Theatre Royal. The famous actress Sarah Siddons, who would later become More's personal friend, took the leading part of Elwina.[68] Siddons also played the role when the play was revived during the 1785–86 season at Drury Lane.[69] The play's renown was seemingly unsurpassed at that time.[70] It was later translated into German and produced in Vienna where Mozart may have been in the audience; a copy of *Percy* was among the seventy-three books and musical scores found in his collection upon his death—perhaps he had thoughts of setting the piece to music.[71] In royalties, the play earned More the considerable sum of six hundred pounds.[72] But More's standard of success was simple: "One tear is worth a thousand hands, and I had the satisfaction to see even the men shed them in abundance."[73]

In the midst of the accolades that poured in upon the play's opening, More wrote, "I had no less than five invitations to dine abroad today, but preferred the precious and rare luxury of solitude."[74] Despite the delight she experienced in her new success as a playwright, she knew such was not most important. "I am at this moment as quiet as my heart can wish," she wrote. "Quietness is my definition of happiness."[75] During this period, More passed many of her days the at Garricks' home, where she penned various verses. David Garrick's special nickname for Hannah was "Nine," by which he meant that More was "the embodiment of all the Muses."[76]

Although not a devout Christian, he was always respectful, protective even, of More's devotion and her scruples about keeping the Sabbath. For example, on one Sunday evening there was a small party preparing to play music; More wrote home, "but before I had time to feel uneasy, Garrick turned round and said, 'Nine,' you are a *Sunday woman*; retire to your room—I will recall you when the music is over.'"[77]

But one January day in 1779, after More had returned from London to Bristol and taken to bed with one of her frequent illnesses, she was summoned back by Eva Garrick with the news of Garrick's death.

More arrived at the Adelphi to be greeted by the new widow with these whispered words: "I have this moment embraced his coffin, and you come next."[78] After paying her respects to the body in the casket, More observed movingly, "His new house is not so pleasant as Hampton, nor so splendid as the Adelphi, but it is commodious enough for all the wants of its inhabitant; and besides it is so quiet that he never will be disturbed till the eternal morning, and never till then will a sweeter voice than his own be heard."[79]

Garrick was much loved by the people of his country. His funeral drew such a crowd that tickets were required for admittance to the service held at Westminster Abbey. The event created a crisis for More when she and her party for a short time were locked within a church tower after attempting to bypass the crowds by entering the church through a back way, and they nearly missed the service. Thanks to the aid of someone who heard their cries for help, they made it out in time for the noble commemoration of a national figure.[80] At the interment in the abbey's famous Poets'

Corner that immediately followed, More reflected solemnly, "This is all of Garrick!" Then, quoting from the book of Job, she added, "Yet a very little while, and he shall 'say to the worm, Thou art my brother; and to corruption, thou art my mother and my sister.' So passes away the fashion of this world."[81]

The friendship between Garrick and More was so deep and so well known that More, along with his widow, received offers and letters of condolence. More and Eva Garrick provided each other with a primary source of consolation during the days, months, even years following his death. "My way of life is very different from what it used to be," More said shortly after Garrick's death. "You must not, therefore, expect much entertainment from my letters," she wrote to her sister from the Adelphi, where she remained with Eva in the room that the couple had always reserved for her during her London stays. The two women withdrew from the world into their own world inside the Garrick home. They took in the occasional visitor but rarely went out in those early days after their friend's departure from life. More wrote to her sisters:

> After breakfast, I go to my own apartment for several hours, where I read, and work; very seldom letting anybody in, though I have a room for separate visitors; but I almost look on a morning visit as an immorality. At four we dine. We have the same elegant table as usual, but generally confine myself to a single dish of meat. I have taken to drink half a glass of wine. At six we have coffee: at eight tea. . . . At ten we have salad and fruits. Each has her book, which we read without any restraint, as if we were alone, without apologies or speech-making.[82]

More remained close with Eva Garrick, who lived another forty-three years following her husband's death.

Their lasting friendship is a foremost example of More's love and embrace of those of different religious and political convictions, a quality not always found in years marked by wars over those very differences. As devoted a Protestant as More was, Eva Garrick's Roman Catholic beliefs never threatened their close friendship. Mrs. Garrick even referred to More as her "domestick chaplain."[83] More did not and would not ever support granting English Catholics political power, but this conviction did not diminish her deep love of and kinship with Mrs. Garrick. Even Johnson teased More, who, he said, as a "good Protestant" shouldn't have been reading books by Catholic authors as she was in the habit of doing.[84] In a country marked by centuries of warring and mutual oppression between Catholics and Protestants, More's personal tolerance was noteworthy.

In the year before his death, following the widely known success of *Percy,* Garrick urged More to write another play. So under Garrick's tutelage, More completed her next tragic drama, *The Fatal Falsehood,* a work centered on the theme of self-conquest. The prologue to the play sets forth unequivocally the priorities to which More consistently adhered as a writer. "The verse though feeble," the prologue proclaimed, "yet the moral's clear":

> *For if to govern realms belong to few,*
> *Yet all who live have passions to subdue.*
> *Self-conquest is the lesson books should preach,*
> *Self-conquest is the theme the stage should teach.*[85]

One biographer remarked that, in writing this play, More seemed to have "in spirit deserted the stage for the pulpit."[86] Perhaps so.

According to a letter of Sally More, this second of More's plays to appear on the London stage "was indeed *greatly* received. . . . When the curtain dropped, the house absolutely shouted."[87] *The Fatal Falsehood* didn't achieve the same level of success as did *Percy*, however. From the start, the work seemed doomed.

More had, nearly on a whim, taken the manuscript for the play to London and placed it in the hands of Thomas Harris, manager at Covent Garden, the spring after Garrick's death. Remorseful almost immediately, More tried to recall it, but Harris was already preparing it for production. It was produced in May while More lay sick in bed with rheumatic gout.[88] One of her sisters wrote home that the play might be staged only three or four nights, and "Hannah seems mighty indifferent about the matter."[89]

Nothing could have prepared anyone for the real drama that occurred the second night of the performance when Hannah Cowley, another playwright who had been under Garrick's mentoring, rose from her seat in the audience and proclaimed of the play, "That's mine! That's mine!"[90] All were astonished, none more than Hannah. The drama only intensified as the controversy continued to unfold in the press and the public eye with Cowley's continued charges of plagiarism and More's adamant denial. All available evidence indicates that the charge of plagiarism was unfounded. Cowley was a fellow protégée of Garrick, and it is possible that he was working with her in a similar vein.[91] The ugliness of the events helped ensure, however, that this would be Hannah's last work for the stage.

More continued to go to London every year and did so for thirty-five years. But the death of Garrick brought with it another kind of death. As we will see, London was losing its luster. She slowly turned her thoughts and her talents to more sober things.

Upon her return from London to Bristol in 1776, family

members and friends noted that More's popularity and acclaim in the city circles had failed to change her deportment.[92] Even after years of successive visits, that same assessment would prove essentially true. While London brought out the bloom, the flower that had taken root in humbler soil remained true to its nature.

CHAPTER 6

LEARNED LADIES

A LUSH PORTRAIT BY FRANCES REYNOLDS PAINTED IN 1780 IS GEN-erally believed to be of her friend Hannah More. The painting captured its subject in the prime of her womanhood and her writing career. She sat at a writing desk. Her head tilted gently downward while her temple rested on the fingertips of her left hand. In her right hand she held a quill pen, poised just above a sheaf of papers on which she wrote. Her long brown hair draped down her shoulder in a long, loosely coiled braid. Her eyes look out toward the viewer but almost imperceptibly to the side. She was deep in thought. Her slight smile seems prompted by something in her mind unconnected to the present scene. The loose draping of her informal dress evokes a sense that is both classical and timeless. Behind her stood a row of heavy volumes of books. The paper More wrote on and the books behind her are visually and symbolically linked by her hand. Altogether, the painting presented More as a writer to be taken seriously.

And she was.

The painting was done at the height of More's association with a like-minded group of serious women writers and intellectuals: the Bluestocking Circle, presided over by Elizabeth Montagu.

During her second visit to London in 1775, More wrote home excitedly about her introduction to Montagu: "I had yesterday the pleasure of dining in Hill-street, Berkeley-square, *at a certain Mrs. Montagu's, a name not totally obscure.*"[1] It's hard to miss the excitement thundering through the words of this letter written so long ago. And no wonder: Elizabeth Montagu was one of the wealthiest and most influential women of the day. In the same letter, More described the awe that Montagu evoked: "She is not only the finest genius, but the finest lady I ever saw: she lives in the highest style of magnificence; her apartments and table are in the most splendid taste; but what baubles are these when speaking of Montagu! her form (for she has no *body*) is delicate even to fragility; her countenance the most animated in the world."[2]

Like her namesake, Queen Elizabeth I, Montagu possessed passions worthy of her wealth, "a passion to rule and a passion for power, as well as a passion for literature," and hers was a "kingdom of arts and letters."[3] Over all the social obligations that came with a woman of her standing, Montagu's favorite role was that of patron of the literary arts. She supported numerous female writers, some still remembered and some long forgotten.[4] Born to a wealthy family, she was twenty-two when she married a rich estate holder and coal-mine owner who was fifty-five years old. They had only one child, a son, who died in early childhood. Following this loss, Montagu became more serious about her Christian faith and devoted herself to helping others through her philanthropy and patronage.[5]

Montagu received More warmly at their first dinner together.[6] More quickly became one of Montagu's protégées. The two developed one of the notable literary friendships of the age, one captured in the many letters they exchanged.

Montagu was known as "Queen of the Blues" for her leading role within the Bluestocking Circle. This loose gathering of intellectuals in the mid-eighteenth century originally included both men and women; increasingly, however, it became known for its female members. Samuel Johnson's friend and biographer James Boswell, in his *Life of Samuel Johnson*, explained the group and the origins of its name in a description that betrays a disdain for learned women:

> About this time it was much the fashion for several ladies to have evening assemblies, where the fair sex might participate in conversation with literary and ingenious men, animated by a desire to please. These societies were denominated *Blue-Stocking Clubs*, the origin of the title being little known, it may be worth while to relate it. One of the most eminent members of those societies, when they first commenced, was Mr. Stillingfleet, whose dress was remarkably grave, and in particular it was observed, that he wore blue stockings. Such was the excellence of his conversation, that his absence was felt as so great a loss, that it used to be said, "We can do nothing without the *blue stockings*;" and thus by degrees the title was established.[7]

Variations on this story fleshed out the origins of the name. An actual blue stocking was a durable, worsted legwear worn as part of informal dress, in contrast to the more elegant black or white silk stockings worn in formal attire. Several explanations have been given for how exactly this term became associated with the circle. According to one source, it arose early on when Stillingfleet declined to come because he felt underdressed; one woman urged him to attend even if he were wearing his blue stockings.[8] Another explanation held that Montagu adopted the term because the French version of the phrase *bas bleu* had been used in France to reference learned women since at least the previous century. At any rate, the Bluestocking Circle it was, and More was honored to be included among them.

The first-generation members of the society included Elizabeth Carter, Hester Chapone, Frances Boscawen, and Elizabeth Vesey, all part of a new class of intellectual women. Despite the later association of the term *bluestocking* with a learned woman, men were part of the gatherings too. They included More's favorites: David Garrick, Samuel Johnson, and Edmund Burke. The circle operated by a patronage system in which new members were added through sponsorship of an existing member. Montagu sponsored More.

Such a patronage system took many forms. Once More had achieved an elevated social position, she, in turn, reached down the social ladder to offer her support to others. One particular outreach of hers did not end well.

A Bristol milk woman named Ann Yearsley befriended More's cook and came to the kitchen to collect scraps to feed her pig. Yearsley, her husband, and five surviving children were destitute, saved from starvation by a well-to-do family. When More learned that this poor, uneducated woman had written a body of poems, she immediately took her on as a project, tutoring Yearsley in writing, editing the poems, and gathering subscribers to fund publication of the poems. The unlettered poet known as "Lactilla, the Milkmaid of Bristol" became something of a sensation. The number of subscribers swelled to more than one thousand and included several duchesses. More wisely invested the astonishing six hundred pounds raised into stocks and established a trust that would provide Yearsley with a yearly income.[9] More also used the funds to have her own publisher, Cadell, produce a collection of Yearsley's work in

1785, *Poems on Several Occasions.* More's protégée was on her way to being the "richest poetess, certainly the richest milkwoman, in Great Britain," as More put it.[10] She also fretted, wisely as it turned out, that such sudden success might go to the woman's head.[11]

When More refused to turn over control from the trustees of Yearsley's fund to Yearsley, the newfound poet rebelled. Yearsley understandably resented More for not trusting her with her own earnings. On the other hand, those earnings came as a result of More's skillful promotion and management of Yearsley's work.

Yearsley retaliated by spreading rumors that More was using her money to fund Cowslip Green, which More was in the process of purchasing. Yearsley published pamphlets against More that created a controversy in Bristol. More was silent in public but shared her disappointment with friends. "Prosperity is a great trial," More wrote to her fellow bluestocking Elizabeth Carter, "and [Yearsley] could not stand it." More admitted, "I was afraid it would turn her *head*, but I did not expect it would harden her *heart*."[12] This experience contributed to More's slowly growing awareness that something more than education, more than wealth, more than influence or power or literary prowess was needed to effect real change in both individuals and society.

Yearsley eventually got her way. More turned over the trusteeship to a lawyer who gave in to Yearsley's demand for control over the funds. In 1788, Yearsley published an anti-slavery poem of her own to rival one by More. She published several more works, but her fame and success quickly passed.

As painfully as the project turned out for More, the experience strengthened her growing influence among members of the upper class who had supported her in it. Even more significantly, More was establishing herself as one uniquely able to bridge the worlds of the great and the low. Her ability to connect the likes of an Ann Yearsley with supporters such as Elizabeth Montagu depended on relationships that were more than superficial. And tellingly, More considered both women—otherwise worlds apart—genuine friends. Crossing such long-established social boundaries was one of the significant examples of the Bluestocking Circle, one More would follow.

The Bluestocking Circle arose from an Enlightenment philosophy that characterized many aspects of this age of reason. The same turn from authority to experience that had wrought the Protestant Reformation, birthed the rise of the individual, and set the evangelical movement in motion expanded liberty for women—and, as we will see, slaves. Rationalism and empiricism questioned some of the age-old prejudices that deemed women as inferior. Observation proved that women could make valuable contributions in art, literature, culture, and conversation and that men and women could relate on an intellectual basis, as could those from different social classes. This was the basis of the Bluestocking Circle and its agenda. Such promotion of mixed society, whether the mixing of men and women or the different classes, was much more progressive then than it seems today. Even Montagu's use of the term *Bluestocking philosophers* indicates the group's connection to the Enlightenment ideals that pervaded the culture.[13] Another of the group's leaders, Elizabeth Carter, was noted by the *Monthly Review* for having intellectual abilities "sufficient to unravel the intricacies of Philosophy."[14] The philosophical outlook of the Bluestocking Circle resulted in a tremendous number of cultural artifacts and projects—publications, paintings, philanthropic activities—that its members produced over the decades of its existence.

The Bluestocking Circle offered a dramatic contrast to the typical social gatherings of the day, as shown in this description of one gathering given in a letter by Elizabeth Carter: "As if the two sexes had been in a state of war, the gentlemen ranged themselves on one side of the room, where they talked their own talk, and left us poor ladies to twirl our shuttles, and amuse each other, by conversing as we could. By what little I could overhear, our opposites were discoursing on the old English poets, and this subject did not seem so much beyond a female capacity, but that we might have been indulged with a share of it."[15]

The Bluestocking Circle offered a much more egalitarian approach to sociability and intellectual discourse. Reason and moderation, prime values of the age, also tempered excesses toward the other extreme, which More noted occurring among some women, such as those in France who were, in their pedantic enthusiasm, prone to "run to study philosophy, and neglect their families to be present at lectures of anatomy."[16]

More's celebration of the Bluestocking Circle, in the form of a poem she was circulating in manuscript form among her friends in 1782, *Bas Bleu; or Conversation*, conveyed the spirit of the gatherings, the personalities of the members against the backdrop of their social and literary relationships, and the character of the group within the context of the times. It demonstrated how the bluestockings "embraced fashionable society while also transforming it."[17] The poem's introduction provided a helpful history of the term *bas bleu*. It also set forth the respectable character of the particular bluestockings the poem was written to celebrate:

The following trifle owes its birth and name to the mistake of a Foreigner of Distinction, who gave the literal appellation of the *Bas-bleu* to a small party of friends, who had been often called, by way of pleasantry, the *Blue Stockings*. These little Societies have been sometimes misrepresented. They were composed of persons distinguished, in general, for their rank, talents, or respectable character, who met frequently at Mrs. *Vesey*'s and at a few other houses, for the sole purpose of conversation, and were different in no respect from other parties, but that the company did not play at cards.[18]

The introduction concluded by describing the gatherings as times "in which learning was as little disfigured by pedantry, good taste as little tinctured by affectation, and general conversation as little disgraced by calumny, levity, and the other censurable errors with which it is too commonly tainted, as has perhaps been known in any society."

It is clear to see from this introduction how the bluestockings came to be associated negatively with an elite, sometimes prudish, conservatism. The group's meetings were in part an imitation of the famous French salons and in part a departure from them. The Bluestocking Circle replicated the intellectual conversation that might be found at the salons but eliminated the drinking, flirting, card playing, and gaming for which the French gatherings were known. Card playing, while popular in all ranks of British society, was strongly associated with the French salons during the reign of Louis XV. Throughout the long, tumultuous history between England and France, even in peacetime, most things associated with France were cloaked with an extra aura of suspicion, particularly among the more conservative English. Society was, lines in the poem complained, "o'er-run" by dancing and games of whist, which More linked to barbarism that robbed culture of conversation and wit. In contrast, the Bluestocking Circle upheld elite standards of respectability and morality. At the same time, it was a rare example of a social activity that transgressed old boundaries of gender and class. Then, as now, even entertainment was tinged with politics. But the Bluestocking Circle created a space to be both fashionable and proper.

Their later reputation for uptight prudishness is surely exaggerated given the membership of Horace Walpole, who, More wrote in her poem, "show'd the way, / How wits may be both learn'd and gay" (lines 62–63). The next lines in the poem recalled Montagu as an esteemed Shakespearean critic, the work that established her literary reputation:

> And she who SHAKSPEARE's [sic]wrongs redrest,
> Prov'd that the brightest are the best. [lines 64–65]

Then More described the critical stance of the collective circle:

> This just deduction still they drew,
> And well they practis'd what they knew;
> Nor taste, nor wit, deserves applause,
> Unless still true to critic laws;
> Good sense, of faculties the best,
> Inspire and regulate the rest. [lines 66–71]

More addressed the poem to one of the three original hostesses of the Bluestocking Circle, Elizabeth Vesey, who was known for her wit and her vivaciousness. Before its publication by Horace Walpole's Strawberry Hill printing press in 1786, More circulated the anonymous manuscript of the poem among friends about a decade earlier, seeking feedback on the work as was customary among writers. It received wide readership and praise from the beginning. Even King George III heard about it and requested a personal copy of the poem, which More wrote out for him by hand.[19] Dr. Johnson was wild about the poem, as Hannah reported to her sister: "He received me with the greatest kindness and affection; and as to the Bas Bleu, all the flattery I ever received from everybody would not make up his sum. . . . He said there was no name in poetry that might not be glad to own it. You cannot imagine how I stared; all this from Johnson, that parsimonious praiser!"[20]

More was so honored by this praise that she confessed to being "ashamed" to even tell it, and she insisted to her sister in this letter that she not tell anyone of Johnson's praise.[21] Even begrudging Boswell, More's usual nemesis, said she had "admirably described" the club in the poem.[22]

The bluestockings' challenge to long-established notions of class, sex, and the rising place of the literary woman translated into important influences on and opportunities for More as a middle-class woman writer during the latter years of eighteenth-century England. More's introduction into and acceptance within the London literary world occurred at a time in English society when women of talent and intellect were just beginning to receive recognition apart from the economic and social statuses into which they were born.[23]

Along with class boundaries, the Bluestocking Circle and More, too, challenged through literary and intellectual pursuits some of the traditional gender boundaries. For her predecessor Montagu, the boundaries of sex were more rigid. "Extraordinary talents may make a woman admired, but they will never make her happy," Montagu wrote to a friend in 1763. "Talents put a man above the world, and in a condition to be feared and worshipped, a woman that possess them must be always courting the world, and asking pardon, as it were, for uncommon excellence."[24] Montagu's wistful concession to the way of the world was rendered more poignant in writing in the same letter: "If I had been a boy, when I had gone a birds nesting, I should have endeavored to have climbed to the Eagles Ayerie."[25]

A generation later, a discernible shift occurred that permitted women fuller participation in various spheres. For example, More sometimes participated in social circles that had been otherwise exclusive to men, such as the so-called Sour-crout Party, a weekly men's meeting that derived its name from the main course[26] and at which More was always welcome.[27] She also attended an annual meeting at the Adelphi where, she said, "nothing but men are usually asked." She reported, "an agreeable day it was to me."[28] These early adventures foreshadowed her later years with the evangelical Clapham Sect where she was the only female member given status nearly equal to that of men.[29]

Though More relished being the only female in the all-male Sour-crout parties and one of only two or three ladies in the learned Oyster Club, she wasn't in favor of crossing all traditional lines.[30] Upon being named an honorary member of the Royal Society of Literature, she demurred. "I have written a strong remonstrance, declining the distinction," she wrote, "partly on the ground that I have no claim to it, but chiefly that I consider the circumstance of sex alone a disqualification."[31] Some gender roles had boundaries that More was unwilling to cross.

Traditional views of family structure were another hallmark of the Bluestocking Circle that neatly fit More's values—despite her choice never to marry. The advancements the members of the Bluestocking Circle sought for women in education and learning were ones that they saw as compatible with the health and vitality of families. More's writings on female education, for example, expressed concern about the kind of education that would prepare a woman to be a good wife rather than merely to land a good husband. She fretted in one letter, "I am acquainted with a great many *very* good wives, who are so notable and so managing that they make a man every thing but happy; and I know a great many others who sing, and play, and paint, and cut paper, and are so *accomplished* that they have no time to be *agreeable*, and no desire to be useful."[32]

More's general view of female education was also reflected in her 1799 treatise *Strictures on the Modern System of Female Education*. Here she argued that the purpose of a woman's education should not be to produce "fashion dancers, singers, players, painters, actresses, sculptors, gilders, varnishers, engravers, and embroiderers." Rather than majoring in frivolities, women should be educated in useful subjects and "be furnished with a stock of ideas, and principles, and qualifications, and habits, ready to be applied and appropriated" in accordance with the roles to which they might be called. For, she continued, "when a man of sense comes to marry, it is a companion whom he wants, and not an artist. It is not merely a creature who can paint, and play, and sing, and draw, and dress, and dance; it is a being who can comfort and counsel him; one who can reason and reflect, and feel, and judge, and discourse, and discriminate; one who can assist him in his affairs, lighten his cares, sooth his sorrows, strengthen his principles, and educate his children."[33]

By twenty-first-century standards, More's assumption that women's roles were limited to those of "daughters, wives, mothers, and mistresses of families"[34] is insupportable. But in the context of her time, More's advocacy of a female education that would furnish women's minds with "ideas and principles" and make them suitable "companions" for their husbands was markedly progressive. Indeed, the companionate marriage—rather than the politically or economically expedient one that had been the norm for all human history—was an idea advanced by evangelicals, including More, who understood marriage to be an institution established to advance the kingdom of God, not property. More believed that "it is almost the worst sort of domestic immorality [in a wife] to be *disagreeable*."[35] In More's mind, being an "agreeable" and "useful" wife was essential for mutual domestic happiness. A happy marriage was a channel for allowing the individual to satisfactorily employ whatever gifts and talents had been bestowed on him or her by God for the benefit of all, both within the family and without. The happiness and success of the marriage partnership would spill over onto the children, who were empowered by the firm foundation of the parents, as was the case in More's upbringing. As one scholar noted, the traditional family structure that More supported in her writings enabled women to "be intelligent, rational, virtuous, and noble creatures, capable of great intellectual and moral achievements. They had the potential for immense influence on their husbands and sons, on their other relations, their servants and the poor."[36] More held, therefore, along with her fellow bluestockings, that "the ideal of rational domesticity helped to liberate the individual within a supportive family framework."[37] This topic was of enough concern to More that it became the theme in the only novel she wrote. It is ironic that More so strenuously argued that women should be educated for the role of wife and mother when she was neither. She was a woman of contradictions as well as convictions.

Nevertheless, More contributed to a shift in the institution of marriage toward a more egalitarian and rational view. This carried with it innumerable implications for other established institutions. More's "conviction of spiritual equality" had a significant part in the role the evangelical movement played in modifying the notion of "separate spheres" for women and men. More's views pointed devout women toward a greater role in public life in pursuit of the public good.[38]

Virtue, both personal and public, characterized the bluestockings. More noted from the start of her involvement with the group that the women were "all ladies of high character and piety."[39] Neoclassical thinkers often made a connection between the harmony and order of beauty and the harmony and order of society. The Scottish Enlightenment thinker David Hume promoted the idea that refinements in art and culture went together and that women were particularly suited to lead in the art of conversation—in which he included the art of the essay. In advancing this view, Hume cited women's natural ability to join "sociable Disposition," "a Taste of Pleasure," and "the easier and more gentle Exercises of the Understanding" in the acts of reflection and observation.[40] In this thinking were the seeds that would later develop, particularly in the Victorian era, into the view that women have a civilizing effect on men. However, at this point in history, this was an advancement of the view of learned women, who often were subject to disdain and ridicule.[41]

For the members of the Bluestocking Circle, learning was a virtue, and all virtues were connected. The virtue of learning could not be separated from sexual morals or religious piety. Thus, the men who were part of the group were valued most not as vehicles of sexual seduction and fulfillment or objects of flirtation—as in the French salons—but as conveyors of intellectual learning and knowledge. Indeed, men introduced these women to higher learning—since the traditional exclusion of women from this realm made men the sole possessors of intellectual understanding. Such was certainly true for More throughout her life, having received a classical education from her father and the encouragement, mentoring, and support of numerous literary men during her writing years. For More and other bluestockings, the most significant role played by the men in their lives was almost exclusively that of mentor and teacher; this profoundly affected the way in which they related with the men who operated for them as arbiters of learning.

The conservative virtues of the Bluestocking Circle, sometimes seen as accommodating to patriarchal views, actually elevated women's status and power. A letter to More from William W. Pepys, one of her many male correspondents, expressed this explicitly: "What I wished you to insist upon principally, is the very extensive influence which your sex might have on ours by an active and judicious use of every fair opportunity to discountenance vice, and encourage the profession of virtuous principles."[42]

One friend bestowed on More the title of "virtuous wit."[43] Balancing these two qualities—virtue and wit—was no easy task in a society that did not tend to view women in such whole and humane terms. More's letters often reflected an uneasy tension between her attempts to promote virtue in her writing and living up to those high standards, as seen in one letter written to fellow bluestocking Frances Boscawen: "Do you know, my dear madam, as I have said before, I feel a little awkward about this same book? I am so afraid that strangers will think me good! and there is a degree of hypocrisy in appearing much better than one is."[44]

A parallel anxiety was reflected in a letter to Elizabeth Carter: "It is so easy to practise a creditable degree of so seeming virtue, and so difficult to purify and direct the affections of the heart, that I feel myself in continual danger of appearing better than I am; and I verily believe it is possible to make one's whole life a display of splendid virtue and agreeable qualities, without ever setting foot towards the narrow path, or even one's face towards the strait gate."[45]

Carter knew this tension all too well. She withdrew from fashionable life once she made the decision to remain single. In order to pursue a life of scholarship and writing, she knew it would be necessary to retain a reputation of propriety and virtue. Retreat from high society was the best safeguard and an example More would eventually follow.[46]

Before she did so, however, More's standing among the blue-stockings rose to such prominence that she was included in a 1779 painting by Richard Samuel. The detail of the painting is referred to as the *Nine Living Muses of Great Britain*. Taken from *Portraits in the Characters of the Muses in the Temple of Apollo*, which hangs in the National Portrait Gallery in London, the detail depicted many women of the Bluestocking Circle gathered in a Grecian-style temple. Elizabeth Anne Sheridan is in the center; to the left are Angelica Kauffman, Elizabeth Carter, and Anna Barbauld. Seated on the right are Catherine Macaulay, Elizabeth Montagu, and Elizabeth Griffith, who are holding manuscripts. Standing behind them are Hannah More, lifting up a chalice, and Charlotte Lennox, who appears to be playing a lute. An engraving of the *Nine Muses* was also included in *The Ladies' Pocket-book*, published in 1778.[47] At this time, More was the least known of all these women, but she had clearly established her place among the fashionable literary set in such a way that everything she wrote from this point forward would be received with respect and, for the most part, acclaim.[48] She was considered the resident poet of the blues, and Hester Thrale said she was "the cleverest of all us female wits."[49] Indeed, in 1782, she was elected membership into the Academy of Sciences, Belles Lettres and Arts at Rouen, France, a prestigious institution devoted to the cultivation of ideas that, opened by King Louis XV in 1744, still exists today.[50] Yet, as noted, More thought herself to be "disqualified" from the honorary membership offered her by the Royal Society of Literature.

The era of the Bluestocking Circle ended with the close of the eighteenth century. For Britain, the century's end was centrally concerned with the Revolutionary War in America followed by the Revolution in France. Polar cultural forces were at work: the spirit of romanticism that would form a revolution all its own, and an antirevolutionary counterresponse of retreat. Both opposed the idea of learned women embodied by the Bluestocking Circle, and both contributed to the decline of the group and its reputation in history.

In symbolizing "the progress of a civilized and commercial nation," the Bluestocking Circle "provoked anxiety about women's proper place in society."[51] The conservative impulse in the face of such violent and dramatic revolution was retreat. Even the modest progress in women's learning was swept up in the wake of this attempt to move the clock back. Learned, strong, outspoken women suddenly smacked of revolution, including as conservative and pious a group as the learned ladies of the Bluestocking Circle. By the end of the century, *bluestocking* became a term of abuse, echoing earlier distrust of learned women's "slipshod" appearance and morality.[52]

Such is the human tendency to overcorrect.

On the other hand, the rising movement of romanticism, with its characteristic idealism, one that tended toward a black-and-white view of the world based on those ideas, preferred for different reasons that women remain untinged by "masculine" traits of learning. Famous romantic writers such as Lord Byron, Samuel Taylor Coleridge, and William Hazlitt criticized the bluestockings. Byron satirized the bluestockings in his famous poem *Don Juan*, Coleridge proclaimed his loathing for "*all* Bluestockingism"; and Hazlitt declared his "utter aversion to Bluestockings," saying, "I do not care a fig for any woman that knows even what *an author* means."[53] Because of the tremendous influence that romanticism gained over the cultural mind-set, the term *bluestocking* came to be a derogatory term applied to learned, pedantic women, particularly conservative ones. The wealth and propriety that made the Bluestocking Circle possible were linked to much that the romantic movement stood against. Furthermore, learned women did not fit in with the romantic notion of a damsel in distress waiting to be rescued by a knight in shining armor any more than they fit in with the antirevolutionary fear of progress.

Dismissed by the polar sides in the culture wars that defined the turn of that century, the bluestockings, women who challenged the traditional view and role of women in society, would all but disappear into obscurity. Though they were forgotten, their legacies were strong and enduring, and Hannah More is credited with carrying that legacy into the nineteenth century.[54]

CHAPTER 7

ALL THAT GLISTENS IS
NOT GOLD

In her poem "Sensibility," published in 1782, More praised fellow poet Thomas Gray with these lines:

> To give immortal mind its finest tone,
> Oh, Sensibility! is all thy own.
> THIS is th' ethereal flame which lights and warms,
> In song enchanys us, and in action charms.
> 'Tis this that makes the pensive strains, of Gray
> Win to the open heart their easy way.[1]

Gray was a professor and classical scholar at Cambridge University and a well-known poet in his own time. Today he is best known for his poem "Elegy Written in a Country Churchyard," published in 1751. More's friend Horace Walpole was Gray's chum. After graduating from the university, Walpole and Gray went together on their European tour—a tradition with which young aristocratic men punctuated their formal schooling. In 1747, at the

request of Walpole, Gray wrote a poem to commemorate the death
of Walpole's cat after the poor thing drowned in an attempt to scoop
up fish in a china bowl.[2] The poem that resulted from Walpole's
lighthearted request was a more than just playful verse, although it
was that too. "Ode on the Death of a Favourite Cat, Drowned in a
Tub of Goldfishes" drew on the classical traditions of the elegy, and
the ode put them to playful use in choosing, rather than the typically lofty subjects reserved for these poetic forms, a cat.

With language that described not only the fallen feline but
was apt to a woman too, the first six of the poem's seven stanzas
described how the demure but "hapless nymph" was fatally tempted
to seize the two golden "angel forms" gliding in the forbidden
waters. The poem concluded with this moral:

> From hence, ye beauties, undeceiv'd,
> Know, one false step is ne'er retriev'd,
> And be with caution bold.
> Not all that tempts your wandering eyes
> And heedless hearts, is lawful prize;
> Nor all that glisters, gold.[3]

On the surface, "Ode on the Death of a Favourite Cat" narrated
the fatal fall of a cat tempted by glimmering goldfish. But beneath
that playful veneer was a morality tale cautioning "beauties" that
even one who was "a favourite" could find herself without a friend
once she took one false step too far and the "lawful prize" was "ne'er
retriev'd." The last line, one that remains familiar today, "Nor all
that glisters, gold," was a commonplace saying in More's day, as is
today its better known counterpart: "All that glitters is not gold."

This axiom captured well More's evolving attitude toward
London life, which was as exhilarating as might be for a young,

provincial woman so well received by the most renowned names of the day. Yet London was becoming for More but fool's gold, its luster steadily losing its appeal.

Over a period of about five years, marked on one end by the death of David Garrick in 1779 and on the other end by her move to her country home, Cowslip Green, in 1785, More gradually withdrew from London life. Some of this withdrawal can be attributed to her growing disenchantment with the trappings of cosmopolitan life. But More had always been bemused—and sometimes amused—by the excesses and superficialities she witnessed there. So while the glistening of the fashionable life grew ever duller over several years, hints of More's doubts about this fool's gold can be found even from her earliest seasons there. It is clear that she was undergoing a greater sense of a calling to more serious work, to more devotion in her faith, and with it to ministry in serving others.

More's enchantment with the theater was also waning. She had considered Garrick, along with his wife, to be her "conscience" in London—as Dr. Stonhouse was when she was in Bristol—testimony to the need of even the naturally good, like More, to be surrounded by positive influences.[4] With Garrick's absence from the scene, More lost her primary, perhaps sole, attachment to the stage, a taste that had been soured by the plagiarism controversy. The objections to the excesses of the theater that had been latent in her all along were unlocked by his departure. She had admitted earlier, "I find my dislike of what are called public diversions greater than ever, except a play; and when Garrick has left the stage, I could be very well contented to relinquish plays also, and to live in London, without ever again setting my foot in a public place."[5]

In turn, the world of the theater was not generally kind to those of conservative and religious leanings. During the negotiations with her publisher, Cadell, for the book rights to *The Fatal*

Falsehood, the publisher remarked to More, "You are too good a Christian to be a dramatic author."[6]

The year after Garrick's death, her friend Frances Boscawen gave More a copy of John Newton's *Cardiphonia.* We will see later the fruit produced in her life by this work, but the event is important to mark here as one step in More's turn away from fashionable life. She was coming under conviction.

On Christmas of 1780, the same year, she wrote home to her family from London, "I would wish you a merry Christmas, as well as a happy New-year, but that I hate the word merry *so* applied; it is a fitter epithet for a *bacchanalian* than a *Christian* festival, and seems an apology for idle mirth and injurious excess."[7]

After Garrick's death, More gave up the theater altogether, neither attending plays nor writing for the stage. Even the revival some years later of her play *Percy* did not shake her resolution. More later stated, "To have gone would have been inconsistent with my publickly professed opinions."[8]

Her shift in thinking was clearly conflicted. It must have been difficult to disavow something for which she had a deep love and in which she had been immersed much of her life. Even long after her decision was made, More occasionally mentioned it in her correspondence, such as in a letter to her sister Martha, reminding her that she had long withdrawn herself from that world.[9] Her most detailed explanation of the change in her views about theater is in the introduction to her collected dramas when she pointed not to inconsistency but to "a revolution in [her] sentiments." More granted that "a well written tragedy is, perhaps, one of the noblest efforts of the human mind." And "of all public amusements," theater, she said, "is the most interesting, the most intellectual, and the most accommodated to the tastes and capacities of a rational being."[10] Yet because she was concerned with the rational side of man and even more the spiritual, she grounded her objection to theater on what she called "a prominent thread of false Principle" woven through "the whole web of the tragic drama." Honor, More charged, "is the religion of tragedy." Emotions such as love, hate, ambition, pride, and jealousy "form a dazzling system of worldly morality," which contradicts "the spirit of that religion whose characteristics are charity, meekness, peaceableness, longsuffering, gentleness, forgiveness."[11] Her struggle suggests that of one for whom theater had been a religious love, that of one who, in not knowing how to love it in proper proportion, felt it best not to love it at all.

More's growing objections to the stage in particular did not extend to her views on literature in general. Indeed, her writings during the period following Garrick's death showed "that she saw no inconsistency between the devoutest piety and the cultivation of elegant literature and taste."[12] Having given up theater, More still recognized the power of dramatic literature and was drawn to employing that influence toward didactic ends.

In 1782, her poem "Sensibility" was published along with a long-term dramatic project, *Sacred Dramas*. The two works together showed how More sought to balance between emotion and reason in an age when many philosophies and people tended toward one over the other. More defined *sensibility* as an "ethereal flame which lights and warms" the human heart.[13] Such a flame was needed to meld relationships together, whether with one's fellow man or with God. *Sacred Dramas* provided a practical application of this idea extolled in "Sensibility." Some objected, as noted previously, to the enhancement of biblical stories by the fires of the imagination used in *Sacred Dramas*. Prior to More's publication of the plays, Samuel Johnson had proclaimed that when it came to the stories of the Bible, "All amplification is frivolous and vain; all addition to that which is already sufficient for the purpose of religion, seems not only useless, but in some degree profane. Such events as were produced by the visible interposition of Divine Power are above the power of human genius to dignify."[14]

But More had, some years earlier, expressed the wise wish, "I hope the poets and painters will at last bring the Bible into fashion, and that people will get to like it from taste, though they are insensible to its spirit, and afraid of its doctrines."[15] She retold with horror that her friend Sir Joshua Reynolds had to identify the subject in his painting of Samuel from the Old Testament. "I love this great genius," More said of Reynolds, "for not being ashamed to take his subjects from the most unfashionable of all books."[16]

Popular opinion, this time, sided with More rather than Johnson. The *Sacred Dramas* collection turned out nineteen editions and was translated into at least one foreign language.[17] Yet the work generated a great deal of controversy among religious conservatives. Ten years after its publication, an attempt to produce onstage one of the stories from *Sacred Dramas* was thwarted when an announcement of the play's upcoming performance "threw the religious people of the town into a frenzy and the preachers 'so barked at and tore to pieces' the proposal of putting Biblical characters on stage that [the producer] abandoned the attempt."[18] Neither the literary elite nor the strict religionists were pleased. More perhaps did something right in striking a balance somewhere in the middle.

The period of More's gradual withdrawal from fashionable society was bookended by the deaths of mentors whom she esteemed and loved. The first, of course, was the death of David Garrick. The other was the death of Johnson in December 1784. During her regular visit to Eva Garrick that December, just before Johnson died, she wrote from Hampton with some alarm, "Poor dear Johnson! he is past all hope." Indeed, the great man was at "the point of death." Johnson was apparently suffering from edema or, as it was called then, dropsy, an accumulation of fluid under the skin. Among More's papers was another letter by an unknown writer offering more details about the last moments of Johnson's life. The account described Johnson's desire to see a clergyman. The minister requested, being in ill health himself, was able only to write a letter. In the letter, he reminded Johnson that whatever despair he might feel over past actions in facing death could be alleviated by considering only the question, "What shall I do to be saved?" The answer to which, the clergyman wrote, was "Behold the Lamb of God!" Johnson was extremely moved and comforted. Thus, the unknown letter writer reported, Johnson appeared at the time of his death "to have been blessed by God" in achieving "renunciation of the self, and a simple reliance on Jesus as his Saviour." Johnson also expressed "that peace," the writer said, "which he had found the world could not give, and which, when the world was fading from his view, was to fill the void, and dissipate the gloom, even of the valley of the shadow of death."[19] His peace offered some solace to her.

For More, London represented the best and the worst of all it meant to be human. The best in London offered her literary friends and fame; the worst, the vanity that tempted and repelled her simultaneously. With the deaths of Garrick and Johnson, the best parts had vanished. The worst seemed to glare at her. She had written after one of her early visits to London that "the more I see of the 'honoured, famed, and great,' the more I see of the littleness, the unsatisfactoriness of all created good; and that no earthly pleasure can fill up the wants of the immortal principle within."[20] Now the truth of this was even more apparent.

Fashion in dress was one example of the many excesses of

London life that tried More's patience. "Simplicity and modesty are things so much exploded, that the very names are no longer remembered," she complained.[21] While the extreme hoops—up to six feet in width—that were all the rage in the first half of the century had been cut down to more manageable sizes, Georgian dress for fashionable women was no simple matter. France, as usual, influenced fashion in England, although English versions tended to be simpler than their French counterparts. One way or another, however, the dress of a fashionable London woman included many accoutrements. An outfit for an afternoon tea, an evening soiree, or a gathering of the Bluestocking Circle might include a muslin neckerchief tucked into the bosom, a bodice and corset that slimmed and elongated the torso, then likely flared out at the hips, perhaps with the aid of a padded false rump or a hoop in the back or a pannier—a voluminous overskirt—at the side of each hip. An abundance of frills would be made from laces, ribbons, and flowers. One popular choice for fashionable ladies, particularly when traveling, was the Brunswick gown, a two-piece outfit consisting of a hip-length jacket with long sleeves that were fitted below the elbow, worn over a matching petticoat, all made of fabric much finer than the working-class versions that inspired the style.

And just as warm air rises, the size of headdresses increased in proportion to the reduction of the girth of hoops. Indeed, fashions for the body were modest compared to those that adorned the top of the head. More wrote in one letter: "I am annoyed by the foolish absurdity of the present mode of dress. Some ladies carry on their heads a large quantity of fruit, and yet they would despise a poor useful member of society who carried it there for the purpose of selling it for bread."[22]

Powdered wigs were often worn by women and men, although more natural hair was coming into style toward the end of the century.

It was fashionable for women to grow their hair tremendously long. Ringlets with ribbons or rope braids—such as More wore in the portrait painted by Frances Reynolds—were popular. And in that same painting, More's clothing displayed a modest, classical simplicity that bespoke her resistance to the excesses surrounding her.

Yet she found herself a bit of the hypocrite, admitting that she needed to try to fit in at least enough not to appear singular. She protested, however, "I detest and avoid public places more than ever, and should make a miserably bad fine lady! What most people come to London *for* would keep me *from* it!"[23]

Other aspects of London social life that confirmed even more her growing convictions included the full menu of Sabbath day activities that More continually had to decline,[24] such as the popularity of card playing and the poor sermons she was subjected to at church.[25] She wrote to Stonhouse from one of her first trips to London that her conscience was nagging her over social appointments on a Sunday. Further, she wrote, she found herself while at the opera ruminating on the biblical admonition, "What doest thou here, Elijah?"[26] "Going to the opera, like getting drunk, is a sin that carries its own punishment with it, and that a very severe one."[27] She could see no end in London of serious things being treated as trivial and silliness undertaken with utmost seriousness. Sermons on a Sunday were poorly delivered. Card playing, however, was a matter of life and death, as one letter More wrote from London showed: "A relation of the Duchess of Chandos died at the duchess's a few days ago, at the card-table; she was dressed most sumptuously—they stripped off her diamonds, stuck her upright in a coach, put in two gentlemen with her, and sent her home two hours after she was dead; at least so the story goes."[28]

With the month-long visit of a troupe of famous actors in town, a Lenten sacrifice from the rest of life ensued: "Everybody goes to the play every night—that is, every other night, which is as often as they perform. Visiting, drinking, and even card-playing are for this happy month suspended; nay, I question if, like Lent, it does not stop the celebration of weddings, for I do not believe there is a damsel in the town who would spare the time to be married during this rarely-occurring scene of festivity."[29]

Though most of the frivolity found More as merely an observer, she didn't manage to be entirely untouched by it. One night in 1781, she and Mrs. Garrick attended a select party hosted by Bishop Shipley. It was attended by a few lords and ladies, Sir Joshua Reynolds, Gibbon, and Johnson as well. James Boswell was also there; he was documenting Johnson's life for the biography he was writing. What happened at this party ensured that More would not be presented favorably in that work. Little is known of exactly what transpired between them except More's brief statement within her larger report on the entire evening. "I was heartily disgusted with Mr. Boswell," she wrote, "who came up stairs after dinner, much disordered with wine, and addressed me in a manner which drew from me a sharp rebuke." More later sensed she may have erred in swatting a fly with a sledgehammer for, she added ruefully, "I fancy he will not easily forgive me." More's prediction seemed to have proved correct. Some believe that the glaring omissions of More from Boswell's *Life of Samuel Johnson* were the result of his "hearty dislike of the woman who dared criticize him."[30] Being largely excluded from this important work and dismissively portrayed in her few appearances therein contributed to the diminishment of More's public favor in later years.

Such an incident—the alloy under the glistening, gold veneer of fashionable life—contributed to More's growing disillusionment with the London literati. Her thoughts during this time about

English society had been expressed a couple of years earlier in a letter to Horace Walpole in September 1788: "In vain do we boast of the enlightened eighteenth century, and conceitedly talk as if human reason had not a manacle left about her, but that philosophy had broken down all the strong-holds of prejudice, ignorance, and superstition."[31] Among the many witticisms of her dear friend Dr. Johnson is this famous gem: "Sir, when a man is tired of London," the urbane critic proclaimed, "he is tired of life."[32] This was not true for More. She simply wearied of London life.

So in 1785, following the death of her father in 1783 and that of Johnson the next year, More moved to Cowslip Green, a one-story, thatched cottage situated between the villages of Blagdon and Wrington, across from the Mendip Hills in the county of Somerset in the west of England. In contrast to the luxury that seemed abundant in London, here More could fulfill her dream of living in a cottage "too low for a clock."[33] Here she could also pursue her lifelong love of gardening, something she spent several hours a day doing. Her labors yielded "pinks and roses" that she boasted of in one letter to a friend.[34] In a letter to John Newton, she wrote about her beloved new home:

> "God made the country, and man made the town," says the delightfully enthusiastic bard you are so near [William Cowper], a sentence to which my heart always makes an involuntary warm response. I have been now some weeks in the quiet enjoyment of my beloved solitude, and the world is wiped out of my memory as with the sponge of oblivion. But, as I have observed to you before, so much do my gardening cares and pleasures occupy me, that the world is not half so formidable a rival to heaven in my heart as my garden.[35]

She continued in the same letter to tell Newton about the slow transformation of her convictions:

> The world, though I live in the gay part of it, I do not actually much love; yet friendship and kindness have contributed to fix me there, and I dearly love many individuals in it. When I am in the great world, I consider myself as in an enemy's country, and as beset with snares, and this puts me upon my guard. I know that many people whom I hear say a thousand brilliant and agreeable things disbelieve, or at least disregard, those truths on which I found my everlasting hopes. This sets me upon a more diligent inquiry into those truths; and upon the arch of Christianity, the more I press, the stronger I find it.[36]

It seems that More was closer to heaven at Cowslip Green. There her thoughts turned from literary acclaim toward service to God and other people. She continued to winter in London for many years but not to the same ends as before. When in the 1785–86 theater season, her play *Percy* revived at Drury Lane—with the role of Elwina played by the famous Sarah Siddons—More did not attend.[37] Her heart had turned elsewhere.

CHAPTER 8

FAITH TO SEE

In 1780, during the height of her high-society years in London, More read a book that changed her life. *Cardiphonia,* sometimes translated by publishers as *The Utterance of the Heart* or *Voice of the Heart,* was a collection of letters penned by John Newton, author of the hymn "Amazing Grace." As was common, Newton's book was published pseudonymously. More was curious to know whom the author of this marvelous and moving book was. She wrote a letter to her friend Frances Boscawen, thanking her for introducing the work to her. "I like it prodigiously," she said. "It is full of vital, experimental religion."[1] Those words, within the context of the times, are telling. By *vital,* More meant "full of life," so opposite the stale, dead religion found in many Church of England members, wearied with centuries of religious conflict. The word *experimental* alluded to the growing emphasis during the eighteenth century on the importance of individual experience in religious practice, the need of each person to have an authentic and personal faith rather than simply to adhere to rote tradition.

Although little known today, *Cardiphonia* is a classic of Christian literature. The volume of personal letters by Newton put forth his convictions concerning human depravity and the sufficiency of Christ to redeem fallen humanity. The book's theme of this vital religion is seen in a passage from the first letter of the collection. "The awakened soul (especially when, after a season of distress and terror, it begins to taste that the Lord is gracious) finds itself as in a new world," he wrote.[2] Who could attest to such doctrines better than this wretch saved by that sweet and amazing grace?

Newton spent the first part of his life following in the footsteps of his father in the seafaring business. Yet even more than the sea, the slave trade defined Newton's early adult life, from being a slave himself to trafficking in human flesh. When he was about twenty, Newton was impressed into naval service. Impressment was a kind of involuntary servitude that was legal in Great Britain, a practice long justified as necessary for a robust national defense well into the nineteenth century. Newton attempted to desert the ship but succeeded only in being flogged, demoted, and transferred to a slave ship that took him to Sierra Leone. There he was handed over to a slave trader and made the slave of an African princess, who abused and mistreated him along with the rest of her slaves. Eventually rescued by another slave trader, he nearly lost his life aboard the *Greyhound* during a horrific storm that almost downed the ship in 1748. Newton cried out to God, his life was spared, and through this he "began to know that there is a God, who hears and answers prayer."[3]

Despite his newfound faith, Newton did not immediately recognize the evil of slavery. He continued to work in the slave trade. In fact, it was *after* his conversion to Christ that Newton became captain of a slave ship. Some of the most detailed records of the horror chambers sailing the Middle Passage are found in Newton's journals. Extracts from his journal detailing a 1754 voyage described the fatal illnesses, suicide attempts, insurrections, and ghastly punishments that characterized the journeys of slaves being transported to the colonies. After one uprising by the slaves, Newton wrote, he and his crew put "the boys in irons and slightly in the thumbscrews to urge them to a full confession." Newton gave an account, too, of one crew member who "seduced a woman slave" and "lay with her brutelike in view of the whole quarter deck." For this, Newton put the man "in irons."[4] The plundering of female slaves was a common part of slavery, constituting one of the industry's greatest attractions for ruthless men, as many descendants of such liaisons attest today.

Newton withdrew from the horrid business only gradually; his failing health was a greater cause for this, at first, than his developing convictions. As his faith matured, he decided to pursue the priesthood within the Church of England. Only when he was no longer immersed in the business could he truly see the slave trade for the evil it was. Newton was ordained in 1764, appointed priest in the parish of Olney, and became rector of St. Mary Woolnoth in London in 1780.[5]

Over the several years that followed her reading of *Cardiphonia*, More became increasingly disenchanted with the trappings of high society and turned more fully toward the Christian faith she had assumed all her life but not embraced with full intention. She couldn't stop recommending Newton's book to friends. "There is in it," she later wrote to her sister, "much of the experience of a good Christian, who feels and laments his own imperfections and weaknesses."[6] In 1787, More trekked to Newton's church, St. Mary Woolnoth, to meet the man.

With Newton as pastor, St. Mary Woolnoth had become one of only a few churches in London sympathetic to evangelical ideas.[7] More visited there on a Tuesday to hear Newton preach. The two talked together after church for about an hour. When she returned home, her "pockets were stuffed full of sermons."[8]

More's meeting with Newton marked one more significant stone on her path toward an increasingly evangelical—and personal—faith. It was Newton—his writings, his sermons, and his friendship—who convinced More to devote her life to promoting spiritual education and reformation across British society.[9] With Newton, in the words of his well-known hymn, More could say, I once "was blind, but now I see."

As a goldfish swimming in a bowl doesn't know what water is, so a person living in eighteenth-century Great Britain—immersed in an economic and social structure built on the slave trade—could not easily, if at all, see slavery for what it was. To do so required, it seemed, a certain kind of perceptiveness of mind and spirit. Hannah More was one of the few who possessed it.

The slave trade seemed so necessary to the material well-being of the nation that even those who could imagine a world without slavery could hardly envision how it might cease. After all, human slavery, in one form or another, had existed for most of human history. In Britain, the slave trade grew most dramatically during the reign of King Charles II, who had been restored to the throne in 1660.[10] Not only were British commerce and prosperity seen as dependent on the slave trade, but so, too, was the kingdom's military prowess. As an island nation, England relied on the health of the navy for its defense. Britain owned more than half of the world's slave ships.[11] The slave trade provided valuable training ground for naval forces. Abolition of the slave trade would "annihilate" an industry that put sailors and ships to work in addition to generating wealth from imports and exports, a 1791 declaration to the House of Commons asserted. A statute was therefore issued declaring that the slave trade was "very advantageous to the nation."[12] One member of the House of Commons admitted that the slave trade was not "an amiable trade, but neither was the trade of a butcher, and yet a mutton chop was, nevertheless, a very good thing."[13] To be sure, when it finally came, the abolition of the slave trade required of the empire what has been called "econocide." The direct cost of emancipation was twenty million pounds, the amount given as compensation to the masters whose slaves were freed according to the Emancipation Bill of 1833. Additional indirect costs included the higher prices paid for goods brought from the West Indies.[14]

Support for the slave trade was couched in more than economic terms, however. Some supporters of the slave trade shrewdly appropriated the appeals by the abolitionists for basic humanity and argued in return that the slaves were better off in the colonies than in their native continent. In 1791, to an abolitionist's appeal for mercy, one earl retorted, "Humanity is a private feeling, and not a public principle to act upon."[15]

Even so, the opposition to slavery began nearly as soon as the slave trade began to thrive in England. Christians were among the leading voices in that fight. The Quaker George Fox proclaimed against the institution of the slave trade in 1671, followed by the Puritan Richard Baxter in 1680. A century later, Granville Sharp, the Anglican son of an archbishop of York, spearheaded efforts to outlaw the slave trade in England.[16] In the middle of the eighteenth century, More's friend Samuel Johnson proclaimed in his *Idler* essay 87, "Of black men the numbers are too great who are now repining under English cruelty."[17] He hated the hypocrisy of American colonists who were chiming for political independence while keeping African slaves in chains: "How is it that we hear the loudest yelps for liberty among the drivers of negroes?"[18] In 1774, John Wesley proclaimed of slavery, "I deny that villainy is ever necessary," and the Methodist Conference decreed the freeing of slaves in the organization's mission outposts in 1780.[19] Even so, Wesley never expected the slave trade to be abolished by law and appealed instead to individual conscience.[20]

This period was dubbed the age of reason. In light of growing changes and developments, the slave trade appeared less and less defensible in a worldview increasingly based on rationalism and empiricism. Furthermore, an economic class between peasant and aristocrat was growing, filling in the gap between high and low. Competing interests—economic, judicial, social, and political— brought new complexities to an issue that had once been determined simply by might and money. Travel, literacy, and communication were making the horrors of human slavery more widely known.

For example, even though only healthy Africans were taken from their native lands, the mortality rate of slaves through the Middle Passage and upon reaching land was about 50 percent.[21] Then came the *Zong* massacre of 1781. One hundred thirty-two African slaves were thrown overboard by the crew of the English slave ship *Zong* in hopes of collecting the funds from the insurance policy that had been taken out on the human cargo. The ensuing legal case was decided based on issues of property, profit, and loss—not humanity or morality. The killing of slaves was ruled to be permissible and the insurers liable for payment for loss. That ruling, issued in 1783, birthed the movement against the slave trade that had been slowly germinating.

The radical abolitionist Granville Sharp tried to have the ship's crew prosecuted for murder but failed. Yet success of another kind was won as more mainstream voices were ready to join the cause. Bishop Porteus, Hannah More's good friend, delivered a sermon against the slave trade in London.[22] James Stephen, a lawyer and great-grandfather of Virginia Woolf, came to despise the slave trade after witnessing an African slave being burned alive; the man had been convicted at a kangaroo court in Barbados.[23] In 1785, Zachary Macaulay wrote home from the West Indies where he was overseer of a Jamaican estate, troubled at how "callous and indifferent" he had become to the suffering of the "cursing and bawling" slaves and "the noise of the whip resounding on their shoulders" as they were beaten mercilessly by their masters.[24] Macaulay's journal revealed the special kinds of horrors of the journey on a slave trip. The ship captain who applied the cat-o'-nine-tails to any slave who refused to dance on command praised Macaulay for refraining from the common practice of cursing.[25] Macaulay's journal entry on May 29, 1795, recorded his troubled reflections on how much more dire the experiences of the slaves were compared to his own on that wretched vehicle:

> ... what must theirs have been whom I saw around me, extended naked on the bare boards; unable when asked to reveal the cause of their complaints; ignorant of the fate which awaited them; filled with fears either of a horrid death or a cruel servitude; and without the distant prospect of ever beholding the face of one of those friends or relatives from whom they had been forcibly torn. Their cup is full of pure, unmingled sorrow, the bitterness of which is unalloyed by almost a single ray of hope.[26]

By 1789, he could take it no longer and abandoned the slave plantations. He returned to England where he joined the evangelical abolitionists.[27]

Of course, if there is one name usually associated with the abolition of the British slave trade, it is William Wilberforce, the member of Parliament who spearheaded the legal effort against slavery and became one of Hannah More's dearest friends.

In 1780, the young man from Hull won his first parliamentary seat at the age of twenty-one. In 1784, William Wilberforce went on to win the representation of one of England's most prestigious seats, the county of Yorkshire. Wilberforce was small in stature and, even more than Hannah, delicate in health. He was gifted with eloquence in speech and a beautiful singing voice for which he was widely known. The description of Wilberforce's eloquence given by James Boswell is famous: "I saw what seemed a mere shrimp mount upon the table; but, as I listened, he grew and grew until the shrimp became a whale."[28]

Wilberforce's journey of faith was, like Newton's, one of fits and starts. After the death of his father when Wilberforce was a boy, he was sent to live with an aunt and uncle whose strong Christian faith and solid teaching greatly influenced him. But as many young men find, young adulthood, university, and independence had a way of turning religious commitment sour. Following his 1784 campaign victory, Wilberforce went on holiday with a friend who was a tutor at Cambridge and a devout Christian. As they journeyed, the two talked of genuine religion. At some point, they picked up a copy of Philip Doddridge's classic work *The Rise and Progress of Religion in the Soul*. Doddridge was a Dissenting minister and hymnist of the early eighteenth century whose informed and intellectual approach to genuine personal faith influenced many for ages to come. Wilberforce was one of them. Before taking that holiday, Wilberforce had all but abandoned the Christian faith of his upbringing.[29] After returning home—having held countless spiritual conversations with his former tutor and having read Doddridge's book—he labored under months of spiritual conviction as he struggled to alleviate his guilt over his youthful excesses and the abandonment of the faith with which he had been raised.

Finally, in 1785, the year after Samuel Johnson's death, and the same year that More moved to her country retreat at Cowslip Green, a downtrodden Wilberforce sought out Newton at St. Mary

Woolnoth. His journal entries showed he had agonized for days before sending a note to Newton requesting a secret meeting. He knew his fame as a parliamentarian would make him all too recognizable, and a meeting with a serious and devout evangelical Christian like Newton would bring controversy. Besides, Wilberforce was still wavering about entering into a true faith commitment. Wilberforce paced about the square outside the church before going in. At last the legendary meeting took place. The old slave trader's counsel to the young politician yielded a crucial swerve in history.

Wilberforce mistakenly thought that religious commitment and worldly affairs could not go well together. He thought that being a sincere Christian required withdrawing from the corrupt corners of human business. Had he gone elsewhere for guidance, had he fallen, for example, under the sway of John Wesley, one nineteenth-century biographer speculated, Wilberforce likely would have followed his inclination to retreat from public life in favor of a course devoted to private piety.[30] But he sought the counsel of Newton. Newton exhorted him to "stay at his post, and neither give up work, nor throw away wealth; wait and watch occasions, sure that He, who put him at his post, would find him work to do."[31] Newton convinced Wilberforce that he need not relinquish his place in government in order to serve God but could do so right where he was if only he set his mind on a worthy goal. From this advice came the course of life that Wilberforce set before himself. On April 14, 1786, Good Friday, Wilberforce attended church and took Communion for the first time.[32] Neither the church nor England would be the same.

Wilberforce was among the first from England's social and political elite to experience conversion through the influence of the evangelical movement. For this reason, he has been identified as "an outstanding instance of the character transformation which the Evangelical Revival wrought on a grand scale."[33] Soon Wilberforce was attending the church of Thomas Scott, a well-known Bible commentator and preacher. He brought with him to church his old friend and cousin Henry Thornton, who would join Wilberforce in efforts for years to come.[34]

Wilberforce had been troubled by the slave trade since he was a youth. At the age of fourteen, he wrote a letter to a local newspaper that criticized the "odious traffic in human flesh."[35] At last he had power and support to attend that conviction.

Wilberforce, as a member of Parliament, knew from the start that his decision to oppose the slave trade would be public and political. More's views developed first in the private sphere. Several years before Wilberforce put his vision for public policy in writing, Hannah More was making her antislavery views known, quietly at first. In 1776, she befriended Charles Middleton, a former naval captain who would help lead the abolitionist movement.[36] By 1782, she referred in a letter to the slave trade as an "old quarrel" between herself and her friend Lord Monboddo. An "extravagant adorer of the ancients," Monboddo embraced the justification of the slave trade offered by the classical world. More protested, demanding to know "how he could vindicate such an enormity." In response to the peer's retort that if slavery was good enough for Plutarch it was good enough for him, More remarked tartly to her sister that "rather than sacrifice his favourite opinion, that men were born with tails, he [Monboddo] would be contented to wear one himself."[37] In another letter home in 1782, More relayed a disturbing tale she'd heard from a ship captain at a breakfast hosted by Middleton. "One day," More reported to her sister, the captain

went out of his own ship to dine on board another; while he was there a storm arose, which in a short time made an entire wreck of his own ship, to which it was impossible for him to return. He had left on board two little boys, one four, the other five years old, under the care of a poor black servant; the people struggled to get out of the sinking ship into a large boat, and the poor black took his two little children, tied them into a bag, and put in a little pot of sweetmeats for them, slung them across his shoulder, and put them into the boat; the boat by this time was quite full; the black was stepping into it himself, but was told by the master there was no room for him, that either he or the children must perish, for the weight of both would sink the boat. The exalted heroic negro did not hesitate a moment; "Very well," said he, "give my duty to my master, and tell him I beg pardon for all my faults." And then,—guess the rest—plunged to the bottom never to rise again, till the sea shall give up her dead.[38]

More afterward told the story to Lord Monboddo, and he "fairly burst into tears." He seemed at last to see that the slavery he supported in the abstract as a classical ideal was far, far removed from the modern reality. More was deeply moved by the story too. She was asked to write an elegy from the event, but she told her sister, "It is above poetry."[39]

In the fall of 1787, More met Wilberforce in Bath.[40] Shortly afterward, she gushed, "That young man's character is one of the most extra-ordinary I have ever known for talent, virtue, and piety. It is difficult not to grow better and wiser every time one converses with him."[41] Although More was fourteen years his senior, her bright eyes and flirtatious demeanor likely helped form a magnetic, if platonic, pull between the two that lasted the rest of their lives. Along with their passionate Christian convictions, they shared a wittiness rare among the faithful. More said glowingly of Wilberforce that he had "as much wit as if he had no piety."[42] They were of such like minds that when More's *Thoughts on the Importance of the Manners of the Great to General Society* was published anonymously, many first attributed its authorship to Wilberforce.[43] More was Wilberforce's link to the world of letters.[44] His influence dissuaded her from following her growing inclination to shrink from the world. More's relationship with Wilberforce would prove to be—apart from those with her sisters—one of the longest lasting and dearest of her life. Their friendship lasted uninterrupted for forty-seven years. They died within weeks of each other, one before seeing the slaves set free, the other departing only weeks after the long-fought victory.

And a long-fought battle it was.

CHAPTER 9

THE LABOR FOR LIBERTY

THE WAR ROOM IN THOSE EARLY YEARS OF THE ABOLITIONIST movement was the Teston home of Sir Charles and Margaret Middleton, whom More had met in 1776. After the death of More's mother in 1786, Margaret Middleton became a mother figure to More.[1] Lady Middleton was one of the first women to take a public role in the movement against slavery.[2] Their dinner party discussions on the topic of slavery have been credited with helping bring about its abolition.[3] At the Middletons' lively and well-attended table, More's instinctive recoil from the slave trade developed into robust conviction.

The Middletons had been influenced in their abolitionist views by their parish's clergyman, Rev. James Ramsay. Ramsay had served as a ship's surgeon under the command of Captain Middleton in the West Indies. While at sea, Ramsay had the opportunity to board a slave ship and saw firsthand the inhumane and cruel conditions of an industry far from the eyes of most British citizens. He left the naval service and took holy orders, choosing to spend the first years of his ministry among the slaves in the Caribbean where he was rector for twenty-seven years.[4] He eventually accepted the appointment in Kent where he wrote about the horrors of slavery, informing many of his country people—the vast majority of them blissfully unaware—about the evils of the business.

The inhumanity of the slave trade was so systemic that its African captives, while subjected to the worst cruelty, were not its sole victims. The industry was steeped in brutality at every level of execution. Slave ship captains were cruel to the sailors; many of these—as in John Newton's case—were taken into service by force and beaten, abused, abandoned, and sometimes sold into slavery. Thousands of British sailors died or were deserted in slave colonies each year. This pervasive cruelty of the entire slave industry helps explain why its inhumanity was so difficult for those living amid it to see it for what it was.

But out of such moral nearsightedness emerged some visionaries. One, Thomas Clarkson, won an essay contest on the topic of slavery while a student at Cambridge in 1785. After winning, Clarkson was convicted to take action on the principles espoused in his essay. He translated it from the Latin in which he'd originally written—customary in universities at the time—and had it published in 1786 as a pamphlet, *An essay on the slavery and commerce of the human species, particularly the African, translated from a Latin Dissertation*. Then Clarkson helped found the Committee for the Abolition of the Slave Trade, begun in 1787.[5]

Meanwhile, surrounded by so great a cloud of witnesses, the Middletons rallied their friends and resources around an extensive political, legal, moral, and social campaign against slavery. They formed the hub of an abolitionist group, dubbed the Testonites, after their meeting place in Teston. The group's passion to abolish the slave trade, fueled by long dinner conversations at the home of the Middletons, grew. Their search for a sympathetic voice in Parliament to lead the campaign to outlaw the slave trade led directly to Wilberforce.[6] In 1786, the Middletons met with Wilberforce and persuaded him that it was time to act. Wilberforce sought the blessings of the prime minister and his good friend William Pitt. Once he received them, Wilberforce was resolved. On Sunday, October 28, 1787, Wilberforce wrote in his journal these famous words: "God Almighty has set before me two great objects, the suppression of the slave trade and the reformation of manners."[7]

In Wilberforce, More found a counterpart. It was as if all she had done and accomplished so far in her life had been merely practice for this historic mission. She wrote home to her sister that she had been called one afternoon by Lady Middleton to come at once and dine with Wilberforce at her house. There she and Wilberforce "had four or five hours of most confidential and instructive conversation, in which we discussed all the great objects of reform."[8]

When More's good friend Beilby Porteus was made bishop of London in 1787, she couldn't contain her excitement. She was thankful to see such a godly leader so strategically placed in "a station in which his hands will be so much strengthened, and his power of doing good so widely extended," she wrote to her bluestocking friend Elizabeth Carter. But even more, it was a coup for the antislavery cause. "I rejoice for many reasons, but for none more than that his ecclesiastical jurisdiction, extending to the West Indies, will make him of infinite usefulness in the great object I have so much at heart,—the project to abolish the slave-trade in Africa."[9]

The More sisters hosted informal meetings of the abolitionists in their Park Street residence in Bristol and received African guests from Sierra Leone at the school, along with sundry curiosities carried in from that land such as insects, cloth, precious metals, and a parrot.[10] "This most important cause has very much occupied my thoughts this summer," she wrote to Carter. Wilberforce, she explained, "who has embarked in it with the zeal of an apostle has been much with me, and engaged all my little interest, and all my affections in it." The matter was to be brought before Parliament in the spring, and she added optimistically, "Above one hundred members have promised their votes." She urged her friend to petition all the people she could for the cause. "It is a subject too ample for a letter, and I shall have a great deal to say to you on it when we meet. To my feelings, it is the most interesting subject which was ever discussed in the annals of humanity."[11]

More soon became known for her passionate campaigning. Friends admired her increasingly for her efforts. "I always rejoice in reflecting on the good you are doing to others," Elizabeth Carter wrote her in 1789. "Most sincerely do I wish and pray for success to your present most benevolent scheme of humanizing and Christianizing those poor savages of whom you give so affecting a description. You know the world too well to expect to do all the good you wish, but you will certainly do some, perhaps a great deal."[12] Carter then offered financial support to the effort, admitting, "Giving money is a very inconsiderable part of such a charity, but my wretched inactivity seldom allows me to do anything more, and therefore I always feel it a duty to do in this instance what I can."[13]

In 1789, More wrote again from London about the group's frenetic efforts toward abolition: "Mr. Wilberforce and the whole junto of abolitionists are still locked up at Teston; they are up *slaving* till two o'clock every morning." They "walked out but once in the three weeks they had been there." Their efforts resulted in evidence to be brought to council, the printed copy of which, More wrote, "was the thickest folio I ever saw." The House of Commons might need to suspend proceedings for a week just to read it, she added dolefully.[14]

Like the other abolitionists, she was naively optimistic that victory was at hand: "I have invited myself to Mrs. Montagu's May-day saturnalia next year," she wrote, but added, "unless I should be engaged by that time to dine with a party of free *negroes*."[15] In one letter to her sister, she apologized excitedly for not writing sooner:

> I did fully intend writing a line on Wednesday, to have told you of the glorious and most promising opening of the great cause of the abolition in the House of Commons, but I could not find one moment's leisure, we had so much meeting, writing, and congratulation. The Bishop of London fully intended to be the first to apprize me of this most interesting intelligence, and accordingly got up so early as to write me a note at seven in the morning; but Lady Middleton forestalled him by writing on Monday at midnight. Pitt and Fox united can do much; "the Douglas and the Percy both together are confident against a world in arms."[16]

The allusion to Shakespeare's *Henry IV, Part I* illustrates how More and her cobelligerents—her partners in this great war—were sustained in their long efforts not only by religious faith but also by the vitality of a moral imagination. In commenting on the power of poetry, Percy Bysshe Shelley wrote in 1821, more than a decade before the abolition of slavery in Great Britain, "The great secret of morals is love; or a going out of our nature. . . . A man, to be greatly good, must imagine intensely and comprehensively; he must put himself in the place of another and of many others; the pains and pleasures of his species must become his own. The great instrument of moral good is the imagination."[17]

It is clear from their letters and journals that these passionate abolitionists had no inkling of the decades-long battle they would face in freeing the slaves. Wilberforce's naive optimism is seen in his early declaration that "there is no doubt of the success."[18] A letter John Newton wrote to More in 1787 betrayed in hindsight his undue optimism. "I think this infamous traffic cannot last long; at least that is my hope," he stated. But Newton's reputation for wisdom and gravity was based in truth, and he went on to issue a dire warning that once the investigation of the slave trade they were calling for was complete, "should it still be persevered in, I think it will constitute a national sin, and of a very deep die." He added forebodingly, "I should tremble for the consequences; for, whatever politicians may think, I assuredly know there is a righteous judge who governs the earth. He calls upon us to redress the injured, and should we perversely refuse, I cannot doubt but he will plead his cause himself."[19]

The evil of the slave trade may have been hard to see at first, Newton conceded. But the abolitionists' efforts would leave the nation without excuse. More firmly believed, however, that people "must never proportion our exertions to our success, but to our duty."[20]

More described the increasing intensity of the struggle in a letter to Horace Walpole, written a few months later in April 1789. "I do, indeed, feel most anxiously, now the moment of deciding the fate of Africa is at hand!" she wrote. She continued, "I was delighted the other day with a new pamphlet on the subject, in which the author applies Dante's inscription over the Inferno to a slave ship."[21] That poignant inscription, written in Latin, is rendered in English:

> *Through me you go to the grief-wracked city;*
> *Through me you go to everlasting pain;*
> *Through me you go and pass among lost souls.*

The abolitionists toiled still, gathering evidence and testimonies they hoped would sway the politicians' and the people's minds, and presenting their arguments and appeals in countless committee meetings and hearings. Fellow abolitionist Zachary Macaulay kept More informed on Wilberforce's progress in parliamentary procedures—women being excluded from these—and sought her advice on the political aspects of the drawn-out campaign.[22] In 1790, More wrote to her sister that she had obtained a copy of one testimony that was to appear before a committee of the House of Commons. The witness was taken to a small gathering of slave traders about to put an infant to death:

> I asked them why they murdered it? They answered, because it was of no value. I told them that in that case I hoped they would make me a present of it; they answered, that if I had any use for the child, then it was worth money. I first offered them some knives, but that would not do; they however sold the child to me for a mug of brandy. It proved to be the child of a woman whom the captain of our ship had purchased that very morning. We carried it on board, and judge of the mother's joy when she saw her own child put on board the same ship; her child, whom she concluded was murdered. She fell on her knees and kissed my feet.

"In what light does this anecdote place this detestable trade!" More concluded in her letter.[23]

One day, Lady Middleton came to call upon More "as soon as she heard" that More had arrived back in London. More hurried over to the Middletons' home and found all in excitement because Wilberforce had announced to the House that he would soon present a bill for the abolition of the slave trade. She spent the next day with the Middletons, a day "given up entirely to negro business, and all other company was excluded." She added, "I enclose Mr. Ramsay's pointed and most sensible pamphlet, and let all the flesh and blood merchants in the world answer it if they can."[24]

More became known for carrying Ramsay's pamphlets around and showing them to everyone she could. With the most horrific parts of the slave trade occurring far from the British Isles, most British citizens had little idea what it entailed. It was easy to imagine modern slavery as something similar to what existed in ancient Greek and Roman culture: a lifelong, humane servitude into which one was born, not violently stolen into, the kind of slavery—the bond servanthood—the Bible talked about. Some people used biblical passages to justify slavery, not understanding that the role of a bond servant described in the Bible, again, was nothing like the violent, forceful bondage of the modern slave trade. James Ramsay's pamphlet *Objections to the abolition of the slave trade, with answers* addressed this very argument. The objection to abolition was given, then refuted by Ramsay:

> *Objection.* Slavery is not unlawful; the bible allows of it.
>
> *Ramsay's answer.* The use of money is not unlawful. But it is unlawful to rob on the highway to procure it. . . . We say men ought not to go to the coast of Africa to kidnap the natives, or to encourage them to kidnap each other; or to bribe them with baubles to go to war, to fight with and enslave each other; to turn every trespass into a cause for enslaving; to subject the unfortunate wretches to the miseries of a West-Indian voyage; to sell them to be half-starved, hard worked, and ill treated. Show us slavery without these attendants, and we shall have little to object against it.[25]

Ramsay's pamphlet wasn't the only arrow in More's antislavery arsenal. In addition to carrying copies of this, she sold prints of an oil painting of an African boy by her friend Mrs. Bouverie.[26] She acted as a liaison for the abolitionist Thomas Clarkson, keeping her London friends informed of Clarkson's research in Bristol's slave-ship ports. She kept a copy of the famous drawing of the slave ship *Brookes*, which had resulted from long, painstaking research by Clarkson, and was in the habit of showing the drawing to guests at social gatherings.[27] The print depicted the appalling manner in which the human cargo in a slave ship was transported: human bodies were packed side by side around the perimeter of the deck and across every inch of the lower hold, jammed tightly enough to hold nearly five hundred human souls. The visual impact of the diagram made it one of the most famous and effective tools of the abolitionist movement. The social conscience had drawn a veil over the horrific business of trade in human flesh. The veil had to be lifted.

Such tactics were politically and socially risky. At one gathering, More quailed: "I was in a large party one evening, showing a section of the African ship in which the transportation of the negroes is so well represented, to Mr. Walpole, &c, when, who should be announced but Mr. Tarleton, the Liverpool delegate, who is come up to defend slavery against humanity. I popped the book out of sight, snapped the string of my eloquence, and was mute at once."[28]

The man who silenced her, General Banastre Tarleton, had made his name as a triumphant and brutal British commander in the American Revolutionary War. After returning home and eventually becoming a member of Parliament for Liverpool, a chief slave-trading city in England, Tarleton earned another reputation as a fierce defender of the slave trade and a ruthless mocker of the abolitionists. Furthermore, he was a longtime lover of a former student at the More sisters' school, the famous actress Mary Robinson.[29] Even the usually bold Hannah was cowed by the notorious man.

More also led a boycott of West Indian sugar—no small gesture in a tea-drinking nation. Those who supported the boycott were ridiculed as "anti-saccharites," criticized as hypocrites, and mocked for their "sanctimonious asceticism."[30] One satirical letter published in both the London and the Bristol press portrayed a young boy questioning how eating sugar was any less "eating Negro flesh," as the boycotters claimed, than putting a fork or spoon made of gold or silver was "putting a dead negro's finger or toe" in one's mouth.[31] A satiric piece, this one a poem in support of the boycott, was published anonymously in a Bristol newspaper in 1792 and is believed to be the work of More's pen:[32]

> I own I am shocked at this purchase of slaves,
> And fear those who buy them and sell them are knaves:
> What I hear of their hardships, their tortures and groans,
> Is almost enough to draw pity from stones.
> I pity them greatly, but I must be mum,
> For how could we do without sugar and rum?
> Especially sugar, so needful we see,
> What, give up our desserts, our coffee and tea?[33]

More's "anti-saccharine" effort had been going on since at least 1788, well ahead of a larger abstention campaign begun in 1791 and spearheaded by the Baptist abolitionist William Fox.[34] Even in her old age, More served only East Indian sugar in her home because it had "no blood on it."[35]

She urged that the Irish playwright Thomas Southerne's adaptation of Aphra Behn's fictional account *Oroonoko, or the Royal*

Slave be produced at Drury Lane. Although a complex work befitting the ambiguity of the slave trade during the time, *Oroonoko* portrayed the slave of the title as a heroic and sympathetic character. "So many go to a play who will never go to church," More said, recommending further that her friend Sheridan write an "affecting" prologue that would rouse antislavery sentiments even more.[36]

More made her own contribution to the literary arm of the abolitionist movement. She produced the poem "Slavery" in 1788, timed to appear just before Wilberforce was to present a resolution at Parliament to consider limits on the number of slaves that could be put on a ship.

"Slavery" was just one entry in an all-out arts abolitionist campaign. Its release coincided with the publication of John Newton's *Thoughts upon the African Slave Trade,* a pamphlet describing the ghastly treatment of slaves from one who knew well. Newton called the pamphlet "a confession, which . . . comes too late."[37] Around the same time, Newton's collaborator on his famous *Olney Hymns,* William Cowper, wrote his poem "The Negro's Complaint." Cowper was one of the most-read poets of the day. Introspective and prone to bouts of depression, he wrote poetry that anticipated the coming romantic age: intense in emotion, vivid in imagery, and humane in temper. More was said to "owe much" to his work.[38] She said of Cowper, "I have found what I have been looking for all my life, a poet I can read on Sunday," when writing to her friend Bouverie.[39]

Cowper was a more literary writer than More. His works had an even greater appeal to the fashionable than hers did. In keeping with the smart strategies to win public opinion adopted by the abolitionists, "The Negro's Complaint" was written to the tune of a popular ballad sung by the lower classes. It was printed on high-quality paper, as well, in order to appeal to upper-class buyers. The poem's simple meter and diction created an easily sung tune. It illustrated the violence and injustice of slavery along with the innocence and virtue of the slave. The year before, the Nonconformist Christian Josiah Wedgwood manufactured the famous jasper medallion topped with a relief of a kneeling slave in chains and emblazoned above him the phrase "Am I not a man and a brother?" The medallion was based on the design of the seal of the Committee for the Abolition of the Slave Trade, founded by Thomas Clarkson earlier that year. The image was imprinted across the empire and could be found on plates, tea caddies, hairpins, bracelets, and snuffboxes. Wedgwood even sent one to Benjamin Franklin in America.[40]

It was a multifaceted campaign that enlisted preachers, poets, and parliamentarians. And it was a brilliant strategy. "You know enough of life," Wilberforce told More, "to be aware that in parliamentary measures of importance, more is to be done out of the House than in it."[41] In other words, changing the minds in Parliament would require changing the heart of the nation first. It was the same idea as that famously expressed in the following century by the romantic poet Percy Bysshe Shelley. "Poets are the unacknowledged legislators of the world," he wrote in *A Defence of Poetry*.[42] The battle against slavery was, in many ways, led by the poets—and other writers and artists—who expanded their country's moral imagination so it might at last see horrors too grave for the rational mind to grasp.

"Slavery" was written in a hurry—even by the standard of More's usual quickness. But it was a crucial moment politically for the cause of abolition. More told her sister, "The slave cause gains proselytes, and of course opposers, every day." She continued, "My little poem on Slavery is too short, and too much hurried; it of course will be very imperfect; for I did not begin it till a fortnight ago. I would on no account bring out so slight and so hasty a thing on any less pressing occasion, but here time is every thing."[43] Yes, time was everything, and it was time for the curtain over slavery to be drawn back.

The poem began with a theological examination of liberty, casting it as a source of heavenly light, one to which Britain had no greater right than Africa. Moving from abstract theological and political ideals to the concrete reality of slavery, the poem slowly built to a passionate pitch:

> Whene'er to Afric's shores I turn my eyes,
> Horrors of deepest, deadliest guilt arise;
> I see, by more than Fancy's mirror shown,
> The burning village, and the blazing town:
> See the dire victim torn from social life,
> The shrieking babe, the agonizing wife!
> She, wretch forlorn! is dragged by hostile hands,
> To distant tyrants sold, in distant lands:
> Transmitted miseries, and successive chains,
> The sole sad heritage her child obtains.
> E'en this last wretched boon their foes deny,
> To weep together, or together die.
> By felon hands, by one relentless stroke,
> See the fond links of Nature broke!
> The fibres twisting round a parent's heart,
> Torn from their grasp, and bleeding as they part.

The slaves' suffering, painted so vividly in these lines, was at once the proof of their humanity and an indictment of the slave trade. The poem demanded empathy from the reader. More exhorted the traders to own how much worse than their own sufferings those of the slaves must be:

> *Hold, murderers! hold! nor aggravate distress;*
> *Respect the passions you yourself possess:*
> *Ev'n you, of ruffian heart, and ruthless hand,*
> *Love your own offspring, love your native land;*
> *Ev'n you, with fond impatient feelings burn,*
> *Though free as air, though certain of return. . . .*
> *Think on the wretch whose aggravated pains*
> *To exile misery adds, to misery chains.*

Finally, the verses linked the love of God and Britain to the cause of universal liberty and closed with an address to God:

> *And Thou! great source of Nature and of Grace,*
> *Who of one blood didst form the human race,*
> *Look down in mercy in thy chosen time,*
> *With equal eye on Afric's suffering clime:*
> *Disperse her shades of intellectual night,*
> *Repeat thy high behest—Let there be light!*
> *Bring each benighted soul, great God, to Thee,*
> *And with thy wide salvation make them free!*[44]

Despite More's doubts, the poem was enthusiastically received. Dr. Horne wrote to her from Magdalen College to thank her for her "excellent and well-timed poem on *Slavery.*" He described how troubled his wife was becoming over "this business of the slave-trade." Yet her response reflected the difficulty of so many in facing the horrors of slavery. Horne told More his wife had questioned a friend who was a native of the West Indies "with the hope that matters might not be quite so bad as they had been represented," returned "much comforted," and then "in the afternoon put into her tea the usual quantity of sugar." Horne continued, "I have not yet ventured to read your poem to her, because, as she knows *you* never say the thing that is not, I am afraid it will be the occasion of withdrawing one lump, and diminishing the other."[45] William Cowper said that he "admired" the poem "as I do all that Miss More writes, for energy of expression as for the tendency of the design."[46] He thought the poem so good that he dropped plans of his own to write one for the cause.[47] The poem's influence lasted into the next century, when it was credited with inspiring missionaries, including the famous David Livingstone, to take Christianity to Africa.[48]

Meanwhile, Wilberforce's planned appeal to Parliament in 1788 was postponed because of one of his frequent illnesses. However, the speech he delivered in 1789 became known as "one of the finest in the golden age of parliamentary oratory."[49] A contemporary described Wilberforce's power of speech as "so distinct and melodious, that the most hostile ear hangs on them delighted."[50] For the next few years, the abolitionists succeeded in building social and political pressure against the slave trade until the French Revolution turned nearly all the nation's attention away from slavery question.

More did her part by continuing to wage war with her pen. In addition to "Slavery," several titles from her later series of Cheap Repository Tracts, written for the laboring classes, addressed slavery: "Babay, A True Story of a Good Negro Woman" (1795), "True Stories of Two Good Negroes," and "The Black Prince, a True Story, being the Account of the Life and Death of Naimbanna, an African King's Son" (1798). Another, "The Sorrows of Yamba; or, the Negro Woman's Lamentation" (1797), was likely an expanded version of a shorter poem that had been circulated and set to the tune of a popular ballad. The poem's story was narrated by an African mother seized from her family and home with one baby at her breast and two others "sleeping by." It continued:

Then for love of filthy Gold,
  Strait they bore me to the sea;
Cramm'd me down a Slave Ship's hold,
  Where were Hundreds stow'd like me.
Naked on the Platform lying,
  Now we cross the tumbling wave;
Shrieking, sickening, fainting, dying,
  Deed of shame for Britons brave.

The African mother-turned-slave went on to describe the suffering and degradation they experienced on the ship, until finally:

I in groaning passed the night,
  And did roll my aching head;
At the break of morning light,
  My poor Child was cold and dead.

The mournful mother found solace in the fact that her child's suffering had ended. She was sold to a cruel master who worked her nearly to death. She managed to escape to the sea where she contemplated suicide, but there encountered an "English Missionary Good," who shared the gospel with her. Yamba put her trust in the Lord and was baptized. She was near death, however, and her heart was still filled with love for Africa. As the poem moved toward its conclusion, Yamba exclaimed:

Cease, ye British Sons of murder!
  Cease from forging Afric's Chain;
Mock your Saviour's name no further,
  Cease your savage lust of gain. . . .

Where ye gave to war it's birth,
  Where your traders fix'd their den,
There go publish "Peace on Earth,"
  Go proclaim "good-will to men."
Where ye once have carried slaughter,
  Vice, and Slavery, and Sin;
Seiz'd on Husband, Wife, and Daughter,
  Let the Gospel enter in.[51]

Some years later, in 1819, More published another antislavery poem, "The Feast of Freedom," written at the request of Sir Alexander Johnstone, chief justice of Ceylon. He had several of her works translated into the native languages where he served and was instrumental in abolishing slavery on the island. The justice requested that More write a ballad to mark the anniversary of the occasion, and this poem was the result. It was translated into the native language and was so well received that Johnstone later wrote to More, "What a pleasure must it afford you, my dear Madam to have the power of producing such moral improvement by your writings, not only throughout Europe, but throughout Asia also! For I am convinced that your writings have had a greater effect, and have been more generally read, than any other works which have been written for the last hundred years."[52]

More's abolitionist efforts over the decades were said to constitute "one of the earliest propaganda campaigns for social reform in English history."[53] Indeed, it could be said that More was the mastermind behind some of the abolitionist movement's most effective campaigns to sway public opinion. Imaginative literature, such as More's antislavery writings, and other arts were essential to the abolitionist movement because, as has been noted, the slave trade was so hidden from the eyes of the people. Even most of the abolitionists had not witnessed firsthand the worst horrors of the trade. While "intense religiosity was at the heart of the abolitionist movement," its primary means were rational.[54] But moral imagination filled in where rationalism stopped short. As the historian James Anthony Froude observed in the following century, "Morality, when vigorously alive, sees farther than intellect."[55]

So More lamented in a letter to Walpole in 1788, "Slavery is vindicated in print, and defended in the House of Peers! Poor human reason, when wilt thou come to years of discretion?"[56] Rather than put his hopes in human progress, Walpole preferred to put his hopes in technological advancements. Like some others, he thought that the rise of machine labor would bring an end to the slave question apart from legislative remedy. Such hopes also provided a convenient excuse to abstain from the debate. But More refused to place the fate of slaves in such hopes and chided her friend Walpole for doing so: "Your project for relieving our poor slaves by machine work is so far from wild or chimerical, that of three persons deep and able in the concern (Mr. Wilberforce among others) not one but has thought it rational and practicable; and that a plough may be so constructed as to save much misery." Then she added with deadpan irony, "But I forget that negroes are not human, nor our fellow-creatures." Even so, she argued, "allowing the popular position that they are *not*, still a feeling master would be glad to save his ox or his ass superfluous labour and unnecessary fatigue."[57]

The Industrial Revolution was not the only revolution diverting attention from the antislavery cause. The French Revolution turned the nation's attention even more. To oppose the British slave industry in such nationally precarious times was seen as unpatriotic; one who supported the weakening of the country by supporting abolition was suspected of likely supporting the French

Revolution too. King George III's opposition to abolitionism grew out of concerns related to the French Revolution, and many of his subjects followed suit.

In 1789, the year the French Revolution began, More and her sister Patty opened a Sunday school in Cheddar, the start of another intense campaign for domestic reform. Within a few years, she began writing tracts for the poor and then treatises for the upper class. Although More and Wilberforce are credited with keeping the abolitionist movement alive after many had given up, she did not limit her efforts at reform to just one cause.[58]

Yet even when she was immersed in other intense labors, the cause of slavery was never far from her mind and heart. In a letter More received from Walpole on August 21, 1792, he described the butchering and beheading of the French queen's staff while the royal family was held as prisoners in the palace. One witness said that "he found the queen sitting on the floor, trembling like an aspen in every limb, and her sweet boy the dauphin asleep against her knee!" But, Walpole continued in his letter, "why do I wound your thrilling nerves with the relation of such horrible scenes? Your *blackmanity* [by which he meant her actions on behalf of the African slaves] must allot some of its tears to these poor victims."[59] A letter she sent home from London in 1794 gave thanks for a victory by Wilberforce with "one clause of the slave bill." Then she added, "Lord! hasten the time when true liberty, light, and knowledge shall be diffused over the whole earth."[60] Many years later, in 1822, she remarked, "When I turn my thoughts upon the world, there are but three things there which deeply interest me—the state of the church—the religious progress of the king—and the abolition of slavery."[61] As she approached her last years, she expressed her greatest wishes: "I think that if I could see the abolition of the slavery of the body in the West Indies, and of the slavery of the soul in Ireland and Popish Europe, I could sing my *nunc dimittis* [the final song of the liturgy] with joy. If they carry their cause in Parliament, we must pray that God may produce good out of this great evil."[62]

John Wesley had warned Wilberforce of the magnitude of the fight against "that execrable villainy, which is the scandal of religion, of England, and of human nature." Wesley told him, "Unless God has raised you up for this very thing, you will be worn out by the opposition of men and devils. But if God be for you, who can be against you?"[63] Wilberforce did face physical assault—twice— as well as ostracism and hatred.[64] It would be more than a dozen years before the British slave trade was abolished in 1807, just a few months before the death of John Newton. Hannah's health was too frail for her to participate directly in the debate or celebration of a hard-won victory. But her wise words had been vindicated: "It should be held as an eternal truth, that what is morally wrong can never be politically right."[65] It would be decades before those in British chains would be set free in 1833.

On July 26, 1833, the Emancipation Bill passed in the House of Commons, decreeing that all slaves in the British Empire were to be freed within one year. Wilberforce died three days later. He was buried in Westminster Abbey near his friend William Pitt. One month later, the House of Lords passed the Slavery Abolition Act. More would die on September 6, two months after Wilberforce's death. For many years, the Church Missionary Society had a policy of naming orphaned African girls after More in honor of her work to abolish slavery.[66]

More was the single most influential woman in the British abolitionist movement. Of course, women's roles were severely limited. They couldn't vote, let alone hold political position. Nor were they granted official membership in the Society for Effecting the Abolition of the African Slave Trade. Even Wilberforce surprisingly, given how closely he worked with Hannah, cautioned against too public a role for women in the abolitionist cause. In a debate with fellow abolitionists over the idea of women forming female abolitionist societies, he argued, "For ladies to meet, to publish, to go from house to house stirring up petitions, these appear to me proceedings unsuited to the female character as delineated in Scripture. I fear its tendency would be to mix them in all the multiform warfare of political life."[67] Such severe limitations make More's contributions to the movement even more remarkable.

History tends to favor the singular public, political acts of those in power, leaving those within the quieter groundswells to obscurity. Although often unrecognized now, through their support of abolition societies, their campaigning in public and private against slavery, their boycotts of products produced by slave labor, and their voluminous writings, More and other women writers were crucial participants in the abolitionist movement that began in the 1780s.[68] In emphasizing the role of women as the keepers of morality and religion, the evangelical movement increased the authority of women to speak on slavery as a moral and religious concern.[69] Along with the evangelical movement, More played a central role in fostering the idea that women were particularly suited to produce antislavery literature that would reach into the hearts of readers where rational arguments failed. By helping to embody the abstract idea of slavery, such imaginative literature was credited with making a significant impact during the first years of the fight against the trade, particularly between 1787 and 1792 when the abolitionist movement was the most popular.[70]

Wilberforce put his hopes in Parliament and politics; he distrusted "agitation" of the masses and was doubtful of boycotts and dismissive of popular sentiments.[71] Later, in 1817, he looked back on this stance and offered a remarkable admission of error: "I really look up to God with renewed thankfulness; I say renewed, for His having by His good providence drawn me to the Abolition business has always appeared to me to call for the most lively gratitude. Individuals who are not in parliament seldom have an opportunity of doing good to considerable numbers. Even while I was writing the sentence I became conscious of the falsehood of the position; witness Mrs. Hannah More, and all those who labour with the pen."[72]

Wilberforce's assessment of More's power was echoed in poet Percy Bysshe Shelley's landmark *A Defence of Poetry*. Here Shelley observed that "a poet essentially comprises and unites" the characteristics of both the legislator and the prophet. "Poetry," he wrote, "strengthens the faculty which is the organ of the moral nature of man, in the same manner as exercise strengthens a limb." It was, in fact, owing to "the effects of the poetry" of Christians, Shelley argued, that the abolition of slavery and the emancipation of women took place. More was one of these "unacknowledged legislators" who helped write the laws that made others free.[73]

CHAPTER 10

TEACHING THE NATION TO READ

IN AUGUST 1789, WILLIAM WILBERFORCE SPENT A FEW DAYS VISITING More in her country cottage, Cowslip Green. More's retreat from London life was prompted as much from her love of the pastoral life as from her slow rejection of the fashionable city life.

Cowslip Green offered generous trees and lush lawns at the foot of the picturesque Mendip Hills looking down on the cottage like a benevolent deity. More spent her mornings working in the gardens and her evenings riding horseback "through delicious lanes and hills."[1] Although much of her life and works reflected the influence of urban neoclassicists like Dr. Johnson, More was perhaps a great-aunt to romantic poets like William Wordsworth and Samuel Taylor Coleridge, for example. Her embrace of nature, children, and the rustic life conformed to the ethical and aesthetic values of that coming age.

If More sought total retirement at Cowslip Green, it was not to be. First was a steady stream of visitors. They included Mrs. Garrick and Mrs. Montagu, all the way from London. John Newton visited, too, later telling More, "I number that week among the happiest in my life."[2] But one visitor in particular put an end to any thought of retirement for the woman in the midst of her middle-age years.

Ostensibly William Wilberforce had come to enjoy a rare and refreshing respite from his usual politician's labors. He had even brought his sister with him, marking the visit as pleasure, not business. But for these reformers, there was no notion of dividing life up in such discrete parts. Nevertheless, More and her sister Patty urged their two visitors to take a day to travel to the beautiful Cheddar Gorge nearby. Reluctant, as usual, to turn his attentions away from the serious thoughts that seemed always to consume him, Wilberforce agreed.

When he and his sister returned to Cowslip Green later that day, Patty greeted him from the parlor, hoping for accolades of the sublime cliffs along with possibly some congratulations to her and her sister for the rightness of their fine recommendation and good taste. However, Wilberforce was distracted and offered only passing praise of the scenery. After speaking briefly to Patty, he retired to his accommodations in the guest room. The dinner his hosts sent to him later was returned uneaten. Hannah and Patty More worried.

Eventually he emerged from his bedroom and joined the sisters, "refreshed," Patty recorded, by "a higher feast than we had sent him."[3] He asked the servant to leave the room and spoke to the two sisters in earnest.

"Something must be done for Cheddar," he expostulated. He had spent the day not gazing on the dramatic cliffs as the sisters had urged him to do, but making inquiries about the condition of the poor people he saw there. He shared his distressing findings with the Mores. "There was no resident minister. No manufactory, nor did there appear any dawn of comfort, either temporal or spiritual," he explained.

The friends spent the next few hours discussing what might be done to alleviate the suffering of the people in the neighboring village. "If *you* will be at the trouble," Wilberforce vowed, "*I* will be at the expense."

"Something commonly called an impulse crossed my heart which told me it was God's work," Patty wrote in her journal later. "We turned many schemes in our heads every possible way" into the later hours of the night. The plan that emerged was the opening of a Sunday school in Cheddar.

The first of these new schools had been started a few years earlier by Robert Raikes in 1780. The first such Sunday schools had appeared as early as the seventeenth century, but Raikes began the Sunday school movement, thus earning him the appellation father of the Sunday school. Sarah Trimmer had followed Raikes's example, establishing the first of several Sunday schools for poor children in 1786. Trimmer, also a writer and publisher of an educational journal, encouraged others to use her model to open more schools. These early Sunday schools weren't then what is meant by the term today—instruction in Bible lessons held at church before or after the main worship service—but simply schools held on Sundays for poor children, who, at a time before publicly funded education, had no means of formal instruction. Sunday was the only day on which those lucky enough to have work didn't labor.

Although famously praised for their potential to reform behavior by Adam Smith—whose 1776 work *The Wealth of Nations* pioneered the field of modern economics—the schools were controversial from the start. The idea of educating the class of people who were born to labor, as most believed, was a radical idea. To do so would have far-reaching consequences for the social order. Of course, they were right.

It's one thing to hatch a plan. Quite another to carry it out. But carry it out More did.

Christians in the British Empire were just beginning to turn their efforts toward widespread evangelism of unbelievers. In the middle of the 1780s, William Carey, later known as the father of modern missions, was beginning to develop a sense of the Christian's duty to take the gospel to all places. Missions had not been an emphasis of the Church of England since its inception during the tumultuous era of the Reformation. But in 1792, Carey published his famous missionary manifesto, a pamphlet titled *An Enquiry into the Obligations of Christians to Use Means for the Conversion of the Heathens*. This work helped form the basis for the kind of global missionary work that continues to this day. As evangelization emerged at this time as a focus for the practice of the Christian faith, those beginning to think about it generally had their sights set on taking the gospel to faraway lands such as Africa and the West Indies—not the remote villages right there at home. But this was exactly where More concentrated her efforts.

And as it turns out, there were similarities between the faraway lands and the villages close at hand, particularly in their spiritual and intellectual states. Over the next several years, Hannah and Patty—the three other sisters remained in their home in Bath—traveled hills and fields, on foot and on horseback, knocked on doors and butted heads with landowners, cajoled, begged, bribed, ate, and fed—all in the attempt to take Christian doctrine to bear in unreached and uncivilized pockets of the world: the villages right outside the doorstep of Cowslip Green.

The conditions of the villages were deplorable. The More sisters were shocked at what they found. The descriptions provided in their letters and journals explained Wilberforce's sober response to what he saw on that trip to view the cliffs.

C.1880 engraving of the school house in Fishponds, Bristol, where Hannah More was born on February 2, 1745, Universal History Archive/UIG/Bridgeman Images

The back side of the school house today, photo courtesy of Roy Prior

Portrait of Hannah More c.1780 by Frances Reynolds / © Bristol Museum and Art Gallery, UK / Bridgeman Images

Mr. and Mrs. Garrick by the Shakespeare Temple at Hampton by Johan Joseph Zoffany, ca. 1762 / Yale Center for British Art, Paul Mellon Collection

Hannah More's country retreat, Cowslip Green, as it appears in the present day, photo courtesy of Kevin Belmonte

An undated print of Hannah More Cottage, the site of More's first Sunday School, photo courtesy of Roy Prior

A plaque commemorating More at Hannah More Cottage in the present day, photo courtesy of Roy Prior

The cover of the second part of one of More's most famous tracts, The Shepherd of Salisbury Plain, Eighteenth Century Collections Online 1795

Engraved portrait of Hannah More c. 1882

A present-day photo of Hannah More Cottage, Cheddar, photo courtesy of Anne Stott

An engraving of More's home, Barley Wood, reprinted in Harper's Weekly, April 8, 1871, photo courtesy of Kevin Belmonte

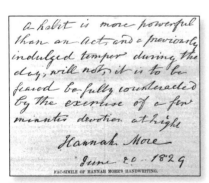
A present-day view from the terrace of Barley Wood, photo courtesy of Kevin Belmonte

Facsimile of Hannah More's writing, photo courtesy of Kevin Belmonte

A portrait of Hannah More reprinted in Harper's Weekly, April 8, 1871, photo courtesy of Kevin Belmonte

Hannah More's last home at Windsor Terrace, Clifton, as it appears today, photo courtesy of Roy Prior

A bust of Hannah More outside the door at Church of All Saints, Wrington, photo courtesy of Roy Prior

A bust of John Locke across from the bust of More at the door of Church of All Saints, Wrington, photo courtesy of Roy Prior

The grave site of Hannah More and her sisters in the church yard of Church of All Saints, Wrington, photos courtesy of Roy Prior

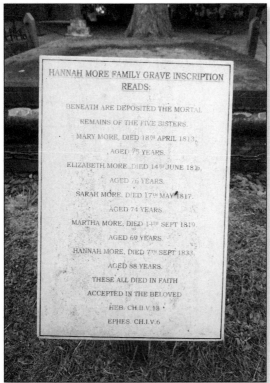

HANNAH MORE FAMILY GRAVE INSCRIPTION
READS:

BENEATH ARE DEPOSITED THE MORTAL

REMAINS OF THE FIVE SISTERS.

MARY MORE, DIED 18TH APRIL 1813,

AGED 75 YEARS.

ELIZABETH MORE, DIED 14TH JUNE 1816,

AGED 76 YEARS.

SARAH MORE, DIED 17TH MAY 1817.

AGED 74 YEARS.

MARTHA MORE, DIED 14TH SEPT 1819.

AGED 69 YEARS.

HANNAH MORE, DIED 7TH SEPT 1833,

AGED 88 YEARS.

THESE ALL DIED IN FAITH

ACCEPTED IN THE BELOVED

HEB. CH.II.V.13

EPHES. CH.I.V.6

The words engraved on the More sisters' gravestone, photo courtesy of Roy Prior

Church of All Saints, Wrington, burial place of Hannah More, photo courtesy of Kevin Belmonte

The poverty was debilitating. The work—for those who had it—among the laboring class in these villages was usually in mining, stone quarrying, glass manufacturing, or farm laboring. Their earnings were usually a mere one shilling a day—about five dollars in US currency today.[5] The poverty in one village was so great that "a single cup of broth cannot be obtained; for there is none to give, if it would save life," More reported.[6] "I am ashamed of *my* comforts when I think of *their* wants," she said.[7]

The immorality also shocked them. Patty More described Nailsea, a village filled with laborers in the glasshouses and mines, as "abounding in sin and wickedness."[8] The people lived in tiny cottages outside the glass factory. Inside where the furnaces blazed, "the swearing, eating, and drinking of these half-dressed, black-looking beings, gave it a most infernal and horrible appearance."[9] No wonder the village inhabitants called the place "Little Hell." In Shipham, efforts to hold morning and evening prayers failed because, Patty More said, "not one could read; but alas! every one could, and did, swear."[10] Patty wrote of one hamlet "so wicked and lawless, that they report thieving to have been handed down from father to son for the last forty years." Where the "churchwardens" themselves feared to tread, they instead sent "two nervous women, really for the above reason of personal fear."[11]

The abandonment of these villages by the church had devastating effects. Cheddar had been without a resident clergyman for forty years, and the results were dramatic.[12] Two thousand poor villagers lived under the virtual rule of several farmers. More reported after their first gathering of all the parents of the parish before the school's opening that it was "a sight truly affecting." They were "poor, miserable, and ignorant," and More witnessed there "more ignorance than we supposed existed anywhere in England."[13] The villagers they encountered were as uneducated "as the beasts that perish," More wrote, "intoxicated every day before dinner [the midday meal], and plunged in such vices as make me begin to think London a virtuous place."[14] In another parish, the clergyman was reported to be in a state of intoxication six times a week and often "prevented from preaching by black eyes, earned by fighting." More said of the same village, "We saw but one Bible in all the parish, and that was used to prop up a flower-pot."[15] The village had no resident minister, and there was "as much knowledge of Christ in the interior of Africa as . . . in this wretched, miserable place," Patty More lamented.[16] Such neglect by the state-assigned clergy was rampant. Collecting tithes while neglecting their parishes was all too common among rectors. In one village where they began a school, More was outraged that the clergyman had "claimed the tithes for fifty years, but had never catechised a child or preached a sermon for forty."[17] In at least one case, the village had no curate, and the farmers told the Mores that although they had the right to appeal for one, they did not "for fear *their tithes should be raised*."[18] No wonder some of the fiercest opposition that More faced came from the clergy. In one village, the laboring men were so feared that "no constable would venture to arrest" one, "lest he should be concealed in one of their pits, and never heard of more."[19] The sisters were warned not to even enter the village, "lest our persons should be endangered."[20]

Many had no knowledge of the Christian faith whatsoever. A girl in one village, "a beautiful young creature about eighteen," More said, was "deeply afflicted with a dropsy." Upon hearing the gospel explained to her, the girl exclaimed, "Oh! Jesus Christ will be very unreasonable if He expects anything of me, for I never heard of Him in my life."[21] Indeed, for a young woman among them to get married in possession of "a fair reputation" was, the sisters said, "an event rare indeed in these villages."[22]

Spirits in the village were so downtrodden that no one could believe that the two ladies who had come to inquire about starting a school would actually do so. After a meeting with the villagers in Yatton about opening a school, Patty More reported, the church bells "were set a-ringing, and the whole village seemed all gaiety and pleasure." When the school opened the following week, one hundred thirty children came.[23] More wrote to John Newton, "It is grievous to reflect, that while we are sending missionaries to our distant colonies, our own villages are perishing for lack of instruction."[24]

Yet the More sisters' attempts to alleviate such oppressive conditions received far from universal acclaim. They were met with suspicion by both the rich and the poor. The wealthy feared that educated members of the underclass would strive beyond their stations, and the poor understandably distrusted the motives of the sisters.

The Mores were savvy enough to know that they couldn't just descend into a village from out of nowhere with grand plans for what would dramatically alter the status quo by changing community conditions for poor and rich alike. The sisters knew they would need local support and cooperation. They began their inquiries concerning Cheddar by chatting with a penniless rabbit catcher who lived nearby. The man, it turned out, was a Quaker and, upon learning what the women hoped to do, "was visibly struck at the prospect of doing good" in the village. "A tear rolling down his rough cheek seemed to announce there was grace in the heart," Patty More wrote in her journal. "You will have much difficulty," the old man warned them, "but let not the enemy tempt you to go back; and God bless the work."[25]

His words proved prophetic. In establishing not one but more than a dozen Sunday schools, More and her sister encountered much difficulty and many temptations to give up. They persevered, however, and their efforts did indeed seem to be blessed by God.

The kindly rabbit catcher informed them exactly whose support would be needed for any effort undertaken at Cheddar, a certain rich landowner whom the sisters proceeded to visit next. They journeyed ten miles "through ploughed fields and shocking roads" and arrived at their destination "almost starved."[26] The man's wife graciously prepared them some refreshment, and the sisters didn't delay in telling the wealthy farmer, whom More described as "very rich, and very brutal," the reason for their call.[27]

He was "very much shocked" upon hearing their plans to open a school for the poor. He told them in no uncertain terms that "religion would be the ruin of agriculture; that it was a very dangerous thing." After all, the members of the laboring class were seen as little more than slaves in these days. Any efforts to introduce them to ideas or possibilities beyond their day-to-day work to survive would upset the apple cart of the social order. The farmer warned the sisters that the introduction of religion in another village had "produced much mischief." More said, "He begged I would not think of bringing any religion into the country; it was the worst thing in the world for the poor, for it made them lazy and useless."[28]

The sisters were unflappable. They took the indignant farmer's expostulations in stride and deftly turned the conversation to more pleasing matters, "as though we had been soliciting a vote at an election," Patty More confessed. They praised the wine he served them, which "put him into good humour" that increased once they assured him they were not seeking his financial support for the school. Finally, confident that they had made some progress with the powerful man, the two sisters "quitted this ignorant, cold, unfeeling rich farmer" and went back to their inn to prepare for the next day's round of visits to more community stakeholders.[29]

The responses to the sisters varied as they made their rounds, but all indicated how radical their idea was for the time. Part of the danger of the Sunday schools would be that educating the lower classes would, even if only to a small degree, narrow the gap between the rich and the poor. Some saw it as thwarting the will of God by upending a social hierarchy ordained by him. The wife of one local landowner declared that "the poor were intended to be servants and slaves. It is pre-ordained that they should be ignorant," she argued. "We cannot alter what is decreed. If a school were to be set up it would be all over with property and if property is not to rule what will become of us?"[30] On the other extreme, another family was supportive but "utterly astonished" at the prospect of "strangers coming there to do good." They liked the plan, particularly if it meant that "their apples would be safer" with the children confined to a schoolroom during their idle hours.[31] Other landowners in the village agreed: orchard robbing was a significant problem, along with other mischief the unsupervised children tended to get into during those few hours of the week in which they weren't sleeping or working. The sisters visited eleven such families, and the responses did not vary more than by a few words.[32]

Following each visit, Hannah More later wrote to Wilberforce, she and Patty returned to their lodgings and practiced their skills "in the art of canvassing" so as to increase their success. "Miss Wilberforce would have been shocked had she seen the petty tyrants whose insolence we stroked and tamed, the ugly children we fondled, the pointers and spaniels we caressed, the cider we commended, and wine we swallowed," she wrote him of their efforts to curry the favor of those whose opposition would have halted the project entirely.[33] "If effect be the best proof of eloquence, then mine was a good speech, for I gained, at length, the hearty concurrence of the whole people, and their promise to discourage or favour the poor in proportion as they were attentive or negligent in sending their children" to the school.[34] Even after the schools opened, in one village "a great lady" tried to bribe the students not to attend by offering a glass of gin to anyone each time he or she didn't go. She outright refused permission to her servant boy to attend, and it was her right to do so within the law.[35]

It wasn't only the wealthy employers and landowners who needed convincing. The poor had to be sold on the idea of being educated. In some villages, the people were so impoverished and oppressed that they feared these strangers had really come in order to sell their children as slaves.[36] In other cases, as More reported in a letter to their benefactor, Wilberforce, "a great many refused to send their children unless we would pay them for it."[37] To attract interest, the sisters had to extol the material benefits of attendance: the opportunities that education would provide for gainful or improved employment. Gaining personal trust would take time.

Once enough support from those who held power in Cheddar had been gathered—and with essentially a blank check from Wilberforce as financial backing—the next step was to find a location. They soon found a suitable house that, with minor renovations, would make a good schoolhouse and took a seven-year lease—"There is courage for you!" More wrote to Wilberforce— in the humble, but spacious, two-story, thatched-roof building on what is now called North Street in Cheddar.[38]

Then they asked around for recommendations until they located an excellent teacher. Mrs. Baber was a woman of some means who had been reduced in possessions and price by a profligate son and, as a result, More reported, had set her mind on more spiritual matters. Baber arrived at the school, bag and baggage, with the "true spirit of a missionary."[39] The sisters chose well. Over her years of service, Baber became so beloved within the village that when she died in 1794, all of Cheddar mourned, and the church could not hold all who came to the funeral.[40] In her detailed account of the project, the *Mendip Annals*, Patty's description of the funeral was hailed later by the novelist E. M. Forster as "a masterpiece of macabre literature."[41]

Just five weeks after the school opened with Baber in charge, Hannah made a visit. Even after such a short term, she found a striking transformation among the students. "Upwards of thirty said the Catechism perfectly, forty could sing three psalms, and several great girls were beginning to know something of the Scriptures," she reported. Even "the face of the village much changed; not a child to be found on the cliffs on a Sunday; the church gradually filling."[42]

Initially, as planned, school was held only on Sunday, a true day of rest in those days because those in the laboring class, including the children, worked the other days of the week. Younger children worked at picking crops, scaring birds, and the like. By the age of twelve, children were considered old enough to do many tasks of the farmers and other laborers. In addition to reading, basic arithmetic, Bible lessons, and the catechism, knitting and spinning were taught to make the students more employable. Eventually, More worked with local manufacturers to adapt the skills taught to local needs and wages.

A year after the Cheddar school opened, More wrote to Wilberforce that "much ground had been gained among the poor," adding, however, that "the success was attended with no small persecution from the rich." She detailed some of the improvements: "Many reprobates were, by the blessing of God, awakened, and many swearers and Sabbath-breakers reclaimed. The numbers both of young and old scholars increased, and the daily life and conversation of many seemed to keep pace with their religious profession on the Sunday."[43] At Cheddar, within the first year, some of the children who had begun school only able to repeat the alphabet were reading the Bible and giving "pertinent answers to any questions which involve the first principles of Christianity."[44] The girl afflicted with dropsy who had never heard of Jesus Christ was asked after being treated if the first visit she would make following her recovery would be to Mrs. Baber, the school mistress. Her spirited response was, "No, it will be my *second;* my first will be to church."[45] Patty More described the conversion of two students in the Cheddar school after observing Baber's teaching: "two grown-up lads, farmers' servants," who "appeared struck to the heart, and shewed [*sic*] truer marks of conversion than any we had met with before." It was reported that the young men sometimes missed dinner in order to pray, and their conversations took on a different tenor and tone: "very striking! so humble, so solemn," Patty More enthused.[46]

Enrollment at the Cheddar school rapidly grew from one hundred forty to three hundred.[47] The Mores decided to open a second school in Shipham. Soon after opening the first school, the two determined women trod on horseback and foot "over a tract of country of ten or twelve miles" to establish more schools in the Somerset region over the next ten years.[48] They sought out the most suitable candidates for teachers they could find: one they tracked down and found milking a cow.[49] Success bred success; each opening generally became easier than the last. By 1796, the schools had 1,600 to 1,700 students in ten parishes.[50] By 1808, more than one hundred students from Cheddar had been "fitted" for domestic service.[51]

The transformations spilled out beyond the schoolhouse walls. Patty's journal reported stories of conversions and spiritual awakenings among farmers and laborers in the villages as well. A church congregation in Cheddar increased from about twenty adults to five hundred, with newly built pews already overflowing.[52] "Here," Patty More wrote, "boys and girls, old and young, men and women. . . . Here the great work evidently goes on—the people hunger and thirst [for God]—the church is filled—families pray—children are easily brought to the knowledge of God."[53] In Cheddar, a Mr. Hyde—"profligate, abusive, depraved"—professed faith in Christ and turned from "a life of wickedness to a life of righteousness."[54]

The sisters monitored the schools closely, traveling back and forth to visit each one during the more temperate months, from May to December, on foot and by horseback. They were subject to ever-changing weather and fickle road conditions. Roads could be impassable; one time, they had to be carried out by the horses of the village men.[55] They often traveled twenty miles between the schools on a Sunday.[56] In a letter to John Newton, More nonchalantly explained that she hadn't written sooner because she had been "a good deal indisposed with a cold caught by walking over our mountains late at night, which I was made to do by a frightful accident of a horse falling, but without doing me the least harm;—not a bone of me was broken."[57] Their days were often more than twelve hours long. When daylight hours were fewer, they often arrived home after dark. "Yet," More recorded in her diary on Sunday, October 26, 1794, "the good providence of God has preserved us from evil, and gives us strength and faith to persevere."[58] The sight of two respectable ladies tramping around the countryside every Sunday became a source of much mockery and ridicule.[59] That, however, was not the sort of thing to deter a woman such as Hannah More. When she was not battling one of her several sporadic bouts of illness, she was otherwise of a robust and determined constitution.

The success of the schools for the children of the poor led to the next logical step: reaching the parents. More undertook efforts toward improving the lives of the adult poor of the villages, but these remained subordinate to the work of the Sunday schools. About six months after the opening of the Cheddar school, the Mores had the idea of teaching the adults on Sunday evenings. In these meetings, a sermon and a chapter of the Bible were read, followed by a song and prayer. The meetings were planned to last only an hour. Only four people attended the first week, but before long the number multiplied to sixty.[60] They also created benefit clubs, or friendly societies, for women. Friendly societies were like local insurance collectives. Members paid a small fee, often on a quarterly basis, and in the case of illness or unemployment received a set payment. Such societies already existed for male laborers but not for women. More opened several of these clubs for the impoverished women in the villages. She tied the women's societies to the work of the schools: membership in the benefit club required certain obligations on the part of its members in support of the school.[61] Members who paid the required dues were given financial payouts upon experiencing illness (three shillings a week) or childbirth (seven shillings, sixpence) as compensation for days spent unable to work.[62] More was shocked when the women protested at one meeting that they preferred to reduce the compensation for a lying-in (childbirth) to increase the amount allotted to funeral expenses. One woman explained, "What [does] a poor woman work hard for, but in hopes she should be put out of the world in a tidy way?"[63] Another rule stipulated that a girl who had been taught in the school and maintained a devout life and good character would be presented with "a pair of white worsted stockings, . . . five shillings, and a Bible." At this, More wrote, "a universal smile graced their ferocious countenances."[64]

Subscription to the club was three halfpence a week, which even at so little was more than many could afford. One club alone raised three hundred pounds, and as was her custom, More invested the funds in government stocks.[65] Therefore, More often gave the neediest women—widows and very poor women—the money to pay the weekly dues.[66] Some parishes had one hundred fifty members in the clubs, More reported to Wilberforce. "You may guess," she wrote him, "who are the patronesses."[67]

More's generosity extended further than the merely economic and utilitarian. She held an "anniversary feast of tea" to which the women were invited, along with some of their wealthier neighbors. There the Mores would "wait on the women, who sit and enjoy their dignity."[68] "It was pleasant," More said after one of these club feasts, "to see them all very tidily dressed in their smart linen gowns, and good black hats; and this is one collateral advantage of the Institution, that, whereas there used to be hardly anybody at church, and the reason assigned was that they had nothing fit to be seen in, now the vanity of having decent clothing to *meet the ladies* [the upper-class women] at the annual festivity makes them industrious and frugal, to buy a gown out of their little earnings; and the churches are now filled with clean and creditable-looking poor women."[69] A delicate, blue-and-white china set that she donated to the Cheddar women's society still sits in a small glass cabinet inside the Cheddar schoolhouse now named Hannah More Cottage.

Another festive tradition that More began as both an enticement and a reward for the children to learn in the schools was a feast, complete with formal procession of all the students, parents, servants, and teachers marching off after the blowing of a horn to a picturesque hillside where all were served generous portions of roast beef, plum pudding, and cake—"as much as their stomachs would hold." Following the meal, the students were given the opportunity to show off the lessons they had learned by reciting the Bible chapters they had memorized, giving the catechism, and singing. One such feast fed 517 children, along with 300 others, and drew 4,000 spectators.[70] No wonder some folks living in that region still talk of the festivities that took place on those lush, green hills generations ago.

Nevertheless, even after the schools had been opened and were operating successfully, they drew continual suspicion. In those days, any hint of goings-on that deviated from the doctrines and teachings of the Established Church were closely scrutinized. Any practice or approach that strayed—or appeared to stray—beyond the clear doctrines and teachings of the Church of England or the Book of Common Prayer was likely to be met with accusations of "Methodism" or "Wesleying."[71] Such a charge was more than mere mockery or annoyance. Throughout the sixteenth, seventeenth, and eighteenth centuries, English citizens whose religious membership or practices lay outside the established Church of England were denied many rights and privileges otherwise granted. Dissenters, or Nonconformists, as they were alternately called, had been for many years prohibited from voting, holding office, or attending a university, and they were restricted in other areas such as owner-ship of land and arms.

More, however, was fiercely committed to the Church of England. She provided ample record of her objections to the irregu-larities of "Methodism," even though she adopted from it—along with an entire movement within the Established Church—some of its evangelical fervor. Nevertheless, it didn't take long for the first school in Cheddar to come under suspicion of Methodism, a charge that meant the kiss of death for any endeavor seeking the support of the Established Church.

In 1800, five years after the opening of the Blagdon school, the teacher hired by More was accused of engaging in "Methodistical" practices, namely, extemporaneous prayer—personal prayers not included in the Book of Common Prayer—during evening services held apart from the school instructions. The national controversy that followed fills a thick volume of letters, publications, and pamphlets produced by the affair. Sides were chosen, and enrollment at the Blagdon school plunged from two hundred to thirty-five students, for the village poor feared incurring the wrath of the curate, a position that wielded almost absolute power over their daily lives.[72]

Soon More was denounced publicly, cruelly, and thoroughly. Some of the worst criticism came from clergymen, particularly Rector William Shaw, who adopted the pseudonym Reverend Sir Archibald MacSarcasm to publish vicious attacks against her. Among the insults hurled at More was the term *She-Bishop*.[73] Periodicals such as the *British Critic* and *Anti-Jacobin*—Tory, as More herself was—joined in, along with proclamations from individual clergymen and bishops. Soon all the More sisters were incriminated. Flyers were posted along the road pointing passersby to where they could see "the menagerie of five female savages of the most desperate kind."[74] More was accused not only of "Methodism," "disloyalty," and revolutionary politics but also, most ludicrously, "not believing one word of Christianity."[75]

It was a sad irony that More held a strong aversion to religious or doctrinal strife. She shunned such controversy and division, remarking it was not her "object to teach dogmas and opinions, but to train up good members of society, and plain practical Christians."[76] "My very soul is sick of religious controversy," she wrote in her diary on July 8, 1803. "Christianity is a broad basis. *Bible* Christianity is what I love . . . a Christianity practical and pure, which teaches holiness, humility, repentance and faith in Christ; and which after summing up all the Evangelical graces, declares that the greatest of these is charity."[77] *Charity* of course, is the old-fashioned term for *love*.

The so-called Blagdon controversy consumed all More's energies and attention over the next few years, from 1800 to 1803. In defense of herself, of her commitment to the Church of England, and of the schools, More wrote a letter to the bishop of Bath and Wells, Dr. Richard Beadon. The bishop, along with many others, came to her defense. Beyond that, More was silent. The lessons she had learned from the Hannah Cowley and Ann Yearsley affairs had sunk in deeply.

After raging for three years, the controversy finally saw vindication for More. But it proved too much to take, even for as tough a woman as she. Additionally, the controversy jeopardized all the other schools. Reluctantly, More closed the Blagdon school, writing that she had been attacked "with a wantonness of cruelty which, in civilized places, few persons, especially of my sex, have been called to suffer."[78]

From 1803 to 1805, she underwent what came to be called her "great illness." On November 27, 1803, she wrote in a journal entry that after meditating on the writings of the seventeenth-century Puritan Richard Baxter, she couldn't help but compare the criticism he faced to hers. "I have to lament that through my want of his [Baxter's] faith and piety, they [the written 'attacks'] had nearly destroyed my life."[79] She probably never fully recovered from the physical and mental toll. Years later, she would still decry such strife within the church body, writing, "Oh, how I hate faction, division and controversy in religion!"[80]

But the good wrought by the Sunday schools is beyond measure. More's approach to education was remarkably creative and progressive. Childhood, as we understand it today, was a concept in its infancy, so to speak—as can be seen, for example, in the way children were depicted in paintings—as miniature adults—until about the middle of the century. More's Sunday schools played a part in cultivating our current understanding of childhood. Well before Charles Dickens portrayed the plight of impoverished children in his Victorian novels, More's schools recognized the particular needs of all children, and those of poor children in particular. Her system of education included different levels of instruction geared toward the needs of the students. She is credited with replacing the accepted method of learning by rote and "deadly monotone" with her markedly varied, lively, stimulating, and dramatic approach to teaching, making effective use of songs and stories within and between lessons.[81] She always began the lessons on the Bible with a parable in order to draw in the students with a story both lively and practical.[82] Later she explained her teaching philosophy in *Strictures on the Modern System of Female Education*, quoting from Shakespeare's *As You Like It*: "Teach, as HE taught, by seizing on surrounding objects, passing events, local circumstances, peculiar characters, apt illusions, just analogy, appropriate illustration. Call in all creation, animate and inanimate, to your aid, and accustom your young audience to 'Find tongues in trees, books in the running brooks, / Sermons in stones, and good in every thing.'"[83]

Rewards such as coins, books, Bibles, and gingerbread for learning, attending church, and exhibiting good behavior were heavily integrated into their approach. The weekly charity schools—such as that where Jacob More had served as master—were known for strict discipline that deterred many a village urchin from voluntary attendance, but More's Sunday schools were kinder operations, drawing even the roughest neighborhood children more readily.

Even so, the education the schools provided was, by More's description, "very limited and strict." When the program expanded beyond the Sunday lessons to school throughout the week, the goal remained to create useful, productive citizens. The students, she explained, "learn of week-days such coarse works as may fit them for servants. I allow of no writing [for the poor]. My object has not been to teach dogmas and opinions, but to form the lower classes to habits of industry and virtue."[84] Just as More's education by her father had gone only a little further than what was considered proper for a girl, More did not believe in educating the poor children beyond their social station. For one thing, to do so would leave them unsatisfied and unhappy in a lot in life nearly impossible for them to escape. For another, the idea of social mobility was still a developing idea. While fluidity was an increasing phenomenon for members of the growing middle classes—such as More—the station of those on the very upper and lower echelons was still viewed as fixed. It would not be until the next century that the more radical concept of social mobility, as expressed in the American Dream, would emerge.

Many now, as then, find basis for criticizing the motives and the methods of the Sunday schools. Some see such efforts not as a means to liberate the masses but as another way of controlling them. Certainly, some of More's language about the poor grates on modern ears even when considered within the context of the times. Descriptions of the students and the villagers as "ignorant," "backwards," and "stupid" crop up in her correspondence. "They have so little common sense, and so little sensibility, that we are obliged to beat into their heads continually the good we are doing them," she wrote, for example.[85] Such a statement does not present a very flattering picture of More's philanthropy. The language should, however, be understood within the entire record of More's work. Despite her use of derogatory terms, More's genuine compassion for the poor was clear. She described, for example, how one gentleman, "bursting with his wealth and consequence, and purple with his daily bottle of port," was so moved at hearing the students repeat their well-studied lessons that he burst out with a spontaneous vow: "Every boy and girl that do mind what the ladies do say I'll give twopence a-piece to!" Such, More said with no small surprise, "was a piece of generosity unknown in the family before."[86]

Her refusal to teach the poor to write demonstrated an adherence to contemporary beliefs regarding class—namely, that the status into which one was born was ordained by God—and is discomfiting by today's standards. On the other hand, many in her time viewed any kind of popular education suspiciously. For example, the esteemed Bishop Horsley pronounced that there was "much ground for suspicion that sedition and atheism were the real objects of some of these institutions rather than religion."[87] Likewise, in 1797, the *Gentleman's Magazine* printed an article that voiced the prevailing suspicions about educating the poor and advocated instead the advantages of keeping the poor man in ignorance and illiteracy so as not to "excite rebellions" or "anarchy and confusion."[88]

From the vantage point of the next century, Leslie Stephen wrote that while what he termed as More's "desire to keep the poor in their place" went out of fashion, her "services to education at a time of general indifference deserve the highest praise."[89] More was not a revolutionary by the standards of her time or ours. In fact, More condemned revolutionary approaches as hindrances to educational reform. Moving too far, too fast, she told Wilberforce, would cause their efforts to backfire because it would only "irritate and inflame the old bigotry which hugged absolute ignorance as hidden treasure not to be parted with," leaving her sober measure of Christian instruction that lay between two extremes to "be rejected by both parties."[90]

More's purpose in reform was, first and foremost, religious, not political. She believed that learning was "the next best thing to religion."[91] In the same letter in which she assured her supporter that she "allow[ed] of no writing," More added, "I know of no way of teaching morals but by infusing principles of Christianity, nor of teaching Christianity without a thorough knowledge of Scripture."[92] The belief in the centrality of Scripture to the essence of Christianity and the incumbent necessity of teaching people to read had been at the heart of the Protestant Reformation. Centuries later, More was getting the task accomplished.

Thus, she viewed her work as being in service of God and her country. One tract she later wrote, called *The Sunday School*, offered a thinly disguised account of the Sunday school effort. In it, the central character explained to a parish farmer why such schools were so necessary: "to teach good principles to the lower classes, is the most likely way to save the country. Now, in order to do this, we must teach them to read. . . . And literacy, as historians frequently remind us, 'was the necessary prelude to democracy.'"[93]

In an effort to more effectively teach Christian doctrine to an audience so deprived of traditional church teaching, More wrote a children's adaptation of the official catechism of the church. Published in 1795, *More's Questions and Answers for the Mendip and Sunday Schools* might be viewed innocently enough as an effective means of reaching her particular audience. From another view, however, it might be considered in far more radical terms as the attempt of a layperson—and a woman, no less—to produce unauthorized church teaching.[94]

If the Sunday schools had not been sufficiently progressive, they would not have received such vehement and widespread opposition from those who feared the schools' potential to challenge social stability. Indeed, despite her clearly conservative beliefs, she was "savagely attacked as a dangerous radical" by many of her contemporaries.[95] More wrote to John Newton in 1796, "One great benefit which I have found to result from our projects is the removal of that great gulf which has divided the rich and poor in these country parishes, by making them meet together; whereas before, they hardly thought they were children of one common father."[96] One biographer observed, "Thirty years before Disraeli, forty years before Dickens, Hannah More did something to make the Two Nations known to one another."[97] More's moderate reforms, although less radical than the educational reforms proposed by Mary Wollstonecraft, for example, were more acceptable and therefore more effective because More successfully positioned herself in the nexus between two worlds at odds. Concerning the proper boundaries of education for the poor, she placed herself against the "ultra-educationist," remarking, "I have exerted my feeble voice to prevail on my few parliamentary friends to steer the middle way between the Scylla of brutal ignorance and Charybdis of a literary education. The one is cruel, the other preposterous."[98]

More worked with the Sunday schools for thirty years. In accordance with her will, the schools were closed six months following her death in 1833.[99] Even so, some of the schools that had been most successful became the first National Schools, the basis for the very same public primary schools educating English children today.[100] Historians estimated that by the 1850s three-fourths of laboring-class children between the ages of five and fifteen were enrolled in a Sunday school.[101] The schools were credited by her contemporaries for having "changed the moral conduct of the labouring classes within their influence" and eradicating "prejudice against the religious education of the poor."[102] Years later, the novelist E. M. Forster said of More's effort with the Sunday schools that "it was good if education is good. She taught the poor how to read and wash, observe Sunday and honour the King, and before her day no one had taught them anything."[103] More helped teach her nation to read.[104]

Chapter 11

An Ample Table

In the southwest of London, just a few miles from St. Mary Woolnoth where More went to hear John Newton preach, sits the historic Clapham district. During More's lifetime, Clapham was a rural village. In 1776, a new place of worship, Holy Trinity Church, opened there in a building erected as a replacement for the old, decaying parish church nearby that dated from the medieval period.[1] At that time, despite being only four miles from London Bridge, Clapham still reflected the agrarian setting of the county of Surrey in which it sat.[2] Because of its proximity to the city, Clapham was quickly becoming an outpost for the well-to-do who were building large, elaborate homes there. In those days, people attended church in their own communities, or parishes, so Holy Trinity quickly became a church for those who were rich and fashionable—but not necessarily devout. However, the evangelical movement that had arisen from the revival sparked earlier in the century by John and Charles Wesley and George Whitefield was bringing change, first to the laboring masses through Wesley and Whitefield's open-air preaching and gradually upward to the higher classes.

In 1792, Henry Thornton, a cousin of Wilberforce, purchased Battersea Rise, a three-story, Queen Anne–style home named after the part of Clapham in which it was located.[3] Henry Thornton, like Wilberforce, was a member of Parliament and, also like Wilberforce, became so at a young age. He started out working in trade but turned to banking, a profession in which he discovered such innate skill that he became one of the most successful and wealthiest bankers in the nation. Wilberforce's vision to reform their society soon became Thornton's vision as well.

As holder of the parish land on which Holy Trinity was built, Thornton's estate held the so-called right of patronage and with it the right to appoint the next curate. The same year he bought Battersea Rise, Thornton offered the curate's position at Holy Trinity to a fellow evangelical, John Venn. When Venn began to preach there, the congregation grew so monumentally that additions had to be made to the church.[4] Some of the rich and empowered in Clapham soon found genuine faith. A circle of these church members then united in their growing commitment to bring the vibrancy of the evangelical Christian faith to every area of life. Clapham—and Battersea Rise within it—became the headquarters for a close-knit group of some of these true believers—believers not only in the Christian faith but also in the idea that serious Christian faith could actually make a difference in the world.

Thornton kept adding to his home, which eventually boasted more than thirty bedrooms and a legendary oval library that served as the meeting room for the community. Dwellings were built on the grounds where other members, including Wilberforce and Hannah More, took up residence for periods of time. The home was part of a great plan of Thornton. "I am in hopes some good may come out of our Clapham system," he explained. Wilberforce was a central part of that plan. Thornton described the young parliamentarian as "a candle that should not be hid under a bushel." He continued, "The influence of his conversation is, I think, great and striking. I am surprised to find out how much religion everybody seems to have when they get to our house."[5] The home was so celebrated that a hymn commemorating it, "Battersea Rise," was written in 1841. It began:

> OLD house, how long I've known thee,
> By high, historic fame,
> By Thornton, Inglis, Wilberforce,
> Each loved and sainted name;
> And now, my pilgrim feet have trod
> Thy consecrated ground,
> And underneath thy sacred roof,
> A pilgrim's rest, have found.[6]

At Battersea Rise, Wilberforce labored on a project that he had been long in the making, his influential book *A Practical View of the Prevailing Religious System of Professed Christians in the Higher and Middle Classes of This Country Contrasted with Real Christianity*, published in 1797. The question Wilberforce posed in the book— asking skeptics of Christianity to consider that those of as great intellect as Sir Francis Bacon, John Milton, John Locke, and Isaac Newton had embraced the Christian religion—suggested just how out of fashion devout Christianity had become. At the same time, the book's instant success—the first edition sold out within days and several more editions were published over the next few months— indicated that a hunger for real faith had not yet been sated.

Besides Wilberforce, Thornton, and More, other members

of the community—not all of whom lived there, but most came for extended stays—included the group's founder, Henry Venn, curate at Holy Trinity and father of the rector John Venn, who was also a member; James Stephen, a lawyer and great-grandfather of Virginia Woolf; Zachary Macaulay, father of the historian Thomas Babington Macaulay; Thomas Gisborne, an author and clergyman; and Charles Grant, chairman of the directors of the British East India Company. While the Clapham Sect is notable for offering expanded roles to the women who were part of its community,[7] More was the only female member who held a status considered equal to that of the men.[8]

The Clapham Sect wasn't really a sect, not in the usual sense of the term, as all its members were respected and committed members of the Church of England. Evangelicalism—whose distinctive tenets emphasize the centrality of the text of the Bible, salvation through the sacrifice of Christ, the need for personal conversion, and the outward expression of one's conversion through acts of service—was by this time a movement occurring both within and outside the Established Church.[9] The fervor of their faith was indisputably fueled by that movement to embrace a religion of the heart, but it was not advancement of evangelicalism that motivated the community at Clapham. Thus, some referred to the group as the Clapham Circle, the Clapham Party, (mockingly) the Clapham Saints, or the Claphamites. The name Clapham Sect stuck only later when in 1844 the son of Claphamite James Stephen, Sir James Stephen, mistakenly thought that one of the group's outspoken critics had referred to them as the Clapham Sect in a critical article. In responding to the article, Stephen used this term. His editor at the *Edinburgh Review* was so taken with it that he used it in the story's headline. Thus, "by misquotation and editorial headlining, the Clapham sect was created," and Clapham Sect it has been called ever since.[10]

Regardless of the name, this fellowship of like-minded believers, "bound together by shared moral and spiritual values, by religious mission and social activism, by love for each other, and by marriage," changed history as they sought to serve God in every area of their lives, personal and public, at home and abroad.[11] As a whole, the Clapham community functioned as a large, extended family, rather like the body as described in the New Testament. If the old, nearly blind John Newton was the soul of the abolitionist movement, Wilberforce its voice, and Hannah its heart and hands, the Clapham community served as the very body, and Battersea Rise was the cloak that offered protection and warmth. They operated as an intimate group that "planned and labored like a committee that was never dissolved" as they decided on projects and issues and mapped out their strategies for accomplishing the group's goals.[12]

Although they operated as one body, the genius of the group lay in capitalizing on the particular gifts of each member. They assigned tasks based on each person's gifts and skills in order to accomplish their common causes.[13] Rather than trying to force all to follow one pattern, each was supported in his or her talents and passions put to the service of the greater vision. Thornton had wealth and connections. Wilberforce was blessed with eloquence. More's powers were wit and pen. Although Wilberforce's charismatic personality had been counted as one of the most effective weapons in the Clapham arsenal, he may have been outdone by the winsome and witty Hannah More.[14]

More was a woman of strong convictions, but she kept a plentiful table. She mixed comfortably and enthusiastically with rich and poor, churched and unchurched, and all in between. It was her habit to eat meals with the poor villagers during the years of the Sunday schools. At the same time, she maintained close friendships with bishops and lords. "How varied is my life," she once observed. "Thursday dining with the Prince-Bishop of Durham—on Sunday with two religious colliers."[15] Her religious tolerance was equally broad in her personal relationships—if not always politically. As committed as she was to the Church of England and even after the renewal of her faith following her meeting with Newton, she continued to befriend those of less or different faith commitments. More had a rare ability to keep strong, unwavering convictions in tension with broad-minded toleration.

Perhaps no friendship reflected More's openheartedness more than the one with Horace Walpole. More was a relatively young thirty-five and Walpole sixty-three when they first met. They bonded immediately and remained close friends—despite bumpy disagreements—until Walpole's death in 1797. Walpole published More's gothic poem "Bishop Bonner's Ghost" in 1789 at his renowned Strawberry Hill Press, which was quite an honor.

Horace liked to refer to her affectionately as "my dear saint Hannah" and "Holy Hannah." Far less conservative than she, he bantered with her about what he considered her overly strict morality. Walpole "rallied me yesterday," More wrote in one letter, "for what he called the ill-natured strictness of my tracts; and talked foolishly enough of the cruelty of making the poor spend so much time in reading books, and depriving them of their pleasure on Sundays."[16] In another letter, one Walpole wrote to her, he teased, "How I admire the activity of your zeal and perseverance! Should a new church ever be built, I hope in a side chapel there will be an altar dedicated to Saint Hannah, Virgin and Martyr; and that your pen, worn to the bone, will be enclosed in a golden *reliquaire*, and preserved on the shrine."[17] Despite his inability or unwillingness to adhere to her moral and religious code, or perhaps because of it,

Walpole seemed genuinely to admire his friend's piety. Many marveled at the odd friendship.

The son of the British prime minister, Sir Robert Walpole, Horace Walpole, later the Earl of Orford, was a confirmed bachelor who never married. Historians and biographers have long speculated about Walpole's sexual inclinations, but in an age in which homosexual behavior was illegal and one in which "homosexual" did not exist as a category of identity, no definitive conclusion can be made. While Walpole exhibited some traits considered now as stereotypically gay—delicate features, flamboyant personality, and an artistic flair—in Georgian England such qualities were often seen as French. Some scholars think that Walpole was simply asexual.

Beyond his literary and political accomplishments as a gothic novelist and a former member of Parliament, Walpole was well known for his keen observations and witty insights, many of which were recorded in his letters. Horace and Hannah had much in common, but probably this shared wit cemented their friendship. His most famous epigram is, "This world is a comedy to those that think, a tragedy to those that feel."[18] Walpole's life reflected that dichotomy, as did the great joys and pains that marked More's life.

Not surprisingly, some people regarded More's friendship with Walpole as irreconcilable. More's first biographer, Roberts, unfortunately felt it "painful" but necessary to apologize for More's extensive and friendly correspondence with a man whose principles "were such as to throw him out of the circle of Christian fellowship."[19] This provincial attitude surely stemmed from an inability to grasp the broader mind of More, one whose confidence in her principles did not require that she demand the same of others. For Hannah, life was a feast, and the space at her table was abundant.

More's friendship with Walpole was marked by a noticeable lack of religious content in her letters to him. This lack did not represent a compromise of principle, however; Walpole's respect for More was evident in the language of his addresses to her in their correspondence and in his continued support of her work over the years.[20] Before he died he gave her a beautifully bound, three-volume Bible in which he had written that she was his "excellent friend," and he had given it with "esteem and gratitude."[21] To Walpole, More was testimony, in the words of one of her early biographers, that "the most implicit faith and the most devoted zeal in Christianity could consist with the highest mental attainments; and that the most devoted piety was no obstacle to cheerfulness and humour."[22] Indeed, despite an apologetic posture toward More's friendship with Walpole, her biographer Roberts expressed the belief that if Walpole had only lived a few years more, he might have been transformed under More's influence.[23] Perhaps, he credited More too much, for More seemed less hopeful about the state of her beloved friend's soul and often fretted about it.

Her camaraderie with Walpole exemplified More's uncommon ability to bridge a cultural gap between the irreligious social elite and the conservative, evangelical community. More considered it to be a "beauty" of Christianity "that it is not held out exclusively to a few select spirits; that it is not an object of speculation, or an exercise of ingenuity, but a rule of life suited to every condition, capacity, and temper." The "characteristic value" of the faith, she wrote, "is its suitableness to the genius, condition, and necessities of all mankind."[24]

Hannah was no separatist, and nor were the Claphamites. Nor were they purists. They were practical. Cobelligerence was the most effective strategy in the Clapham Sect's program for reform. Where there were opportunities to partner with others who shared their goals, they did. They betrayed no conviction nor violated any conscience in seeking common cause with those outside the circle of their personal convictions. They sought and gained cobelligerents in every battle within the war for the soul of their nation. And this ability to put aside differences to pursue shared goals was Hannah More's forte.

She was a committed member of the Church of England, yet served as a bridge between two worlds, that of the high church and that of the more fervent evangelical upstarts on the church's outskirts. She asserted that she was "most sincerely attached to the Establishment, . . . not, as far as I am able to judge, from prejudice, but from a fixed and settled conviction."[25] She continually declared—using terms common to the doctrinal debates of the day—her hatred of "enthusiasm, cant and sectarian phrase."[26] In other words, More did not hold, as some did, to a "vain belief in personal revelation," as her friend Samuel Johnson defined *enthusiasm* in his 1755 *Dictionary of the English Language*. The kind of transformation that More experienced was referred to as a "religion of the heart," a phrase that doesn't quite carry the connotations of the much-later phrase in common use by evangelicals, "personal relationship with Jesus." The idea of personal revelation from God apart from the Bible or church doctrine was seen as irregular at best, dangerous at worst, by a faithful member of the Church of England. Likewise, *cant* and *sectarian phrase*—jargon and divisive doctrinal terms, respectively—were decried by an Anglican such as More for isolating the user and his or her faith from the rest of society in a way that was useless at best, seditious at worst. "How I hate the little narrowing names of Arminian and Calvinist," More groused.[27] She shunned the evangelical label largely because she wished to avoid the swirling doctrinal controversies. An Anglican such as More was obliged to adhere to the prescribed prayers and practices outlined in the Book of Common Prayer. Extemporaneous prayer was something practiced by Methodists, not faithful members of the Established Church—which the Blagdon controversy painfully made clear. Even the family prayers routinely offered by those living at Battersea Rise—and which would become characteristic of later evangelicals—felt uncomfortable to More.[28]

One historian gave an unverified account stating that sometimes More took the carriage of her friend Bishop Porteus to Clapham to visit Venn, the evangelical rector at Holy Trinity. When she did, the carriage dropped her off at a public house a mile from the rectory because it wouldn't do for the bishop's vehicle to be seen at an evangelical rectory.[29] Of course, Clapham was not part of the bishop's diocese, so perhaps it was more a matter of good manners for the bishop of London to refrain from interfering in the domain of the bishop of Winchester.[30] At any rate, Hannah More need not toe such denominational or diocesan lines; nor did she. As a result, although More remained committed to the Established Church, she played a significant part in advancing the evangelical movement both within and without it.[31]

While theologically conservative, the Clapham Sect's religious tolerance was moderate for the times. They were particularly sympathetic to Dissenters, those of denominations characterized by more Puritan or anti-Catholic doctrine and practice. As with most conservatives, the position of the Clapham Sect—and More, increasingly so—toward Catholics was less tolerant. Years of civil wars and unrest over the Catholic and Protestant divide lent a basis for the victorious Protestants to be wary of enfranchising those with ties to the Roman Catholic Church. Catholics were granted freedom of worship in Britain in 1791, but religious rights were one thing, civic rights another. Full emancipation, namely, the right of Catholic citizens to serve in Parliament, was a bridge deemed too precarious to cross by many conservatives, including More and other members of the Clapham Sect. Time would fade these residual fears of Catholics holding political power—Wilberforce would eventually vote in support of Catholic emancipation—yet More would not go that far. In 1819, upon hearing the news of one more defeat of the Catholic Bill in the House of Peers, More exulted to a friend that "we have beaten the Romanists."[32]

Despite such shortcomings as individual members and as a collective community, the Clapham Sect was remarkable for crossing rigid barriers of class, party, and creeds.[33] They moved easily among and with liberal Christians, freethinkers, and unbelievers alike in pursuit of their prodigious goals.[34] More affectionately referred to the gatherings at Wilberforce's quarters as being like "Noah's Ark, full of beasts clean and unclean."[35]

Their cobelligerency was not without risk. Although "thoroughly Anglican," they met with suspicion from many in the Established Church who were not evangelical.[36] Newton in particular was criticized for his camaraderie with the common people and condemned by the church hierarchy for associating with Dissenters and occasionally permitting Baptist ministers to share the pulpit with him.[37] But the members of Clapham recognized that the reformation of society required the cooperation of many from within that same society. Such mutual support would be needed far more than they ever realized over the forty years it took to abolish slavery.

Today what is remembered and counted greatest among the accomplishments of the Clapham community is the abolition of the slave trade, but such a victory would likely not have been won without the group's successful attempts at reformation of the entire society, from high to low, from Sabbath to Saturday. The efforts of the Clapham community were three-pronged: they aimed at alleviating the suffering and oppression of the lower classes, reforming the excessive and negligent behaviors of the upper classes, and advancing Christianity at home and throughout the world.

The Claphamites' campaign to reform the upper class was often described as one to "make goodness fashionable." While their efforts at reform were aimed at every level of society, they saw the greatest need for change among the "fashionable." Their reformation would, in turn, affect reform of the lower orders by both example and influence.

An early victory came in 1787 when Wilberforce succeeded in convincing King George III and the archbishop of Canterbury to issue an official proclamation in favor of improved morals and better enforcement of existing laws against vices such as gambling, drunkenness, impiety, Sabbath breaking, prostitution, and profanity. The Proclamation Society was thus formed. The effort garnered the expected criticism, but it also received broad-based support that was the beginning of social consensus that would help the Clapham Sect in later efforts, which proved much harder to advance.

Despite the devout personal faith of the Clapham members, their reformation campaign was not religious as much as it was moral, social, and political.[38] Most of their strategies employed corresponding tactics. They developed "launchers," ways to turn discussion and social gatherings to serious topics.[39] They conducted research, circulated petitions, undertook boycotts, and published pamphlets, treatises, and poems. Such efforts helped not only to accomplish their goal of reforming members of the upper classes but also to bring the support of the newly reformed to the other efforts at reform.

As part of these efforts, More published her *Thoughts on the Importance of the Manners of the Great to General Society* in 1788, followed by *An Estimate of the Religion of the Fashionable World* in

1791. Despite the general unpopularity of religious books among the upper classes, More's "wit and brilliance" are credited with producing impressive sales and wide readership of these works. Leslie Stephen claimed they were "the most widely read books of the day."[40] Each work went through several editions in a short time, and it was widely believed that the improvement of the example set by the great and the fashionable was marked due to the books' influence.[41] Other Claphamites made similar contributions, particularly Wilberforce's *A Practical View of the Prevailing Religious System of Professed Christians, in the Middle and Higher Classes in this Country, Contrasted with Real Christianity.*

Another significant literary effort by the sect was the founding in 1802 of the journal the *Christian Observer,* edited by Clapham member Zachary Macaulay. With the rise of literacy and print culture, newspapers, periodicals, and journals were wildly popular, and an array of publications could be found across the political and religious spectrums. As an evangelical periodical, the *Christian Observer* staked out a territory that was "more cultured" than was typical of other such journals and therefore was more read and more respected by members of the social elite its founders sought to influence.[42] In particular, the journal challenged other conservative religious journals' positions against the arts as mere "worldly pursuits." One contributor to the *Christian Observer* explained in making the case against the "excessive scrupulousness indulged in by many" of those overly pious folks, "Straining at gnats is the very best preparation for swallowing camels."[43] Not only was More a contributor to the journal, but she helped, in the words of Wilberforce, prevent the publication from "sink[ing] under its own solemnity" by bringing some of her wit and vivacity to its pages.[44] The journal was a success, holding a solid presence within the evangelical community for at least a generation.[45]

Encouraging Sabbath observance was another matter the sect pursued among the upper classes. While Sunday was ostensibly a day set apart by law throughout the empire as a day of rest, many activities violated the spirit of that law: ordering servants to work on hair dressing, attending Sunday concerts, and going for strolls after worship where all thoughts of the sermon would quickly dissipate. The ramifications for neglecting observance of the Sabbath rippled down to every class in the example set by the superiors and by their frequent requirements of the working class to work on that day. Wilberforce attributed the suicides of three colleagues, in part, to increased stresses that might have been alleviated by one day of rest a week.[46] For people in the laboring classes such as those served by More's Sunday schools, Sabbath day observance was their only rest from grueling workdays that were twelve to eighteen hours long—attendance at Sunday school was very much restful for those toiling in hard labors. Lip service and law were still on the side of Sabbath observance, yet Sunday parties, dinners, concerts, and drawing room gatherings were common invitations that More had to decline, even from such a dear friend as Mrs. Montagu.[47]

Dueling was a serious vice of the upper class against which the Clapham Sect campaigned strenuously. The ancient practice persisted; even worse, it was on the increase. As late as 1804 in America, Alexander Hamilton was killed as a result of his duel with Aaron Burr, who was charged with murder. More's old hero Richard Sheridan had fought in a duel, as did Prime Minister Pitt—Wilberforce's close friend. Even the diminutive Wilberforce had been challenged to a duel by a slave ship captain.[48]

If the justice of the duel seemed harsh, even more so did the rule of law, particularly for the poor and powerless. The society that countenanced human slavery did not treat its own citizens in prisons much better. Prison conditions in eighteenth-century

England were cruel and inhumane, to say the least. The most notorious prison in Great Britain was London's Newgate. Here people having debt, those awaiting trials, and those facing execution were housed in tiny, crowded cells. Debtors were often accompanied by their family members. Prisoners slept on straw on the floor and had to pay for their bedding and clothing. The sanitary conditions were so bad in Newgate that the smell was often unbearable to passersby outside. Not surprisingly, dozens of prisoners died in Newgate every year. Before the end of the century, the prisons were so crowded that some prisoners were kept in old ships, called hulks—as famously depicted in the next century by Charles Dickens in *Great Expectations*. So many offenses were punishable by execution in the eighteenth century that its justice system came to be called the "bloody code." Stealing was often punishable by death, with transportation to the British colonies—including America until 1776—meted out as a merciful alternative. For example, one woman from Blagdon was sentenced to death for stealing butter.[49] Individuals with means had numerous recourses, so the poor carried the brunt of the harsh justice system. The sheer brutality and quantity of public hangings had a deleterious effect on the whole of society, as the Claphamites saw it. Public executions had become a grisly form of entertainment and drew large crowds. All this went against the virtue of benevolence the Clapham Sect sought to advance, and Wilberforce supported fellow parliamentarians' proposals for abolition of the death penalty for lesser crimes.

Even more crucial than penal reform was prevention of crime and its harsh punishments. The Clapham Sect believed that popular education was a central means of preventing many of the petty crimes committed by the oppressed and listless poor. Thus, they promoted an array of approaches to popular education in an age that had not yet instituted public, compulsory education. Thornton and Wilberforce lent their support, for example, to the Society for the Support and Encouragement of Sunday Schools in 1785. As its name indicated, the purpose of the society was not to run schools but to support the people who did and to promote those efforts—much as Wilberforce did for the More sisters' schools. John Newton delivered "charity sermons" to raise funds for the schools.[50] Conservative in their politics, members of the sect shared the concerns that teaching the poor to read could have the unintended consequence of exposing them to radical literature and thereby cultivating revolutionary spirits. But rather than keeping the poor illiterate, as many of the upper classes wished, the Claphamites produced literature that would appropriately fill the appetite for reading that they themselves had helped to whet. Indeed, the Claphamites took a progressive view regarding literacy as "the necessary prelude to democracy" and pursued it.[51] In a speech before the House of Commons in 1819 advocating for more education for the poor, Wilberforce argued that "if people were destined to be free, they must be made fit to enjoy their freedom."[52] More's Cheap Repository Tracts, as we will see later, offered a dramatic solution to this problem. This project by More and her fellow Claphamites to provide reading material to the poor that was both affordable and edifying advanced significantly the idea that the poor should be taught to read—and the support of literacy itself. Writing, as we have seen, was another matter and was during this period considered a discrete skill that was taught separately. It would be some time before the idea that the poor should be taught to write as well as to read would become universally acceptable. Only in the more radical Methodist schools was writing taught, and More strove to distance herself from such schools, particularly after the Blagdon controversy.[53] As long as the poor were unable to write, the means of production of reading material would remain in the hands of those in power; continued pressure from foreign wars and revolutions ensured such control would remain a concern among conservative and moderates alike for decades to come.

The Clapham Sect didn't limit its efforts to domestic reform but reached outward on the globe. One of its earliest and most ambitious projects was the establishment in 1791 of the Sierra Leone Company, which founded the British colony of Sierra Leone on the west coast of Africa for the purpose of resettling former American slaves who had fought on behalf of the British during the American Revolution. Henry Thornton was chairman of the company, while Wilberforce served as director alongside other members of the Clapham Sect and the abolitionist movement. Eventually, Claphamite Zachary Macaulay served as governor for several years. As a business venture formed to defeat the slave trade, the project combined two kinds of freedom in which the Claphamites believed: freedom for slaves and freedom of trade. Yet the project was fraught with economic, political, and practical risks that reaped considerable failures.[54] Still, it was a brave and bold endeavor. The long-lasting results of the company and its resettlement project included putting in place trade systems that would flourish after the abolition of the slave trade. Through their presence and their practices there, Christian influence spread farther into the continent.

Since its inception, the East India Company had forbidden evangelization as a way of quieting the bark of colonization's bite. The missionary aspect of colonization was another fruit of the Clapham Sect's labors. One of the sect's greatest victories in international missions came in 1813 when the decision to renew the East India Company's charter included a missionary clause the sect had developed. At Wilberforce's request to "stir up a petition in Bristol" on the matter, More published an unsigned letter in the

Bristol Journal arguing for the merits of taking the gospel to India "in a gradual and prudent way." More's efforts soon produced petitions in Bristol, Manchester, and elsewhere collected to bolster Wilberforce's successful appeal in the House of Commons.[55] In his speech on the East India bill, Wilberforce attached the account by a missionary to India of his witness to the burning of a woman alive along with the corpse of her recently deceased husband: "It was a horrible sight. The most shocking indifference and levity appeared among those who were present. I never saw anything more brutal than their behavior." The account described in dreadful detail the agonizingly slow burning of the woman over a small fire, how "the legs of the poor creature [were] hanging out of the fire while her body was in flames." The spectators then beat her legs until they were broken and could be bent toward the fire. "Such were the confusion, the levity, the bursts of brutal laughter, while the poor woman was burning alive before their eyes," the witness wrote, "that it seemed as if every spark of humanity was extinguished by this accursed superstition."[56] The parliamentary decision in favor of the missionary clause went down in history as "the greatest evangelical vote on any single issue ever recorded in the House of Commons."[57]

The longest-standing project of the Clapham Sect is perhaps the Church Mission Society (CMS), still in operation today. This evangelistic arm of the Anglican Church was founded in 1799 as the Society for Missions to Africa and the East by Wilberforce, Thornton, and Babington, among others. The mission work of the CMS began in Sierra Leone but extended across the globe as a marked presence throughout the colonial and postcolonial ages.[58]

The Claphamites didn't give just time and words toward missions and reform—they gave their money too. More's Sunday schools were supported by monies from the Claphamites. Until he married in 1796, Thornton gave an incredible six-sevenths of the income he had inherited from his father to charity.[59] He was not unique among the members of the Clapham Sect. Zachary Macaulay gave away nearly all his wealth on behalf of African slaves. Wilberforce was involved in nearly seventy philanthropic societies, and one year, he gave away three thousand pounds more than he made.[60] The Clapham Sect was also instrumental in founding or supporting countless philanthropic societies. Besides the Proclamation Society that began it all, others included the Church Mission Society (mentioned above), the Anti-Slavery Society, the Abolition Society (a largely Quaker effort), the Sunday School Society, the Bettering Society, the British and Foreign Bible Society, and the Small Debt Society. No wonder Wilberforce, in a letter to Thomas Jefferson, called the generosity that characterized the Clapham Sect a "concert of benevolence."[61]

All their efforts and resources were crystallized in one quiet, simple domestic scene back in Clapham. While serving as governor of Sierra Leone, Zachary Macaulay sent some African children to England for an education. Some died shortly after their arrival, but the others were sent to school in Clapham where More was found catechizing one of the youngsters. She expressed delight with his quick answers.[62]

Yet despite their generosity, benevolence, and sharp moral vision, the Claphamites had blind spots too. Historians today note their dearth of attention to conditions for the factory workers closer to home.[63] This lack owed at least in part to their support of free market economics and the movement toward mass production it was bringing to Great Britain.[64] Wilberforce believed that "the interests of the manufacturers and those of humanity were not at variance" and reluctantly supported parliamentary intervention.[65] In the early nineteenth century, Wilberforce voted in favor of modest reform measures, but when one considers the sect's zeal for abolishing slavery and advancing foreign missions, it is difficult now not to see such efforts as minimal in comparison. Even so, while the Clapham Sect's first efforts at improving conditions for factory workers were small and ultimately ineffectual, they laid the groundwork for the more dramatic reforms later in the century.[66]

Despite its shortcomings, the "silent revolution" begun by the Clapham Sect infused society with benevolence and compassion that had not before existed on such a scale.[67] Indeed, "in proportion to numbers," the Claphamites "achieved perhaps more than any other group in English history" by influencing Britain's political and social policies, particularly those that affected the poorest classes of people.[68] The reforms they sought and achieved set the tone for the coming Victorian age with its emphases on religion, morality, family, and duty. Indeed, for her central role in this, Hannah More has been called "the first Victorian."[69]

CHAPTER 12

BURDENED FOR THE BEASTS

The culture into which More was born imagined and had imagined for many centuries all creation, from top to bottom, as bonded together from heaven to earth like the links of a chain. Every category of creation was seen as a link on this great chain of being, as it was called. Human beings were the middle links, each order of angels ascended as the upward links, and each order of animals, plants, and minerals descended along the lower ones. This hierarchical view extended into the general categories as well. Within the category of human beings, all were hierarchically arranged by class, with royalty and nobility on the links above commoners and so on. This image of the great chain of being held powerful sway over the image by which More's society viewed the relationships of human beings with one another and the rest of creation. People were only beginning to imagine a world that did not consist of rigid hierarchical boundaries.

From today's vantage point, one in which equality is valued, the problems with such a controlling image are readily apparent.

Yet the strength of such a view as the order of creation was the belief that each link, whether placed high or low on the chain, was equally important to the strength of the entire chain. The well-being of society as a whole depended on the well-being of each link in the chain and on maintaining each link's proper place in the chain. While members of More's society found it difficult to envision a form of equality that would not upend all order, they valued the importance of each link in the chain.

The understanding that on the great chain humans held a higher place than animals had a twofold implication for the reform efforts by More and her friends. First, human beings were understood as superior in moral significance and value in the chain of being; however, their elevated place on the chain was accompanied by profound responsibility toward the lower creatures. By the same thinking, the upper classes were likewise responsible for the well-being of the lower classes. Hannah and her like-minded reformers, therefore, saw the reform of one part of society as having ripple effects for all society. The work that More undertook in educating the poor was not an endeavor separate from her attempts to elevate the morals of the upper class. Nor were these efforts separate from her quieter endeavors to promote kindness toward animals. In strengthening the separate links, each of these activities strengthened the entire chain.

The image of the great chain of being made the interconnectedness of all creation impossible to ignore to those with minds of moral clarity and integrity. A famous series of engravings printed in 1751 by the eighteenth-century artist William Hogarth dramatically portrayed this kind of interconnectedness within the scales of both creation and morality. The *Four Stages of Cruelty* depicts a central figure who goes from torturing small animals as a boy, to beating a fallen horse as a corrupt coachman, to murdering

his lover, and finally to receiving his just reward of public dissection after being tried, convicted, and hanged. Each print is highly
detailed—including the depiction of various acts of horrific cruelty perpetrated on animals—expanding the story as it unfolded
through the sequence of pictures, creating a visual narrative that
sets forth a holistic moral vision. In the previous century, Descartes
and his followers viewed animals as mere machines to be used by
humans with no regard in the name of science; Hogarth's work
reflected a shifting attitude. Kindness toward animals was a growing concern in the eighteenth century.

The evolution of More's views on animal welfare reflected both
this societal shift and her strengthening faith convictions. In her
earlier literary career, More criticized poetic expressions of sentimentality toward animals as a form of rhetorical excess and emotional
self-indulgence in her poem "Sensibility," published in 1782 in the
same volume as *Sacred Dramas*. During the so-called long eighteenth
century (1660–1830), a "cult of sensibility" arose that exalted the
outward manifestations of emotional sensitivity—weeping, fainting, and the like—as the marks of morality and refined character,
to the point that signs of sensibility became more important than
benevolent or moral actions. In addressing the virtues and limits
of sensibility in the poem, More cautioned against the hypocrisy of
an overly sentimental view of animals that neglected higher moral
obligations:

> There are, who fill with brilliant plaints the page,
> If a poor linnet meet the gunner's rage;
> There are, who for a dying fawn deplore,
> As if friend, parent, country, were no more;
> Who boast, quick rapture trembling in their eye,
> If from the spider's snare they snatch a fly;

There are, whose well-sung plaints each breast inflame,
And break all hearts—but his from whom they came.
He, scorning life's low duties to attend,
Writes odes on friendship, while he cheats his friend. [lines 267–76][1]

When More's interests and work later shifted in response to her growing Christian conviction, her view toward animal welfare underwent a parallel expansion. Despite the excesses of sensibility that concerned More, sensibility helped foster her growing opposition toward cruelty in all forms, whether that of slavery, prison and labor conditions, or animal mistreatment. Sensibility was part of a larger social and theological framework that encompassed all society and creation. This meant that the welfare of animals was an important issue for the reformers. "England is a paradise for women, and hell for horses," Robert Burton, the famous seventeenth-century Oxford scholar wrote as far back as 1621 in *The Anatomy of Melancholy*.[2] More was joining others in attesting the truth of the latter point.

William Cowper—the poet More described as one she could read on Sunday, and coauthor with John Newton of the *Olney Hymns*—reflected both emotional sensibility and evangelical conviction in his poetic treatment of animals. Indeed, Cowper has been called the "eighteenth-century poet of animal welfare" for his poetic—and personal—identification with suffering animals, most famously in *The Task*.[3] Here Cowper likened his pain to that of a struck deer, which he then linked to the crucified Christ:

> *I was a stricken deer, that left the herd*
> *Long since; with many an arrow deep infix'd*
> *My panting side was charged when I withdrew*
> *To seek a tranquil death in distant shades.*

There was I found by one who had Himself
Been hurt by th' archers. In his side he bore
And in his hands and feet, the cruel scars.[4]

Such cultivation of the moral imagination through art and literature undergirded the efforts of the reformers across a range of concerns. The same empathy for slaves that More and her friends sought to develop through a moral imagination ran along the entire chain of being, all the way down to the brutes. The abolitionists' inclusion of animal welfare in their attempts to cultivate benevolence across society went back at least to More's friend and fellow abolitionist Margaret Middleton, who was an early role model to Hannah in the animal-welfare concern. More said of Middleton that "her kindness, which you would think must needs be exhausted on the negroes, extends to the suffering of every animal."[5] Imaginative identification with others illuminated, More and her friends believed, the relationship of humanity in relationship to God.

In the views of a reformer like More, a society that mistreated animals presented a distorted image of God's relationship to his human creation. Such an argument was made by Soame Jenyns, a writer and member of Parliament for Cambridgeshire, in his 1782 work *Disquisitions on Several Subjects,* which included the essay "On Cruelty to Inferior Animals." In this essay, Jenyns objected, "No small part of mankind derive their chief amusements from the deaths and sufferings of inferior animals; a much greater, consider them only as engines of wood, or iron, useful in their several occupations." He then catalogued the varieties of cruelties toward animals common in eighteenth-century society, from the forms stemming from the necessary uses of animals to the more horrific forms that served as entertainment:

The carman drives his horse, and the carpenter his nail, by repeated blows; and so long as these produce the desired effect, and they both go, they neither reflect or care whether either of them have any sense of feeling. . . . The social and friendly dog is hanged without remorse, if, by barking in defence of his master's person and property, he happens unknowingly to disturb his rest. . . . The sluggish bear, in contradiction to his nature, is taught to dance, for the diversion of a malignant mob, by placing red hot irons under his feet: and the majestic bull is tortured by every mode which malice can invent, for no other offence, but that he is gentle, and unwilling to assail his diabolical tormentors. These, with, innumerable other acts of cruelty, injustice, and ingratitude, are every day committed, not only with impunity, but without censure and without observation; but we may be assured, that they cannot finally pass away unnoticed, and unretaliated.[6]

These blood sports, as they were called, were deeply woven into the fabric of English life, from high to low. Lacking land and horses with which to hunt in a more genteel manner, the rural villagers participated in blood sports that seem particularly brutal, if differing only in degree.

Bullbaiting was the most popular of these violent entertainments, one often incorporated into seasonal festivities, religious celebrations, or more solemn events such as wakes.[7] It was so common a form of entertainment that in some towns, an iron ring to which the bull's rope was tied was a permanent fixture.[8] The county of Staffordshire had a particular notoriety for its bullbaiting events, to the point that it developed a recognized breed of bullbaiting dogs, the Staffordshire bull terrier.[9]

An early nineteenth-century publication recorded one particularly depraved event:

> Some years ago at a bull-baiting in the North, a young man, confident of the courage of his dog, laid some trifling wager: that he would at separate times cut off all the four feet of his dog, and that after every amputation he would attack the bull. The cruel experiment was tried, and with success. . . . At a bull-baiting in Staffordshire, after the animal had been baited by single dogs, he was attacked by numbers let loose at once upon him.—Having escaped from his tormentors, they again fastened him to the ring; and with a view, either of gratifying their savage revenge, or of better securing their victim, they actually cut off his hoofs, and enjoyed the spectacle of his being worried to death on his bloody and mangled stumps. These facts speak more than a volume against the sophistic arguments of the advocates for exciting brave and manly courage by the exhibition of bloody and barbarous sports.[10]

Bearbaiting and badgerbaiting were sometimes used in contests similar to those staged between bull and dog, although these animals were less available than bulls.[11] Dogfighting also existed but drew less attention and therefore less controversy. In 1839, James Macaulay, a student at Edinburgh University, won the award for best essay from the school's theology faculty. In his winning piece, *Essay on Cruelty to Animals,* Macaulay described the violence of the dogfights. Witnesses to one organized fight described how dogs were tortured in order to goad them into fighting, then "told of the laceration of the dogs; of their distressing cries and yells of pain . . . of the pit being at the end quite a pool of blood." Macaulay's paper also exposed the fact that such cruelty was not limited to the ignorant poor. Although held in rural outposts, organized dogfights were participated in and supported by the "men high in rank and station in society." One event in particular included "several noble lords and members of parliament."[12]

Bull running was popular in England for hundreds of years, sometimes drawing hundreds of participants and spectators in some locales. Unlike the more formal running of the bulls in Spain, a religious ritual rooted in the honoring of Saint Fermin, this popular version was essentially a free-for-all bullfight with only staffs or sticks as weapons, if those. Entire towns participated, with shops and businesses closed, roads barricaded, and church bells ringing at the start of the run. The chaos that followed the release of the bull created a carnival atmosphere in which revelers either tormented and teased the bull before running off or stood back and watched from as safe a distance as might be found. The festivities lasted into the afternoon and ended when the exhausted bull was caught and slaughtered.[13]

Cockfights were also popular. They were advertised frequently in newspapers as taking place in villages and towns, although the larger fights were hosted at actual cockpits or at inns that had their own pits.[14] Cocks were altered to maximize both blood and sport: their wings and tails, their natural defenses, were clipped; their beaks were filed and sharp spurs placed on their legs. A visitor to England from Germany witnessed the events and reported on how the birds "peck at each other, and especially how they hack with their spurs. . . . Their combs bleed terribly and they often slit each other's crop and abdomen with the spurs." The bloodbaths whipped up the human spectators. "There is nothing more diverting" to the crowd, the tourist reported, "than when one [cock] seems quite exhausted and there are great shouts of triumph and monstrous wagers; and then the cock that appeared to be quite done for suddenly recovers and masters the other."[15]

Like dogfighting, cockfighting was a sport all classes shared in common: avid participants could be found from high to low, as illustrated in another painting by William Hogarth depicting men adorned in ruffled shirts and powdered wigs joined with men and women wearing crumpled caps and woolen coats, all gathered in a frenzy around the cockpit containing two feathered creatures meeting in battle. In the arrangement of its figures before the tableaux of the pit, the painting perversely alluded, it is commonly noted, to Leonardo Da Vinci's *The Last Supper*, with a betting nobleman seated where Christ sits in that holier scene. Cockfighting was frequently attended by drinking, brawling, shouting, and betting men. Much of the crime, begging, and misery found in the rural districts was attributed to "this cruel sport."[16]

Yet another sport involving birds was cockthrowing. This popular entertainment was sometimes incorporated into the traditions of Shrove Tuesday, the day before Ash Wednesday, a day originally dedicated to shriving or confessing in preparation for the Lenten season.[17] In a cockthrow, the bird's owner tied the bird to the ground by a cord the length of four to five feet attached to the creature's leg. The owner charged a few pence for three throws. Competitors stood about twenty feet from the bird and tried to knock it down by throwing a stick or club at it. One observer reported that "their legs are broken and their bodies bruised in a shocking manner."[18] The bird was won if the thrower succeeded in knocking it down and could run and grab it before it got up. Birds deft enough to avoid this fate fetched considerable earnings for their owners. Often the winner of the bird would turn around and use the prize bird for his own cockthrowing enterprise.[19] A witness reported in the mid-eighteenth century, "Scarcely a churchyard was to be found but a number of those poor innocent birds were thus barbarously treated."[20]

Cockthrowing was the first blood sport to go out of vogue, partly because it was seen as the least sporting of all. The efforts by the famous and influential clergyman Josiah Tucker, who wrote a tract against the sport around the middle of the century, helped bring disfavor to cockthrowing. By the early 1750s, cockthrowing was increasingly condemned as "evil." Despite local orders against it in various locations resulting in arrests of participants, it took nearly a century to abolish it.[21]

Toward the end of the century, an increasing number of essays, tracts, and sermons were being written against all the blood sports and in favor of humane treatment of animals.[22] Opposition to blood sports was not always rooted solely in concern for the animals. Rather, some began to recognize the way such activities affected the human participants. Wanton cruelty to animals dehumanized its participants and, in turn, hampered "enlightened morality" and intellectual progress. One 1789 newspaper reported blood sports served to "degrade mankind beneath the barbarity of a savage" and were "totally inconsistent with the laws of nature, the laws of religion, and the laws of a civilized nation."[23] Another writer argued, "Cruelty towards Men is most confessedly an Offence against God, and can the same Disposition towards brutes be otherwise? Did not the same Hand which made Them make Us?"[24] An anti-bullbaiting tract proclaimed that the "monster, who can willfully persevere to torture the dumb creation, would feel little or no compunction, to serve a purpose, in aiming his bludgeon at the head, or ingulfing [*sic*] the murderous blade within the warm vitals of his fellow creature."[25]

Furthermore, the dehumanizing effect on participants in blood sports was seen as fostering a host of other vices: impiety, social disorder, riot, drunkenness, mischief, and immorality.[26] "If

we eagerly stimulate brutal fierceness, we are guilty of a most bar-
barous impiety," said one critic.[27] "Every act that sanctions cruelty
to animals must tend to destroy the morals of a people, and consequently every social duty," said another.[28] Training people "to
delight in scenes of cruelty" was harmful to public order and "cor-
ruptive" to youth, one newspaper opined in 1801.[29]

Efforts by Wilberforce, More, and like-minded activists against
animal cruelty were directly linked to their other efforts at social
reform. Benevolence toward all lower creatures was a characteristic feature of the evangelical movement from its beginnings, and
Christians, including many clergymen, led the way in informing and organizing opposition to the blood sports.[30] Early in the
century, John Wesley made an appeal on behalf of animals in his
*Compendium of Natural Philosophy, Being a Survey of the Wisdom
of God in the Creation,* pointing out that animals "that want the
help of man, have a thousand engaging ways, which, like the voice
of God speaking to his heart, command him to preserve and
cherish them."[31] Later in the century, Sarah Trimmer, one of the
founders of the Sunday school movement, put animal welfare at
the forefront of her program for moral education. A clergyman
for the Staffordshire district fought zealously for twenty years to
put an end to bullbaiting before the practice was ended there.[32] In
The Task, quoted earlier, the evangelical hymnist William Cowper
denounced such "detested" blood sport:

> *That owes its pleasures to another's pain;*
> *That feeds upon the sobs and dying shrieks*
> *Of harmless nature.*[33]

The poet later linked benevolence to essential humanity in
these famous lines:

I would not enter on my list of friends
(Though graced with polish'd manners and fine sense,
Yet wanting sensibility) the man
Who needlessly sets foot upon a worm.[34]

Wilberforce, too, was a "great lover of animals." In *A Practical View,* he decried the blood sports, designed, he said, "to fill up the void of a listless and languid age."[35] He included bullbaiting among the "multiplied plague spots" on England's complexion, "sure indicatives" of a "falling state."[36] He and his friends were known for confronting animal cruelty when they encountered it. Once, in his later life, Wilberforce was walking with his young grandson on a hill near Bath when the two encountered a cart driver cruelly whipping his horse as the beast haltingly pulled a heavy load of stone up the hill. When Wilberforce intervened on the animal's behalf, the carter swore and told him to mind his own business. But upon realizing who was before him, the man paused and said, "Are you Mr. Wilberforce? . . . Then I will never beat my horse again!"[37]

As More's Christian convictions grew, so, too, did her conviction that benevolence toward animals was part of a holistic Christian worldview, and her writings came to reflect these evolving views. She and her fellow reformers considered reading in particular as central to moral reform because of the ability of reading to cultivate empathy deeper than what the senses can communicate, whether the issue was slavery or animal welfare.[38] For example, following the defeat of a parliamentary motion by Wilberforce to abolish the slave trade, a poem by Anna Barbauld lamented that even the "sight" of "the Negro's chains" had not been enough to sway the nation.[39] To be sure, images—such as those of the inside of a slave ship that More was using to expose the horrors of the slave trade—had their place. But reformers whose faith centered on the written word naturally tapped into its particular ability to transform thinking.

In a ballad More composed for the Cheap Repository, "The Hackney Coachman; or, The Way to Get a Good Fare," she described an exemplary figure whose morality was characterized by kindness toward animals: "I am a bold coachman, and drive a good hack," the song began. "Though poor, we are honest and very content," the coachman sang in later lines. The ballad conveyed the sincere piety of someone who avoided drinking and "mischief" and stepped into church on Sundays when hired to take a lady there. Then the verses said:

> Though my beasts should be dull, yet I don't use them ill;
> Though they stumble, I swear not, nor cut them up hill;
> For I firmly believe there's no charm in an oath,
> That can make a nag trot, when to walk he is loath.[40]

Although animal welfare was never a central focus of her work, More shared Wilberforce's conviction against cruelty to animals, most dramatically in her Cheap Repository Tracts. The tracts explicitly correlated kindness toward animals with Christian piety and virtue. For example, in *Black Giles the Poacher*, a host of crimes and vices were perpetrated by this ne'er-do-well. Among them was the fact that he "kept two or three asses, miserable beings, which, if they had the good fortune to escape an untimely death by starving, did not fail to meet with it by beating." The children of the lazy, cheating Black Giles naturally followed in their father's ways. Rather than tend their own poor creatures, Giles's sons stole their neighbor's geese and cruelly "[plucked] the quills of the down from these poor live creatures." Later, in part two of the tale, Giles and his sons ferried stolen apples out of town, whipping "the asses till they bled."[41]

The tract *The History of Tom White* offered a more extended treatment of the animal welfare concern. At the beginning of the tale, Tom was characterized as "one of the best drivers of a Post-chaise on the Bath Road." While working for a faithful farmer, Tom was required to attend Sunday school and "to read his Bible in the evening after he had served his beasts." However, after Tom fell in with local hooligans, he took to drinking and swearing, and his character was corrupted. In a passage describing Tom's growing habit of swearing, the narrator of the tale remarked, "And here I cannot but drop a hint on the deep folly, as well as wickedness of being in a great rage with poor beasts, who, not having the gift of reason, cannot be moved like human creatures, with all the wicked words that are said to them; but who, unhappily, having the gift of feeling, suffer as much as human creatures can do, at the cruel and unnecessary beatings given them."

After being injured in a chaise accident because he was "a little flustered with liquor," Tom fell under conviction and turned to God. When he returned to work and was required to labor on Sunday, he realized that taking proper care of his horses—allowing them to rest—would allow him to attend church during their respite. "A man who takes care of his horses will generally think it right to let them rest an hour or two at least," he said. Piety and proper care of the beasts went hand in hand. While his old rascally friends made fun of Tom for his newfound fastidiousness, he paid them no mind. Instead, he was careful, the tract explained, "in never giving his horses too much water when they were hot; nor, whatever was his haste, would he ever gallop them up hill, strike them across the head, or when tired, cut and slash them in driving on the stones." The narrator went on to explain:

What helped to cure Tom of these bad practices was that remark he met with in the Bible, that a good man is merciful to his beast. He was much moved one day on reading the Prophet Jonah, to observe what compassion the great God of heaven and earth had for poor beasts: for one of the reasons there given why the Almighty was unwilling to destroy the great city of Nineveh was, "because there was so much cattle in it." After this, Tom never could bear to see a wanton stroke inflicted. Doth God care for horses, said he, and shall man be cruel to them?[42]

After growing financially successful, Tom returned to the old farmer for whom he had worked in his youth, who reported that "many horses" were saved because of Tom's attentive care.

The approach to animal welfare taken by More and her evangelical friends was distinguished by its moderation. The cult of sensibility that influenced some of their contemporaries' views—and that More criticized—produced a perspective about animals rooted not in duty, ethics, or stewardship but in emotional indulgence. One 1766 novel, for example, described a character who meted cruel punishment to her slaves but wept over the injury of a pet dog.[43] Some conservatives criticized sentimentality toward animals for its philosophical connection to the egalitarianism of radical Jacobites and French *philosophes*.[44] Such thinkers charged sentimental animal lovers with inverted priorities, loving the lowest creatures most. Inordinate affection for pets like lap dogs and little monkeys was linked to the liberal values of the French Revolution by some conservative thinkers and therefore was linked to the decline of British culture.[45] Thus, for some antirevolutionaries, the blood sports were necessary diversions from seditious activities such as reading—as More was teaching in the Sunday schools—which was linked to revolution.[46]

Ironically, both of these extreme views toward animals—sentimental and utilitarian—were self-serving. Neither considered animals as creatures designed as part of God's order and sovereign purpose, one for which humans held significant responsibility. More's view moderated between the extreme conservative view that disdained affection for animals and the other extreme of an absurd sentimentality that turned a blind eye on human suffering. So while promoting human responsibility toward animals in the tracts, she criticized the opposite extreme.

On this theological and social basis, she and her fellow Claphamites, particularly Wilberforce in his role of parliamentarian, helped establish England's first animal welfare laws. Eleven bills on animal cruelty were brought before Parliament between 1800 and 1835.[47] The first attempt was a bill to prohibit bullbaiting, sponsored by Sir William Pulteney and supported by Wilberforce. The bill never made it to a second hearing. It wasn't until 1822 that the first animal-welfare legislation passed, despite Wilberforce's faithful support of each legislative attempt. This first victory was Richard Martin's bill to prevent cruel and improper treatment of cattle. As he had been for each previous attempt at animal-welfare legislation, Wilberforce was one of the bill's sponsors. Two years later, at an 1824 coffeehouse gathering, the Society for the Prevention of Cruelty to Animals was formed, largely under the leadership of activist Christians. Wilberforce was appointed, along with fellow members of Parliament and several clergymen, to superintend the publication of sermons and tracts on animal welfare in hopes of influencing public opinion toward their unpopular position. Not surprisingly, the first animal-welfare groups were regarded as "meddlesome" and "fanatical," as were most attempts at moral and social reform.[48]

Nevertheless, by the year of More's death in 1833, bullards were reporting difficulty in raising funds for the next bull run. When an opponent who attempted to prevent that year's run showed up in town, he reported receiving threats of personal violence and having "the most horrid imprecations" uttered against him by "the ferocious and blood-thirsty bull-baiters" because kindness toward the beasts had prevailed.[49]

The novelist E. M. Forster, whose great-aunt, Marianne Thornton, was More's goddaughter, described years later in 1925 a picture of More that faced him as he sat, writing, in a chair that had belonged to her. The picture, titled "Mrs. Hannah More and her Favorite Squirrel," depicted an elderly More seated at a Chippendale table with a squirrel upon it. "They face one another," Forster wrote, "they bend their necks with identical gesture, and the calm light of a hundred years ago flows in through square panes of glass upon the letter and the nut that they are opening."[50]

CHAPTER 13

REFORM, NOT REVOLUTION

"FROM LIBERTY, EQUALITY, AND THE RIGHTS OF MAN, GOOD LORD, deliver *us*!"[1] More wrote exasperatedly to Horace Walpole in January 1793. While More was working to improve the lives of rural English laborers through her Sunday schools, a revolution was brewing in France, one flamed by atheism. More could not imagine those ideals of the French Revolution—"liberty, equality, and the rights of man"—apart from sedition, tyranny, and god-lessness, so she rejected them out of hand.

Some among the fashionable in England, however, were drawn to the ideals and underpinnings of the French Revolution. Even More applauded, along with nearly everyone else, the storming of the Bastille on July 14, 1789. But by the next year, French liberty had taken religion as its prisoner: the landholdings of the church were seized by the government, monastic orders were destroyed, and the Civil Constitution of the Clergy subjected the country's Catholic priests to the dictates of the French government. In 1790, More wrote in a letter to William Wilberforce that she "conceived an utter aversion to liberty according to the present idea of it in France."[2] A Tory in politics and thus a believer in Great Britain's limited monarchy, More had a conservative approach to reform centered on expanding responsibility, not rights, and promoting duty, not democracy. Despite her devoted labors in the rural villages in western England, More believed, as did her collaborators in Clapham, that social transformation had to begin at the top. "Reformation must begin with the GREAT, or it will never be effectual," she argued. "Their example is the fountain whence the vulgar draw their habits, actions, and characters. To expect to reform the poor while the opulent are corrupt, is to throw odours into the stream while the springs are poisoned."[3]

This idea of the responsibility of the upper classes to set the example for the rest of society would become a defining characteristic of the later Victorian age—to the point of being later satirized famously by Oscar Wilde in his work *The Importance of Being Earnest*—but this was an embryonic idea in More's time. The prevailing notion was expressed by one popular clergyman who told the aristocratic members of his congregation that they were not expected to uphold high standards of virtuous behavior because they could make up for such lapses with generous charitable giving. More was infuriated. She "could not accept that there was one law for the rich and another for the poor."[4] How could one expect the lessons in pious, responsible living she brought to the poor to have any lasting effect when every day their "betters" acted worse? She became convinced that the upper classes needed reform too.

Who better to lead the attempt than Hannah More? The bishop of London encouraged her to do so. Where, he asked her in 1787, "can we find any but yourself that can make the 'fashionable world' read books of morality and religion, and find improvement when they are only looking for amusement?"[5] Similarly, Dr. Horne told her, "We can tell people their duty from the pulpit; but you have the art to make them desirous of performing it, as their greatest pleasure and amusement."[6] Even John Wesley sent Hannah a message through her sister: "Tell her to live in the world; there is the sphere of her usefulness; they will not let us come nigh them."[7]

During the summer she spent at Cowslip Green in 1787, More reflected on the frivolity, excess, and impiety she daily witnessed during those seasons spent in London. The result was *Thoughts on the Importance of the Manners of the Great to General Society*, published the following year. She released the work anonymously, admitting to a friend that she wished her authorship would remain undetected because, she confessed, "I was conscious that I did not live up to my song." Further, she explained, with her usual humility, "I was seriously persuaded that my insignificant name could not add weight or strength to the book, but might *diminish* it." The antithesis of modern celebrity authors, she sought to promote the ideas in the book rather than herself. Undetected, she hoped, the book "might be supposed to be the work of some wiser and better person than a discovery [of the author] would prove it to be."[8]

The first edition of *Thoughts on the Importance of the Manners of the Great* sold out like ice in a sweltering heat; the third edition sold out within hours;[9] seven editions were published within three months.[10] Guesses about its authorship ranged from William Wilberforce to the bishop of London.[11] Of course, Bishop Porteus knew the secret because More sent him a draft of the book just before its publication, and he roundly approved it. "Upon the whole, I must say it is a most delicious morsel," he wrote her, "and I almost envy you the good that it will do." He was "charmed and edified with it," he wrote, and "impatient to see it in the hands of every man and woman of condition in London and Westminster."[12]

John Newton praised her, writing in a letter after receiving a signed copy from her, "You could easily write what would procure you more general applause; but it is a singular privilege to have a *consecrated* pen, and to be able and willing to devote our talents to the cause of God and religion."[13] Bishops across England were reading and discussing *Thoughts on the Importance of the Manners of the Great*. Queen Charlotte read one of the first copies and promptly recognized it as More's work. Convicted by More's exhortations therein, she vowed to cease her practice of sending for a hairdresser on Sundays.[14] The queen loaned a copy of the book to the novelist Fanny Burney, who recorded in her journal her admiration for the book's design but complained she thought the duties outlined by More were too strict.[15] More's friend Walpole teased More, as usual, for promoting "monstrously severe doctrines" in the book.[16]

By "manners," of course, More was talking about more than politeness and table etiquette—as was Wilberforce in setting forth his second great object, she meant morality. Manners were understood to be more than mere surface matters; outward manners expressed and helped shape the inward spirit. The book challenged the very lifestyles of the rich and famous of eighteenth-century Georgian England. Then, as now, the habits and values of those in the most elevated positions of society were on display for all to see, whether they wished it or not, thereby setting the example; whether for good or ill, they set the example. *Thoughts on the Manners of the Importance of the Great* served as an exposé of the habits of the fashionable, not by uncovering what was unknown but by holding up a mirror by which the powerful might see themselves.

What was considered polite, More contended, had been long confused with what was right. She set out to draw the needed distinction. "Politeness," she said, was often a "screen" for hiding "so many ugly sights."[17] In "polite conversation," More contended, "the most grave offences are often named with cool indifference; the most shameful profligacy with affected tenderness and indulgent toleration. The substitution of the word *gallantry* for that crime which stabs domestic happiness and conjugal virtue, is one of the most dangerous of all the modern abuses of language. Atrocious deeds should never be called by gentle names."[18]

Another objectionable practice too common within the polite world—so rampant that even the scrupulous didn't seem to give it a second thought—was the widely accepted practice of ordering servants to tell visitors that their masters and mistresses were not at home when, in fact, they were. While the reasons for such a lie might be considerable, ultimately, More argued, the habit would only chip away abhorrence for lying altogether.[19]

She challenged, too, the popular attitude that bad behavior could be negated by charitable giving. "Is it not almost ridiculous," More asked, "to observe the zeal we have for doing good at a distance, while we neglect the little, obvious, every-day, domestic duties, which should seem to solicit our immediate attention?" She wrote pointedly, "It is less trouble to subscribe to the propagation of the gospel in foreign parts, than to have daily prayers in our own families."[20] In other words, true religion, like charity, begins at home.

A common excuse for impiety among the fashionable—who tended still to claim a nominal Christianity in those days—was the desire to avoid religious extremism. But More wasn't buying it: "'We must take the world,' say they, 'as we find it; reformation is not our business; and we are commanded not to be righteous overmuch,'" she wrote. "But these admonitions are contrary to every maxim in human affairs. In arts and letters the most consummate models are held out to imitation. We never hear any body cautioned against becoming too wise, too learned, or too rich."[21]

Besides, More argued, the risk of extreme piety among the fashionable was a phantom. Indeed, "he who declaims against religious excesses in the company of well-bred people, shews [*sic*] himself to be as little acquainted with the manners of the times in which he lives, as he would do who should think it a point of duty to write another *Don Quixote*."[22]

Yet More cautioned against true extremism and warned against religious excess in the other direction as well. A consequential impediment to the embrace of religion was, More argued, "that garment of sadness in which people delight to suppose her dressed; and that life of hard austerity, and pining abstinence, which they pretend she enjoins her disciples."[23] The "mischief," she wrote, "arises not from our living in the world, but from the world living in us; occupying our hearts, and monopolizing our affections."[24]

Thoughts on the Manners of the Importance of the Great was a striking success, particularly considering the unpopularity of the subject. At least one of More's contemporaries claimed that the book resulted in "the abandonment of many of the customs which it attacked."[25] In sweet irony, the book "itself became *fashionable*."[26]

More knew that changes in externals could reap only so much fruit, however. With events still simmering in France and with irreligion at the root of it, it was time to dig beneath the surface of manners to the root of the matter: religious faith. In 1791, she followed *Thoughts* with *An Estimate of the Religion of the Fashionable World. By one of the Laity*. Again, no name was attached to the work. Her friend Boscawen chided her for such a useless attempt, given her prominence: "Like Saul, you are higher than any of the people from the shoulders and upwards, you must be conspicuous; if your energy, your style, your piety is so superior, you must be discovered through all the veils that are so carefully thrown over you."[27]

John Newton solved the mystery immediately, and upon receiving a copy signed "from the author," he wrote immediately to praise her work as "a light shining in a dark place," for which he predicted the fashionable would thank God and the writer.[28]

More's first tack in the book was to defend the Established Church:

> Perhaps there has not been, since the age of the apostles, a church upon earth in which the public worship was so solemn, and so cheerful; so simple, yet so sublime; so full of fervour, at the same time so free from enthusiasm; so rich in the gold of Christian antiquity, yet so astonishingly exempt from its dross. That it has imperfections, we do not deny; but what are they, compared with its general excellence? They are as spots on the sun's disk, which a sharp observer may detect, but which neither diminish the warmth, nor obscure the brightness.[29]

If she had skirted matters in *Thoughts on the Importance of the Manners of the Great*, here she undertook them full on. She did not mince her words. "Religious duties are often neglected upon more consistent grounds than the friends of religion are willing to allow," she wrote. "They are often discontinued, not as repugnant to the understanding, not as repulsive to the judgment, but as hostile to a licentious life."[30] Those who had—whether by deliberation or default—abandoned the faith could not see their inconsistency: "While we glory in having freed ourselves from the trammels of human authority, are we not turning our liberty into licentiousness, and wantonly struggling to throw off the *Divine* authority too?" she asked pointedly. "Freedom of thought is the glory of the human mind," she continued, but only if "it is confined within its just and sober limits."[31]

As much as More and her friends in the Clapham Sect sought to advance benevolence, it was, More believed, no substitute for true religion. One of the "reigning errors among the better sort," she argued, was "to reduce all religion into benevolence, and all benevolence into alms-giving."[32] While virtue is "her own adequate reward,"[33] she claimed, morality is "not the whole of religion."[34]

There was perhaps no one more able to make an appeal for religion to the fashionable than More. John Newton explained to her, "Zeal, perhaps, sufficient to attempt something in the same way might be found in many; but other requisites are wanting. If a prudent minister should attempt such an extensive inroad into the kingdom of darkness, he might expect such opposition as few could withstand. But your sex and your character afford you a peculiar protection. They who would try to trample one of *us* into the dust will be ashamed *openly* to oppose *you*."[35]

Newton's analysis was accurate. More's sex and character made room for her in places denied to others. A remark by Leslie Stephen in his biography of More seems inspired by this period of her writing. If she "showed a little self-complacency," he wrote, "the wonder is that her strong sense kept her from being spoilt by the uniform flattery poured upon her by her contemporaries."[36]

She had written plays produced by England's premier stage manager. She had written verses extolled by the country's most revered literary critic. She had turned from that world to the church and written serious treatises that had been praised by royalty and bishops. Yet few of such accomplishments would do what Hannah More did next: she gathered together all the talent and experiences she had gained thus far in life—her literary skills, her experience in the Sunday schools, her political savvy, and her social finesse—and poured them into a pamphlet for the poor. She never could have dreamed that stooping so low would eventually lead to her most influential and most highly praised work. She now plied her pen to advance reform among the common readers with not a book, but a pamphlet.

England was awash in a sea of pamphlets, the seventeenth- and eighteenth-century equivalent to today's blog posts: quick and cheap to produce and easy to circulate. "I wonder if I shall ever live to read a book again," More complained to Walpole. She was immersed in reading—and soon in writing—endless specimens from the war of words that served as ammunition for the real war going on.[37]

Hundreds of pamphlets had been published about the revolutionary ideas stirring in France. One was Thomas Paine's *Rights of Man*, published in two parts appearing in 1791 and 1792. Writing to counter an earlier argument by Edmund Burke against the French Revolution, Paine argued in favor of the people's right to revolt and questioned the heredity rule that had governed society for virtually all humankind. Because many of the arguments against the divine right of kings and government by hereditary succession, particularly those arguments undergirding the French Revolution, were antireligious, it was difficult for many at the time to see democracy and equality apart from atheism and sedition. Paine's views were taken as an attack on the Christian religion, tied as it had been for centuries to the monarchy. The second part of *Rights of Man*, even more radical than the first, was printed cheaply and therefore gained wide readership among the lower classes, who were soon talking of rights and revolution.

Urged by her friends William Pepys and Elizabeth Montagu, More made a counterstrike against revolutionary politics that would mark a new direction in her literary career.[38] *Village Politics Addressed to all the Mechanics, Journeymen and Day Labourers in Great Britain, by Will Chip, a Country Carpenter* appeared at the end of 1792. She furthered her usual attempt at anonymity this time by using a publisher other than her usual to deflect detection.[39] In *Village Politics,* More brilliantly combined allegory and narrative in the form of a dialogue that presented an alternative story—the conservative one—about revolutionary politics. Taking the form of an extended dialogue between two main characters, the town blacksmith, Jack Anvil, and the mason, Tom Hod, this story portrayed the English form of government as superior— more stable, rational, and just—to the revolutionary one. Setting it against a rural backdrop of people with believable minor characters and scenarios and using the colorful but clear language of the common people, More recounted and refuted—in the terms of her intended audience—the most appealing arguments for revolutionary politics. When Tom said he wanted "a new constitution," Jack suggested that Tom go to the doctor. When Tom said he wanted "a *general* reform," Jack answered that "the shortest way is to mend thyself."[40] The exemplary Jack sent his daughter to a charity school from which she brought home her reading lessons and books to her family. The best route to reforming society was reforming oneself.

Village Politics portrayed the inseparability of politics, religion, and morality and addressed not only the concerns raised by Paine's pamphlet but also the entirety of More's social agenda, from high to low. While promoting England's present form of government, the pamphlet, ironically perhaps, offered progressive views of charity institutions and religious toleration and depicted the poor as having a voice.

Horace Walpole judged the work as "infinitely superior to anything on the subject, clearer, better stated, and comprehending the whole mass of matter in the shortest compass."[41] Furthermore, by pricing the pamphlet well under Paine's, it achieved phenomenal circulation. Parliamentarians and clergy members purchased it in the thousands and then distributed it freely.

Soon More made another offering to the pamphlet wars, this one targeted at the politically connected. About the same time that *Village Politics* appeared, an address was made to the national convention in France by Jacques Dupont, who called for the establishment of national public schools that would remove religion from its curriculum. "Nature and Reason," Dupont declared, "these ought to be the gods of men! These are my Gods! Admire *nature*— cultivate *reason*."[42]

When the speech was translated into English and published, it caused an outcry among the conservatives across the channel in England. "The object of this oration," in More's view, was "not to dethrone kings, but HIM by whom kings reign."[43] The speech "stuck in my throat all the winter," More wrote to Walpole. "I have been waiting for our bishops and our clergy to take some notice," she said impatiently, but to no avail. Rather, "blasphemy and atheism have been allowed to become familiar to the minds of our common people, without any attempt being made to counteract the poison."[44] She decided to take matters into her own hands. "The attempt *I* have presumed to make, I need not tell your lordship, is a very weak one," she admitted.[45] But she had done something when others had done nothing.

Remarks on the Speech of M. Dupont appeared shortly afterward. In it she warned that the "liberty and universal brotherhood, which the French are madly pursuing, with the insignia of freedom in one hand, and the bloody bayonet in the other, has bewitched your senses, is misleading your steps, and betraying you to ruin." It was but "madly pursuing an illusory perfection of human freedom."[46] The atheism at the root of the French Revolution, "which destroys all belief in, and of course cuts off all love of, and communion with God," More proclaimed, "disqualifies for the due performance of the duties of civil and social life."[47] She added, "If we would fly from the deadly contagion of atheism, let us fly from those seemingly remote, but not very indirect paths which lead to it. Let France choose this day whom she will serve; 'but, as for us and our houses, we will serve the Lord.'"[48]

The pamphlet was extensively circulated and produced a profit of two hundred forty pounds, which More donated in support of French emigrant clergy, driven out of the country by the antireligious spirit that permeated the Revolution.[49] Thousands of French Catholic priests arrived in England homeless and hungry. The More sisters opened their home in Bath to some of them, and Hannah supported various efforts to provide them with relief. Devoted Anglican that she was, More easily defended her humanitarian support of these Roman Catholic clergy on biblical grounds, even against fellow Anglicans who claimed that the atheist Dupont was doing the work of God by expelling Catholicism from France.[50]

More returned to more domestic concerns and followed up a vein of thought begun earlier in her *Estimate of the Religion of the Fashionable World*. In 1792, another revolutionary, this one at home rather than abroad, had written a treatise on the rights of women: *A Vindication of the Rights of Woman* by Mary Wollstonecraft, who is considered today to be the mother of feminism. More was not much taken with Wollstonecraft and shared her exasperation over this talk of women's rights in a letter to Walpole in 1793:

> I have been much pestered to read the "Rights of Women" [*sic*] but am invincibly resolved not to do it. Of all jargon, I hate metaphysical jargon; besides there is something fantastic and absurd in the very title. How many ways there are of being ridiculous! I am sure I have as much liberty as I can make a good use of, now I am an old maid; and when I was a young one, I had I dare say, more than was good form. If I were still young, perhaps I should

not make this confession; but so many women are fond of government, I suppose, because they are not fit for it. To be unstable and capricious, I really think, is but too characteristic of our sex; and there is perhaps no animal so much indebted to subordination for its good behaviour as woman.[51]

More's conservative view toward rights needs to be considered within the context of her conservative antirevolutionary views. Having adopted some of the traditional, aristocratic positions, More focused concern on duty and obligation over rights.

Wollstonecraft's shocking personal life was no small obstacle to More's interest in reading her work. A radical in politics, Wollstonecraft had gone to France in support of the Revolution, and having denounced the institution of marriage, she took up with an American scoundrel who later abandoned her and the little girl he fathered with her. In despair over her lover, Wollstonecraft made two dramatic suicide attempts. Eventually, despite her continued rejection of marriage as an institution, she married the political radical and anarchist William Godwin when she became pregnant by him. She died in 1797 from complications after giving birth to another daughter, Mary, who grew up to be Mary Shelley, author of *Frankenstein.*

Yet had she read *A Vindication of the Rights of Woman,* More might have found that she and Wollstonecraft shared many concerns, particularly related to a voguish female education that rendered women weak, vain, and frivolous.

This was the theme of More's 1799 work, *Strictures on the Modern System of Female Education, with a View of the Principles and Conduct Prevalent among Women of Rank and Fortune.* As the title suggests, the intended audience was the upper class, but many among the middle class read it too.[52] Unlike her earlier conduct books, this one was published with her name and was the most influential and significant of these. In it More sought to bring balance to the prevailing approach to the education of young women. She criticized two extreme philosophies of education: one influenced by the doctrine of sensibility, which treated women as frivolous creatures of mere emotion and sentiment, and the other influenced by the radical politics espoused by Mary Wollstonecraft, which placed too much emphasis on the French notions of rights, liberty, and equality.

Linking frivolous female education to apostasy, More argued that the un-Christian nations denied women "light, liberty and knowledge." She noted, "It is humbling to reflect, that in those countries in which the fondness for the mere persons of women is carried to the highest excess, *they are slaves* . . . their moral and intellectual degradation increases in direct proportion to the adoration which is paid to mere external charms."[53]

A useful education served women best, More thought. To "learn how to grow old gracefully is perhaps one of the rarest and most valuable arts which can be taught to woman."[54] Yet, when beauty is all that is expected or desired in a woman, she is left with nothing in its absence. It "is a most severe trial for those women to be called to lay down beauty, who have nothing else to take up. It is for this sober season of life that education should lay up its rich resources," she argued.[55]

The vanities More sought to combat were deeply rooted, beginning early in a girl's life. Particularly pernicious was the fashion of "Baby Balls," late-night parties that featured four- to eight-year-old children being adorned in fancy clothes to dance French minuets.[56] More offered strong words against these events—the eighteenth-century version of today's child beauty pageants—which not only cultivated vanity but also robbed children of their childhoods:

They step at once from the nursery to the ball-room; and, by a change of habits as new as it is preposterous, are thinking of dressing themselves, at an age when they used to be dressing their dolls. Instead of bounding with the unrestrained freedom of little wood-nymphs over hill and dale, their cheeks flushed with health, and their hearts overflowing with happiness, these gay little creatures are shut up all the morning, demurely practising the *pas grave,* and transacting the serious business of acquiring a new step for the evening, with more cost of time and pains than it would have taken them to acquire twenty new ideas. . . . Thus they lose the amusements which properly belong to their smiling period.[57]

This shallow but fashionable approach to educating women that began at such a tender age continued through their later years, toward one of only two ends, More complained: "either to make their fortune by marriage, or, if that fail, to qualify them to become teachers of others." The results were disastrous for women as individuals and for society: "the abundant multiplication of superficial wives, and of incompetent and illiterate governesses."[58]

Strictures called for greater emphasis on knowledge and less on decorous accomplishments, upholding a spiritual as well as a rational purpose for education. Its regimen covered a range of educational concerns from language, history, and geography to public amusements and the proper use of time. More argued for a rigorous education for women, one that would "elicit truth," foster "precision" in thinking, and cultivate "an exact mind." Female education should "bring the imagination under dominion" and lead women "to think, to compare, to combine, to methodise." It should "confer such a power of discrimination," that the student "shall learn to reject what is dazzling, if it be not solid; and to prefer, not what is striking, or bright, or new, but what is just."[59]

A proper education fits the mind for fulfilling one's duties to society as a body, just as exercise fits the body for the same purpose.[60] More wrote, "The chief end to be proposed in cultivating the understandings of women, is to qualify them for the practical purposes of life."[61] For this reason, contrary to popular opinion of the time, More asserted that "a woman cannot have too much arithmetic."[62]

Naturally, More saw a central role for religion in a proper education. Genuine religious conviction should distinguish between belief and morality, between internal conviction and external conformity. Education should, therefore, impart "clear views of the broad discrimination between practical religion and worldly morality; in short, between the virtues of Christians and of pagans. Shew [sic] them that no good qualities are genuine but such as flow from the religion of Christ. Let them learn that the virtues which the better sort of people, who yet are destitute of true Christianity, inculcate and practis [sic], resemble those virtues which have the love of God for their motive, just as counterfeit coin resembles sterling gold."[63]

The inculcation of the Christian faith, More argued, should not be left to personal whim or mere chance. "Do young persons, then, become musicians, and painters, and linguists, and mathematicians, by early study and regular labour; and shall they become Christians by accident?" she asked. She cautioned, too, against a sugar-coated Christianity that made false promises of ease and pleasure from its embrace. She called such deceptions an "error into which even some good people are apt to fall" in their eagerness to attract adherents to the faith. "In order to allure" young people to Christianity, she cautioned, "they exhibit false, or faint, or inadequate views of Christianity; and while they represent it, as it really is, as a life of superior happiness and advantage, they conceal its difficulties."[64] The results might ultimately result in abandonment of the faith: "May it not be partly owing to the want of a due introduction to the knowledge of the real nature and spirit of religion, that so many young Christians, who set out in a fair and flourishing way, decline and wither when they come to perceive the requisitions of experimental Christianity? requisitions which they had not suspected of making any part of the plan; and from which, when they afterwards discover them, they shrink back, as not prepared and hardened for the unexpected contest."[65]

Strictures received "congratulations and compliments" from every corner, including church and court.[66] By now, More had written so many works that they filled volumes. The year 1801 brought the first publication of her collected works, a beautifully bound set of eight octavo volumes. The year brought a new personal as well as a professional turn. More moved into Barley Wood, a large home she had built on a sloping lawn outside the village of Wrington. Barley Wood offered more suitable accommodations for her many visitors and friends. Here More stationed herself for battle in the Blagdon controversy, and here she both suffered and recuperated from the long illness that ensued. The Blagdon controversy nearly bested her. She retreated for a long while. Stronger people would not have done so. But weaker never would have emerged.

"Battered, hacked, scalped, tom-a-hawked as I have been for three years, and continue to be, brought out every month as an object of scorn and abhorrence, I seem to have nothing to do in the world," she told one correspondent in declining an invitation.[67] During this time, she confessed that writing had become "irksome" to her, in part because of the discomfort of sitting for long periods but also because of her inability to shake off the ugliness of the Blagdon affair.[68] Even so, in the midst of her illness, she published patriotic ballads to bolster a nation in fear of a French invasion, along with a delightful, satirical poem "The White Slave Trade," skewering the frivolities of the fashionable world, published anonymously in the *Christian Observer*.

In 1804, the same year she finally emerged from this long illness, her sisters sold their home in Bath, where they had lived since 1790, and moved in with Hannah at Barley Wood. They had all long ago retired from teaching. Endless visitors and correspondents provided her with little rest. For multitudes of her admirers, a visit to Barley Wood was a pilgrimage, its resident a patron saint.

Published in 1805, the first work she produced upon regaining her health was the treatise *Hints Towards Forming the Character of a Young Princess*, advice for raising Princess Charlotte, the only child of the Prince of Wales, the future George IV, and heiress presumptive to the throne. (Sadly, the princess did not live long enough to become monarch, dying at age twenty-one while giving birth to her first child.) A few years earlier, More met the little princess and wrote to her sisters:

> She is the most sensible and genteel little creature you would wish to see. I saw Carlton House and gardens, in company with the pretty Princess, who had great delight in opening the drawers, uncovering the furniture, curtains, lustres, &c. to show me; my visit was to Lady Elgin, who has been spending some days here.
>
> For the Bishop of London's entertainment and mine, the Princess was made to exhibit all her learning and accomplishments: the first consisted in her repeating the "Little Busy Bee," the next in dancing very gracefully, and in singing "God save the King," which was really affecting, (all things considered) from her little voice. Her understanding is so forward that they really might begin to teach her many things. It is perhaps the highest

praise, after all, to say, that she is exactly like the child of a private gentleman; wild and natural, but sensible, lively and civil.[69]

Along with the success of *Strictures,* this personal connection to the girl likely emboldened More in tackling a topic of national significance: the education of a future monarch.

She sought her friend Wilberforce's approval by sending him a draft of the manuscript.[70] When she published the work anonymously, the author was assumed at first to be a "gentleman"—who else would be so bold?[71] The book was praised by many, including the Queen, although the increasingly unruly young Charlotte declared her detestation of it.[72]

More purposely avoided the word *education* in the title in order to set the work apart from the flood of works on that topic—to which, of course, she had already made contribution.[73] Moreover, the title suggested the central concern More always had in her educational philosophy: character. In this case her curriculum considered the magnitude of a monarch as a moral as well as a political leader and proposed studies emphasizing classical and English history as well as Christian doctrine.

Years later, when informed by one of her correspondents that her *Hints Towards Forming the Character of a Young Princess* had received wide acclaim in the United States, More is said to have exclaimed, "I have conquered America!"[74] For the royalist More, this was sweet victory indeed.

CHAPTER 14

AN IMAGINATION THAT
MOVED THE WORLD

IF MORE HAD WRITTEN ONLY DRAMAS, VERSES, AND TREATISES, her mark on the world would have been deep enough. But her inkwell wasn't empty yet. Her greatest contribution to the world of letters was yet to come: stories.

It is difficult today to understand why the dry didacticism of More's essays and treatises was so appealing in her day. Hers was an age of ideas, an age grappling with redefinitions of a radically shifting world. Still, More understood that more than ideas, imagination moved the world. She'd written stories for the stage, but drama was considered a form of polite literature while novels and tracts were not. She'd already descended into the world of popular literature with her antirevolutionary tract *Village Politics* and found a new form and audience for her stories. The idea of writing more stories, many more, was one, she recorded in her journal two years later, that "engages my whole heart."[1] The idea now captivating her—one with the full support of the Clapham Sect—was the Cheap Repository Tracts.

In More's words, the purpose of the tracts was to "improve the habits, and raise the principles of the common people, at a time when their temptations, moral and political, were multiplied beyond the example of any former period."[2] It would turn out to be one of the most successful projects of the Clapham Sect. Henry Thornton served as treasurer, and William Wilberforce provided finances. Although not a member of the sect, Bishop Porteus wholeheartedly lent moral support. According to the plan approved by Henry Thornton, the goal of the repository was "to supplant the corrupt and vicious little books and ballads" sold by hawkers everywhere.[3]

Traditionally, street literature offered either ideas or escape, either instruction or entertainment. Tracts, chapbooks, broadsheets, and ballads from hawkers, peddlers, and booksellers glutted the streets. Some were political, such as Paine's *Rights of Man*. But many were sheer amusement. A staple in the reading diet of the newly literate, the most common cheap literature offered bawdy songs, love ballads, folk tales, and tales of superstition—and notoriously lacked religion, morality, or even good manners. Between the two main kinds of street literature—political and entertaining—readers could have their fill of either medicine or sugar. The Cheap Repository Tracts would offer both in one serving. It was an ingenious plan.

The real innovation of the Cheap Repository was to combine the entertainment and teaching so as, in the famous dictum of Horace in his *Art of Poetry*, to both "instruct" and "delight."[4] As More and her friends saw it, providing edifying but amusing reading material to the newly literate poor could accomplish two things at once. First, the tracts could reach an otherwise unreached audience with lessons in religion, thrift, and morality. Second, by offering an alternative to the unwholesome street literature circulating in abundance, More hoped to reform the appetite of the masses, "to abate their relish for those corrupt and inflammatory publications" and develop in its place a taste for wholesome reading.[5] Thus, the stories, songs, and poems of the Cheap Repository Tracts offered reading that was simple, substantive, and fun, all written at the reading level of the newly literate. Interwoven in them were many of the causes and concerns of More and the Claphamites. For example, in one a minister modeled a catechismal approach to biblical instruction, similar to that used in More's Sunday schools. Another character's moral behavior was rewarded by being promoted to Sunday school teacher. Pious characters attended church and refused to read bawdy literature. Habits of thrift and industry were rewarded. Well-to-do characters were portrayed negatively or positively depending on how well they fulfilled their social duties and set good examples.

The allure of the tracts began with the covers, designed to look like the existing popular tracts with eye-catching illustrations and attention-grabbing titles such as *Sinful Sally*, *The Gin Shop*, *The Roguish Miller*, and *Tawney Rachel*, modeled after the most popular of the tracts that More considered corrupting. *Tawney Rachel* was a particularly clever specimen. The full title was *Tawney Rachel: Or, the Fortune Teller, with Some Account of Dreams, Omens, and Conjurors*. Rachel was the pipe-smoking wife of the title character of another set of tracts, *Black Giles the Poacher*. Rachel only pretended to be employed in legitimate work selling books, ballads, laces, and such, but her peddling was an opening for telling people's fortunes. The tract revealed the tricks and stratagems she used to take in innocent people like tenderhearted Sally Evans, who was fooled by Rachel into thinking she was fated to marry a man other than the one she loved and thus married a worthless wretch with another wife. Sally's story revealed many lessons that More wanted to impart to readers about vanity, superstition, and romanticism.

Some titles from the Cheap Repository were more sober: *The History of Diligent Dick* and *Patient Joe, The Newcastle Collier,* for example. But the titles, colorful as some might be, were not the most innovative part of the tracts' design. The cover art was most groundbreaking. While the scandalous tracts the Cheap Repository sought to replace used generic woodcuts generally related to the theme again and again, More employed one of the best engravers in London to make original woodcuts for individual tracts, each one featuring details that illustrated the song or story within, some even with details from other tracts in the series.[6]

In fact, the Cheap Repository was an early example of modern mass marketing. In addition to the appealing packaging of the titles and illustrations on the covers, the price of each was set to under-cut significantly those of the corrupting forms of street literature, expanding the potential of the tracts to wield even wider influence. The Cheap Repository also anticipated modern advertising strategies. Often a tale ended with a hint about an upcoming tract so as to entice readers to buy the next installment in the series, a precursor to the serial publication that would be expertly employed in the next century by Charles Dickens.[7] The illustration for one tract included the cover from an earlier tract, a form of cross promotion that exhibited modern marketing acumen as well as postmodern intertextuality. More cozied up to the booksellers and hawkers so they would add her tracts to their sales offerings. Some distributors offered trade-ins of the corrupting tracts for the edifying versions of the repository. Circulation was further increased by the support of local societies, which purchased and distributed the tracts. Military commanders distributed the tracts to their troops, widening the tracts' influence even further.[8] Distribution was increased when More published more expensive versions for wealthier readers, whose purchases helped to underwrite those sold at lesser cost to the poor.[9]

New tracts were issued for three and a half years, from March 1795 through September 1798, numbering more than one hundred editions. Hannah wrote about half of them but oversaw the entire production. Their sales and influence are considered unprecedented by nearly any measure of similar literature. Within the first few months, the publisher was unable to keep up with demand. Two million were circulated in less than a year.[10]

The tracts were remarkable, little works of art that garnered praise then and continue to do so. In comparing the tracts to the work of Sir Walter Scott, Wilberforce—who harbored more than a little bias for his friend—asserted, "I would rather go to render up my account at the last day, carrying up with me *The Shepherd of Salisbury Plain*," one of the most praised tracts of the Cheap Repository.[11] One tract, a ballad comparing the front and back of a carpet to our limited understanding of God's plan, was praised by Bishop Porteus, who said, "Here you have Bishop Butler's Analogy all for a halfpenny."[12] One scholarly journal claimed that the tracts were surpassed in popularity only by *Pilgrim's Progress*.[13] Most critics today judge the tracts to be More's most significant and skilled literary accomplishment.

The art of the tracts seemed to have been matched by their usefulness, as reports of the tracts' positive effects flowed in. Rev. John Venn, rector of Clapham, reported that one person in his parish had been converted through a tract.[14] Some attributed the singing of the ballad *The Riot, or Half a loaf is better than No Bread* to stopping a riot in Bath. *Patient Joe, The Newcastle Collier* was said to have solved an industrial problem in northern England.[15] Decades after the tracts' publication, the publisher of the 1853 edition of *The Works of Hannah More* credited the project with an "astonishing moral change" and added that still "the pieces which then accomplished such wonders have not lost their interest."[16]

As with any endeavor so innovative and influential, the tracts garnered controversy. On one side, some charged that mixing moral and religious instruction with entertainment was dangerous. The bishop of Worcester, who had opposed More's Sunday schools, thought it too risky to teach the poor to read. While he considered the Mores to be "good Ladies . . . with a good design, no doubt," the bishop fretted about "who shall hinder them from reading bad books as well as good."[17] Others considered More and the tracts' supporters as "kill-joy puritans."[18] Such seemingly contradictory judgments point to the truth in the middle. The tracts were politically and religiously conservative but socially liberal. They supported traditional hierarchies and work ethics, yet empowered the poor in arguably radical ways by providing reading material that improved literacy with the use of elevated language accessible to readers. And the tracts included not only lessons in morality and religion but also recipes, thrifty hints, and tips for self-improvement. The last section of *The Cottage Cook*, for example, was a list of "friendly hints":

- The difference between eating bread new and stale, is one loaf in five.
- If you turn your meat into broth it will go much farther than if you roast or bake it.
- A bit of leek, or an onion, makes all dishes savory at small expence.
- If the money spent on fresh butter were spent on meat, poor families would be much better fed than they are.
- If the money spent on tea were spent on home-brewed beer, the wife would be better fed, the husband better pleased and both would be healthier.
- Keep a little Scotch barley, rice, dry pease, and oatmeal in

the house. They are all cheap, and don't spoil. Keep also pepper and ginger.
- Pay your debts, serve God, love your neighbour.[19]

Empowering the poor to achieve self-improvement, even on such modest terms, was progressive in an age in which the very notion of progress was still strengthening. All in all, the project situated More as not only one of the first social critics to recognize and critique popular culture but also one of the first to put popular culture to use for a greater end.[20]

But another class of readers was unreached: the swelling ranks of the middle class. And what this growing audience wanted to read wasn't tracts, treatises, or verse; they craved novels.[21]

With the advent of the circulating libraries, increasing rates of literacy, and more abundant leisure time than ever, novel reading was on the rise. Like popular street literature, novels were not considered part of the class of polite letters. Serious writers disdained association with the form, but More saw a ripe opportunity. Since readers of novels hungered for stories about love, why not offer a work that offered just that—but much more?

Novels are so much a part of most people's reading diet today, so central to the cultural imagination, that it's hard to imagine when they weren't. But the novel as a literary form was still developing during More's lifetime into the form we know today. During the first decades of More's life, when she was writing more polite literature in the forms of verse and drama, some of the pioneering novels in English were being published: Samuel Richardson's tragic masterpiece about that paragon of Christian virtue, *Clarissa*; Henry Fielding's romping, panoramic comedy *The History of Tom Jones*; Laurence Sterne's baffling and experimental *Tristram*

Shandy; Horace Walpole's gothic trendsetter *The Castle of Otranto*; and Frances Burney's sentimental coming-of-age novel *Evelina*. While history has come to recognize these titles as works of literary worth, during More's lifetime, the novel as a literary form was not the respected art form it is today. When novels first emerged in the early eighteenth century, they were base, even bawdy, forms of entertainment, akin to today's most titillating reality television shows. For one thing, novels were written in common prose rather than the lofty poetry of esteemed writers including John Dryden and Alexander Pope—and that which was used by More in her earlier works. When writers such as Richardson and Fielding began to elevate the form by using it to tell stories of more serious import, they refused even to call their works novels and presented them as histories or real letters. Despite the success of midcentury novelists like Richardson and Fielding, many periodicals and critics refused to include novels in the category of literature. It didn't help that many novelists springing up were women, ensuring that the genre was viewed as a literary form of inferior worth. After all, women were not permitted to receive a classical university education; therefore their writings could not rise to the standard of polite literature. Neither could the novel. Novels were viewed as merely popular and low, at best, and corrupting, at worst.

Even More's good friend Samuel Johnson had worried about the dangers to impressionable, young readers presented by this newfangled approach to fiction that portrayed realistic characters rather than the idealized ones found in the old romances. Johnson feared that "for the sake of following nature," in striving for realism, novelists painted characters that, like people in real life, had a mixture of positive and negative characteristics. Such works "so mingle good and bad qualities in their principal personages, that they are both equally conspicuous; and as we accompany them through their adventures with delight, and are led by degrees to interest ourselves in their favour, we lose the abhorrence of their faults, because they do not hinder our pleasure, or, perhaps, regard them with some kindness for being united with so much merit."[22]

In other words, Johnson feared a desensitizing effect that realistic characters would have on readers, one that might foster greater social acceptance of negative characteristics in people as long as these were accompanied by more pleasing ones. It is not "a sufficient vindication of a character, that it is drawn as it appears, for many characters ought never to be drawn," Johnson warned. Johnson likely had Fielding's novel *The History of Tom Jones* in mind in writing this essay, a novel in which the good-hearted, young hero bedded numerous women before gaining his rightful place in society and the wisdom and continence necessary to maintain it. When More mentioned a passage from *Tom Jones* during one of their London soirees some years before, Johnson was appalled.

"I am shocked to hear you quote from so vicious a book," Johnson scolded her. "I am sorry to hear you have read it; a confession which no modest lady should ever make. I scarcely know a more corrupt work."

More was abashed. She conceded her error in judgment and, in later writing about the conversation, explained, "I thought it full as ill of it now as he did, and had only read it at an age when I was more subject to be caught by the wit, than able to discern the mischief."[23]

Their exchange demonstrated the changing tides of the age as well as More's increasing sense of propriety. The earlier eighteenth century had still exhibited some of the decadence of the earlier Restoration period, its shedding of the old Puritan restraints and a putting on of celebratory—and sometimes excessive—exuberance in all things. The swing of the pendulum was making its return stroke toward a more conservative culture—owing in large part to the influence of the evangelical movement and More's part in it.

More was not one to be confined by the boundaries of social class or literary snobbery, however. She had reached above her station with polished verse and drama, along with treatises aimed at improving the religion of the great. She had reached down by writing for the poor with the Cheap Repository Tracts, her most successful writing project yet. Even so, Wilberforce and Thornton had to plead with her for some years to write a moral novel, something along the lines of the Cheap Repository Tracts but for a middle-class audience.[24]

However, More had come to possess the general polite disdain for novels. She had condemned such works in *Strictures on Female Education*, proclaiming that the "corruption occasioned by these books has spread so wide, and descended so low, as to have become one of the most universal, as well as most pernicious, sources of corruption among us."[25] Her reading diet consisted of the poetry of William Cowper and Sir Walter Scott, the philosophical works of William Paley, and a wide variety of sermons from clerics of the seventeenth century, as well as some from the contemporary age.[26] She did read the occasional novel but was chagrined more often than not by what she found in it. Her words against novel reading in *Strictures* were harsh: she called for no less than the banishment of novels, "mischievous in a thousand ways," from dressing rooms and libraries alike.[27] One novel she read was written by an old friend, Madame de Staël, the former Germaine Necker. More had first met this famous hostess of French salons and proponent of romantic political and literary theory when the latter was just a girl and had accompanied her parents to a gathering at the home of David Garrick while More was staying there.[28] In 1807, Madame de Staël published a loosely autobiographical novel,

Corinne, showcasing a lifestyle of marital infidelity and revolutionary philosophy. More read the novel raptly, unable to resist its lure, despite her dismay at the values it promoted. Realizing this pull, More could no longer deny the power a novel could hold over the imagination, a power that might just as well be harnessed for good rather than ill.[29]

Inspired by her new understanding of the force of the novel form and emboldened by her success in adapting cheap tracts toward a similar end, More finally heeded her friends' implorations and set out to redeem the novel. If cheap street tracts could be cleaned up to make entertainment instructive for the lower orders, why not this growing form of literature for middle-class readers? She explained in a letter to William Pepys: "I thought there were already good books enough in the world for good people, but that there was a larger class of readers whose wants had not been attended to,—the subscribers to the circulating library. A little to raise the tone of that mart of mischief, and to counteract its corruptions, I thought that was an object worth attempting."[30]

Coelebs in Search of a Wife, More's only novel, was released anonymously in December 1808. Even she was not bold enough in this daring undertaking to attach her name to the work. She confided ahead of time in only one friend, Ann Kennicott.[31] She dared not tell even her Clapham friends.

A hubbub ensued. The world went crazy over *Coelebs*—most likely pronounced "Caleb." The bookseller was prepared to publish a second edition within a few days of the first, but it wasn't soon enough. Before the next edition could even be put to press, the first was out of print.

Everyone wanted to know the identity of the author. The booksellers in Bath couldn't bear the pressure and, to More's dismay, soon surrendered the secret. Henry Thornton had no idea that his partner in reform was behind the sensation. But Wilberforce knew Hannah too well and exulted in guessing the book's authorship correctly.[32]

Within two weeks, "booksellers, all over the country, became clamorous for copies," and ten more impressions were sold in the first six months, twelve in the first year.[33] By 1817, More was called upon for a corrected copy for the fifteenth edition.[34] The novel was viewed in France favorably by Madame de Staël, whose salacious novel had left More so dismayed. Over the next ten years, the novel became a cause *célèbre* all over Europe, being translated into French and German and appearing in Iceland and Sweden.[35] Across the ocean in America, thirty editions were printed before More's death.[36]

The novel was second only to the Cheap Repository Tracts in sales of More's works. Its success was "unprecedented in the annals of English literature," and it was one of England's earliest bestsellers.[37] "From all indications, *Coelebs* was the most widely read of the first quarter of the nineteenth century"[38] and was the most popular of all More's works.[39] It brought More two thousand pounds in profit in the first year.[40]

More tapped into the formula followed by the most popular novels by making the search for love and marriage the central theme of the work—*coelebs* is the Latin root word for "celibate" or "bachelor." In the novel, however, the main character went by the name of Charles. The title of the novel—apart from the irksomeness of the Latinate name—seemed shrewdly calculated to appeal to More's target audience: the patrons of the circulating libraries that catered to those readers' insatiable appetites for stories of love and intrigue.[41] Then as now, nothing appealed more to most than the search for love. This was what More's novel offered. But more than what appeared on the surface was under the cover.

For what *Coelebs in Search of a Wife* offered was less a sensational novel than a narrative treatise on the selection of the right marriage partner. The notion of choosing a marriage partner was rather new in More's time, one evolving alongside the emerging middle class. When society had been stratified into essentially two main classes—rich and poor—marriage partners were far less matters of personal choice than of economic expediency: the rich married someone who would enhance one's position in society, and the poor married out of their narrowly conscripted social pool. Choice played little part in the matter. But with the increasing social mobility that produced the middle class came more freedom to choose a partner—and more responsibility to make a wise choice.

Paralleling this development, indeed contributing to it as previously noted, the evangelical movement promoted the religious factor in the choice of a marriage partner. In contrast to the prevailing view, the evangelicals understood marriage to be part of the Christian vocation, the means by which a man and a woman could support each other in mutual spiritual growth and minister to society through that growth. In other words, the purpose of marriage was perceived as far greater than political or economic. It was personal and spiritual. Thus, the evangelicals were instrumental in advancing the ideal of the companionate marriage, one built on shared faith and mutual affection, a revolutionary notion in an era in which forced marriages were a not-so-distant memory— the subject of Samuel Richardson's 1748 novel *Clarissa*. It was also the kind of marriage exemplified by More's dear, nonevangelical friends from years before, David and Eva Maria Garrick.[42]

What better instrument to teach those given this new freedom of choosing a marriage partner—and a whole host of other social and religious lessons—than the literary form they turned to for entertainment? This was exactly what *Coelebs in Search of a Wife*, a didactic novel, attempted. As with More's previous works, the novel was centrally concerned with the influence of education and religion on character and conduct and their ramifications in this world and the next.

The novel began with Charles as a young man whose godly, Christian parents were deceased. His mother had previously advised him that when he did someday seek out a wife not to be attracted merely by exterior qualities since character and conduct lead to "rational happiness."[43] Charles met the woman who would become his wife, Lucilla, before the novel was half over. But because the model of marriage the novel advanced was the companionate marriage, and because Lucilla's humility and modesty prevented her forwardness or self-revelation, Charles's search turned unintentionally into a quest to learn from others the true nature and character of Lucilla. Only this knowledge would let him know—let them both know—whether they were suitable marriage partners for each other.

Along the way, Charles encountered a host of other people and families who exposed him—and readers—to an array of educational methods both good and bad, religious doctrines both true and false, along with various approaches to education, child rearing, and philanthropy that offered lessons through positive and negative examples. Indeed, *Coelebs in Search of a Wife* bore much in common with More's favored genres: the essay and the conduct book. The result was a work that equally resembled all these—conduct book, essay, and novel.

The work employed numerous ingredients from popular novels of the day: a tale structured around a quest; an orphaned hero; a dramatic scene of deathbed repentance; a scandalous elopement; competition—perceived, at least—in love; and an ending with a marriage. While such incidents increased the novel's interest, they did not really advance the plot in any way. Rather, such occasions served as vehicles for instruction, usually through the voice of Mr. Stanley, who was ready to turn any event or observation into a lesson for his family, for Coelebs, for his guests, and, of course, for the reader. Thus, *Coelebs in Search of a Wife* not only cultivated the new ideal of marriage based in companionship rather than political or economic expediency but also promoted More's ideals for female education, parenting, and morality. Although it was the only novel she would write, in many ways, *Coelebs in Search of a Wife* was her most representative work.

It's strange perhaps then that *Coelebs in Search of a Wife* is practically unreadable for most readers today. Tastes have changed, and the art of the novel has progressed toward more nuance and complexity than the plain didacticism of More's novel. In *Coelebs*, dialogue drowned what little dramatic action was contained in the plot. Character conceded to concept. Ideas overwhelmed artistry, and much of the novel read like the periodical essays that More loved to read. Even some of More's contemporaries found the novel insufferable. *Coelebs in Search of a Wife* was among the books given to Catharine in Jane Austen's unfinished novel of that name by Catharine's prudish aunt, Mrs. Percival, in hopes of encouraging the girl's modesty and virtue. In his satirical poem "Don Juan," George Gordon, Lord Byron, described Don Juan's prim and learned mother as straight out of *Coelebs in Search of a Wife*.

Yet even with its flaws in characterization and plot, the work employed many features that had come to characterize the novel by this time in its development. Some of the techniques More employed in it anticipated those that would be developed and perfected by later novelists. The ironic authorial distance she employed in a few scenes anticipated the approach that Austen would take in her satirical attacks on the tastes and values of her society. Similarly, the portraiture of Dickens's characters was hinted at in some scenes depicting poverty and injustice met by kindness.

In combining didacticism with artistry, teaching with delight, *Coelebs in Search of a Wife* helped lift the genre of the novel from base entertainment to respectable literature. Further, its commercial and critical successes created new readers of novels. The many praises heaped on *Coelebs in Search of a Wife* by those who usually disdained novels made way for the renowned Victorian novels that would be written later in the century. The foremost literary genre of that age was the novel. More's novel was a beginning in the genre's transformation from lowbrow to high art in the hands of historic nineteenth-century novelists such as Charles Dickens, the Brontë sisters, and William Makepeace Thackeray.

More's stories showed how to combine the moral and the imaginative in a new way.

Chapter 15

We Shall Be Equal

More was strong, but she was sensitive. When she was strong, she was very strong. When she was weak, she was debilitated. More's desire for approval was the source of her strength and her weakness. Gaining approval motivated, in part, her writing and good works. Losing it took devastating tolls on her emotional and physical health and filled her with self-doubt. In 1802, in the wake of the Blagdon controversy, she confessed to Wilberforce, "I have been so batter'd daily and monthly for the past two years about the wickedness and bad tendency of my writings, that I have really lost all confidence in myself, and feel as if I never more cou'd write what any body wou'd read."[1]

She then underwent a period that likely would be diagnosed today as depression. Her sisters rallied around; she stayed home from London that winter and emerged from one of her worst illnesses yet.[2] Although nearing sixty, More had another phase of life ahead and volumes yet to write. Renewed vigor overtook her.

At beautiful Barley Wood, the five sisters lived out their

remaining days together. Hannah pursued her lifelong passion for gardening and beauty in cultivating the expansive grounds spreading out from the village of Wrington. A gallery of drawings, paintings, and prints lined the parlor walls.[3] This would be her home for more than twenty years, a pleasant and peaceful estate, the bounty of her pen. The garden at Barley Wood featured monuments to Bishop Porteus and John Locke, the latter a gift from her old friend Elizabeth Montagu.[4] A replica of the Locke bust hangs today at All Saints' Church in Wrington, where More and her sisters are buried and where a bust of Hannah is mounted opposite Locke's at the church door. She had expressed as a little girl the wish that someday she would be rich enough to own an entire quire—four sheets folded in half to make eight leaves—of paper. She was now.

Throughout her life, More belied the stereotype that equates dourness with devotion. Even after her turn from fashionable society, she exhibited a jubilant wit and encouraged others to live exuberantly. Her friend Sir William Pepys told her, "Mrs. Montagu and I used always to agree that you had more wit in your serious writings than other people had when they meant to be professedly witty."[5] Often criticized for her severity, More seemed rather to have struck a balance between the extremes of puritanical severity and libertine excess that characterized her age. "I have refused," she declared at one point, "to publish a severe edict against the sin *of wearing flowers*." To do so "would be ridiculous enough in me who so passionately love them."[6] She found it necessary, she said, "to encourage cheerfulness" among those who insisted on austerities.[7] One of her many correspondents wrote her to ask whether she thought it was one's "duty to indulge the gayety of your temper among strangers?" In answer, she asserted that "it is a part of Christianity to convert every natural talent to a religious use." She continued, "You are serving God by making yourself agreeable, upon your own views and principles (for the motive is the act), to worldly but well-disposed people, who would never be attracted to religion by grave and severe divines, even if such ever fall in their way. Those who can adorn the doctrine of God their Saviour by cheerful manners, defeat the end of the Giver by assuming a contrary character. It is an honest bait, by which they will at last be attracted to like you for some better part of you."[8]

Such an exhortation was honestly derived, for no one needed it more than she did. More's naturally cheerful character, strong as that character was, could not withstand entirely the attacks on her character and beliefs that the Blagdon controversy generated. She wrote in her journal in the spring of 1803:

> One ill consequence I experience from my long trial is, that whereas I used to watch for all occasions for introducing useful subjects, I am now backward to do it, from the idea that all I say may be called enthusiasm. Alas! it is a difficult case;—I know not how to act—Lord! direct me by thy Spirit. The low tone, too, of common conversation is very unfavourable to a spirit of devotion. I seize, however, what time I can to be alone, and that is the time I most truly enjoy. I do not get weary of holy reading; but meditation and prayer too soon fail.[9]

She admitted sadly at the conclusion of that event that she "had hung up my harp on the willows, never more to take it down."[10]

But she was soon convinced by petitioners to play again, this time to write patriotic ballads to bolster national courage in the face of a possible invasion from France. A few years later, she was emboldened enough to write *Coelebs in Search of a Wife*. Then her quill took its final dip into sacred territory. Nearly all the works More wrote during her last years of publication were purely devotional: *Practical Piety* (1811), *Christian Morals* (1812), *Character and Practical Writings of Paul* (1815), *Moral Sketches of Prevailing Opinions and Manners, Foreign and Domestic, with Reflections on Prayer* (1819), *Bible Rhymes* (1821), and *The Spirit of Prayer* (1825). *Practical Piety* exceeded *Coelebs* in sales and was widely circulated, even finding its way into the hands of two visitors from the Middle East who declared that "they would translate [it] into their language immediately on their return home" and that it would be the first work printed in their home country, using the printing press they were taking with them.[11] Jane Austen wrote in a letter that some of her acquaintances were reading More's most recent work—which would have meant *Practical Piety*—"with delight."[12] Despite advancing age, More was still a quick scribbler, as she'd always been. Astonishingly, her "thick" *Moral Sketches,* more than five hundred pages long, was, she said, "first thought of in January, entirely written, printed, and published at the end of August."[13] She wrote *The Spirit of Prayer,* at once a devotional and a criticism of nominal Christianity, in her eightieth year. It went through eleven editions and was immediately translated into French.[14]

These works seemed to mean more to her than those of her early literary acclaim. She confided to a friend that "the only remarkable thing which belonged to her as an author was, that she had written eleven books after the age of sixty."[15] Her continued influence as a writer, and now in her last decades, as a philanthropist and spiritual mentor to many, led the *Christian Observer* to write of her, "What Wilberforce was among men, Hannah More was among women."[16]

Barley Wood became a destination for visitors from all over the kingdom. More told Wilberforce that she had not found there the retirement she had sought. "I never saw more people known and unknown in my gayest days," she wrote.[17] A steady flow of guests, which included various bishops and other clergymen, visited her home. So many churchmen frequented it that it was described as "a minor Evangelical centre."[18] One week she had eighty visitors in total.[19] Following his visit there in 1813, it is described in *The Life of William Wilberforce* as "the favoured seat of intellectual and religious sunshine."[20] One biographer explained, "She was the nearest a Protestant culture could come to a holy woman," and no evangelical who was in the vicinity could forgo a visit to "the mother of the movement."[21] Barley Wood was a veritable pilgrimage for the devout, some from as far away as America. Even after her death, strips from her dresses, cut up by her servants for distribution,[22] were treasured by believers like holy relics.[23]

Her fellow evangelicals were not the only visitors: foreigners, the famous actress Sarah Siddons, possibly Jane Austen and her sister Cassandra, and even the infamous Thomas Malthus, father of the population control movement, were among those who darkened her doorstep.[24] She could not find reason to turn any away, despite the admonitions of friends concerned that such hospitality was exhausting her.

Hannah was particularly welcoming to the many children who came and played on Barley Wood's undulating lawns.[25] One of these children, Marianne Thornton, recalled in later years her time with the five women as one in a home "full of intellect and piety and active benevolence" characterized by "uninterrupted harmony," tasty treats, and "merry stories."[26] Besides hosting such youngsters at Barley Wood, More took in the child of a widowed servant and, later, two orphans.[27] All the while she continued to care for children through the Sunday schools, which were "flourishing," she reported to Wilberforce.[28]

Her concerns for the poor extended beyond the children of

those mining towns to the laborers as well. In the aftermath of the war with France, when deprivation and hunger were rampant in the poor villages of the nearby Mendip Hills, More interceded on the laborers' behalf, soliciting money from her wealthy friends for their support.[29] She helped widows too. She raised further funds by publishing several new ballads and tracts and issuing a reprinted version of *Village Politics*. She contributed so much of her own funds to alleviate the suffering of the poor, even purchasing ore from the miners, that her purse grew slender, she said, and she expressed fears of going bankrupt.[30]

Her philanthropy extended to young clergymen. She used the profits from her investments to provide books of religious instruction and general support to needy members of the clergy. She also served as an informal mentor to many of these young clergymen who sought out her advice and counsel.[31]

Even as More's writing slowed and then ceased, she served as a role model for like-minded Christians. She embodied benevolence. She intervened on behalf of a local servant girl dismissed for sexual impropriety by pleading on her behalf for her to find employment, not wanting the girl to starve.[32] She once gently chided the Reverend Mr. Jay, whose Congregationalist church she sometimes attended in Bath—a bit scandalous for a Church of England woman. When Rev. Jay offered a complaint on Hannah's behalf about someone's ingratitude toward her, Hannah pointed out that "instances of ingratitude" serve to "show us our motives" and offer a mirror by which to see "our ingratitude towards our infinite benefactor."[33] Rev. Jay observed later that More's conversation was always characterized by "the law of kindness."[34]

Not everyone was so kind. In 1817, the radical journalist William Cobbett, who traveled to America to bring back the remains of his deceased friend Thomas Paine, mockingly called her the "old bishop in petticoats," a remark that took hold among her enemies and was highly insulting in those days with its suggestion of behavior highly improper for a woman.[35] Ironically, though, the term speaks highly of the strength of her character and convictions. Yet she was ever humble. Her piety and humanity are poignantly expressed in a letter to Wilberforce, written in the midst of a royal scandal involving Queen Caroline cheating on the also unfaithful King George IV: the queen's sins, she wrote regretfully, "occupy my thoughts more than my own."[36]

Her continued and strengthening adherence to the central evangelical conviction—that salvation depends on faith in Christ alone—and her disavowal of some teachings of high church Anglicanism—particularly her disbelief in the regenerative power of baptism and the necessity of bishops to the unity of the universal church—put her out of favor with some churchmen.[37] She had long expressed tolerance for Dissenting Christians, those such as Baptists and Methodists who worshipped outside the Church of England. But she never was able to overcome her opposition to Catholic emancipation. Despite the humanity More showed toward the Catholic clergy exiled during the French Revolution, she remained steadfast in her political opposition to Catholic emancipation at home. Even after Wilberforce came around to support the rights of Catholics to sit in Parliament, she could not shake the old fears of Catholic tyranny that had plagued her nation centuries before. More maintained the old conservative position and remained opposed.[38]

Her convictions and passions changed not a whit in her last years. In 1822, she wrote, "When I turn my thoughts upon the world, there are but three things there which deeply interest me—the state of the church, the religious progress of the king, and the abolition of slavery."[39] At age eighty-three, she joined the newly formed committee for the Female Anti-Slavery Society for Clifton, remarkable not only because of her age but also because such female-run societies were to many, Wilberforce included, a controversial assertion of power.[40] The fact is, however, women's participation and effectiveness in such societies rivaled those of men. More was one of the most esteemed members of this local group,[41] committed to supporting "the cause of our oppressed and degraded African Brethren."[42]

Her convictions may not have changed, but her world was rapidly changing. The last two decades of More's life were marked by loss after loss. She nearly lost her life in 1814 when, after an illness lasting for months, she was standing in front of the fireplace in her room, and she suddenly heard what sounded like "the roaring of the wind in the Chimney." When she turned around, she realized that she was "all in flames." A woman staying with her saved her life by grabbing her and rolling her on the carpet to put out the flames, burning her own hands in the process. The accident was reported in the newspapers, and More received many well wishes from friends.[43] She survived to outlive not only all her most beloved friends but also each of her sisters.

The first sister to depart the world was Mary, the eldest, who died in 1813. Her death was followed by Betty's in 1816 and then Sally's the next year. For the next two years, it was just Hannah and her favorite, the youngest, Patty, with whom she had organized the Sunday schools. The two sisters were both in fragile condition. "My own health and that of my sister Patty is broken and infirm," she wrote in one letter, "yet we are still, except in severe weather, able to attend our school." She then reported how they continued to support seven hundred children and their parents in the Sunday schools.[44]

Patty was almost like life to Hannah by that time. She was, she said, her very "hands, eyes, and ears."[45] In 1819, during a long illness, Patty experienced a night of intense physical distress. The Wilberforces were visiting and offered comfort to Hannah. Patty's final hours that morning were thankfully more peaceful. Her last words were about "ordering shoes and stockings for the poor."[46] Hannah was then alone.

Then Hannah's almost-sister, Mrs. Garrick, died in 1822. More would face another decade of life with most of her closest companions gone. She expressed regret for some of the time she had spent in her later years writing instead of being with those who had passed away: "I have lost so many of my contemporaries within the last year, particularly in the higher classes, that I am ready to ask with Dr. Johnson, where is the world into which I was born?—they taken, I spared—they of great importance in society, I of little or none; but by thus extending my life, God has been pleased to give me a longer space for repentance and preparation. May it not have been given in vain."[47] Of her dearest friends, only Wilberforce remained.

There were new friends, however, and More continued to receive visitors, who numbered in the hundreds, and since she had outlived family members and old friends, she was perhaps constantly rejuvenated by the flow of new friends from the younger generations, although poor health kept her from leaving Barley Wood for a period of years and confined her to her bedroom upstairs for two years.[48] Some of the friendships she developed included members of the royal family. Princess Sophia, with whom Hannah was quite close, and her brother, the Duke of Gloucester, were among her most famous visitors to Barley Wood. No wonder Joseph Cottle honored Hannah in his 1820 poem "An Expostulatory Epistle to Lord Byron" by including her as one of the "names sent embalmed to every age and shore, / like Howard, Thornton, Wilberforce, and More."[49]

The famous romantic poet Samuel T. Coleridge—who, as we saw earlier, called More the "first literary female he had met" and who was also an active abolitionist—visited her at Barley Wood in 1814. However, More's long-standing tendency to ingratiate herself with her social superiors marred Coleridge's visit. Two hours into an engaging conversation with the notable poet, a titled guest arrived, and More abandoned Coleridge's party, leaving them to withdraw "to a snug window" and fend for themselves while she entertained the visiting viscountess.[50]

A scurrilous attack against More was published in 1820 by Henry Hunt, a radical activist and labor movement leader who had made a name for himself in Bristol politics. From the jail in Somerset county where he was serving time for his role in the protest for parliamentary reform known as the Battle of Peterloo, Hunt wrote his memoirs wherein he characterized More as a fanatical "female saint" who was an "imposter." During "her younger days," Hunt claimed preposterously, More "had been a very frolicsome lass" before she all "at once converted into a saint, and set up for a severe and rigid moralist; and she had the merit of establishing the gang generally known by the title of the SAINTS, amongst our politicians." Hunt then charged that "it has been whispered, but that, of course, must be a calumny, that, from the well-known character of some of these gentry, who were very frequent in their visits, the buxom dame (who had now assumed the title of Mrs.) contrived, like the friars of old, to indulge in the gratification of those passions to which it is said real saints are not prone. Some of her neighbours were in consequence so ill-natured as to say, that her conversion was not sincere, but that it was a mere cloak to cover certain practices."[51]

Hunt then slyly closed his nearly libelous account with the disclaimer, "But my readers are aware that we must not believe *all* that the world says."[52] Hunt's *Memoirs* does not appear to have been widely read or taken seriously by any who did read it. By now, More was accustomed to such attacks and could hardly take one such as this seriously. Despite all her significant accomplishments, there was plenty to keep More humble.

In response to the attacks leveled against her during the Blagdon controversy, More lamented, "I believe that the false witness borne against me, has caused my works to be much less read and more condemned." But, she added, "God can carry on his own work, though all such poor tools as I were broken."[53] Later, offering advice for the Christian writer in *Christian Morals*, More acknowledged that even purity of motive does not assure a writer's humility. More must have sensed this struggle in herself. The goal, she stated, of making even small improvements in one's "immediate sphere is a duty out of which he should not be laughed by wits." Rather than "indulging unfounded hope of improbable effects, the Christian writer will be humbled at the mortifying reflection, what great and extensive evil the most insignificant bad man may effect, while so little comparative good may be accomplished by the best."[54] Despite advocating such humble aims, More saw good effects. She wrote, "It is a singular satisfaction to me that I have lived to see such an increase of genuine religion among the higher classes of society."[55] By the testimony of many, her works contributed considerably to this increase.

In 1825, her health recovered, and she enjoyed more wellness than she had experienced in some years, this near the age of eighty-two. But, she wrote to Wilberforce that same year, "I am feeling the common effect of those who live to an advanced age,—that almost all my contemporaries are dropping before me."[56] She kept up with events going on in the nation and world until senility began to set in during her last years.[57]

Her increasing illnesses were treated with opiates, as was common.[58] More's servants increasingly took advantage of her weakened health and amiable temperament. They pilfered and caroused once she was the sole, enervated mistress of Barley Wood. In 1828, friends intervened, insisting More relocate from the isolation of the rambling estate to the city where her friends and doctor could keep closer watch on her and the staff of servants, reduced from eight to four.[59]

Reluctantly but resolutely, she consented. The day her friends came to take her to her new home, "she descended the stairs with a placid countenance, and walked silently for a few minutes round the lower room, the walls of which were covered with the portraits of all her old and dear friends, who had successively gone before her; and as she was assisted into the carriage, she cast one pensive parting look upon her bowers, saying, 'I am driven like Eve out of Paradise; but not, like Eve, by angels.'"[60]

The new abode sat in an elegant row house on Windsor Terrace in the Bristol parish of Clifton, a fashionable neighborhood of cliff houses "perched daringly" atop the Avon Gorge.[61] More had come a long way metaphorically—less so geographically—from that humble schoolhouse home in Fishponds. She would spend her last days not far from the school she and her sisters ran so many years ago but elevated socially and spiritually from those meager beginnings.

Admirers, friends, and flatterers continued to call so steadily that it was necessary for More to limit her visiting days to just two each week.[62] Her old friend Thomas Babington Macaulay arrived in 1830 for what would become an ill-fated visit. In his youthful zeal, Macaulay made a passionate argument in favor of widespread parliamentary reform, a recurring national issue that conservatives such as More had long opposed. After Macaulay went on to support these efforts as Member of Parliament, More retaliated by writing him out of her will.[63] Nevertheless, Macaulay reflected later in his life only with fondness and affection for the woman he called his "second mother."[64] In 1831, Wilberforce came to see her, and they had a lively visit. When he called again in 1832, she seemed at first not to recognize him until she heard his voice.[65] When he died in July of the next year—just weeks before her death—his passing did not likely register, given the confused state of her mind by then.[66]

Despite the weakening and wandering of her mind and the loss of her taste and smell from a fever some years before, her bright eyes for which she was so well known did not fail.[67] She was able to read without spectacles until she read no more. Neither did her hearing falter much. One day, a servant asked to read a passage from the Bible to her. More asked, "What are you going to read?" When the servant replied that the passage would be on the resurrection of Christ, More exclaimed, "If we meet at his feet we shall be equal!"[68]

Her physician reported that until the end "her features were not shrunk, nor wrinkled, nor uncomely."[69] In November 1832, her bodily and mental health took a sharp downward turn that continued to decline gradually for the next ten months. "Prayer was the last thing that lived in her,—every breath was prayer," reported one witness to her last days.[70] Two weeks before her death, she lost her appetite and ceased to eat. In the last week, she seemed unable to recognize most of her friends.[71]

The day before she died, her friends held the morning devotion at her bedside: "She was silent, and apparently attentive, with her hands devoutly lifted up. From eight in the evening of this day, till nearly nine, I sat watching her. Her face was smooth and glowing. There was an unusual brightness in its expression. She smiled, and endeavouring to raise herself a little from her pillow, she reached out her arms as if catching at something, and while making this effort, she once called, 'Patty,' (the name of her last and dearest sister,) very plainly, and exclaimed, 'Joy!'"[72] These were her last words. She took her "last gentle breath" the next afternoon on September 7, wrote William Roberts, who sat beside her.[73] She was eighty-eight.

The church bells throughout Bristol rang during the funeral procession. People from high to low, from city and country assembled at Barley Wood to follow the procession to the church in the village of Wrington.[74] She was buried next to her sisters in the churchyard there. A headstone under a mighty tree commemorates the lives of these five sisters: "These all died in faith."

Epilogue

More's life spanned the reign of four kings. She witnessed the American, French, and Industrial Revolutions. She died mere weeks after England abolished slavery for good. At the time of her death, she had amassed nearly thirty thousand pounds, an amount unknown to women writers. Most of this went to about two hundred charities, including many she founded. The beneficiaries of her wealth included numerous schools, mission societies, and outreaches to orphans, slaves, and the poor.[1] More's biographer Henry Thompson was granted permission to dedicate his *Life of Hannah More* to Queen Victoria.[2] The Church Mission Society instituted a policy of naming orphaned African girls after her.[3] In 1835, the American novelist Catharine Maria Sedgwick described More's work as "a poetic emission of light from the star just risen above the literary horizon."[4] A school in Resiterstown, Maryland, in the United States also has her name. Her pen left virtually no area of her society unmarked: literature, education, morality, religion, and abolition. She reached high and low in her nation and across the globe.

Within a couple of generations of her death, however, More's reputation fell into disfavor. Her style of writing and morality were replaced by more modern modes. It didn't help that William Roberts's biography, the first published, flattened the rich textures of her personality and faith. Roberts's emendations of her letters and records re-created More in a saint's image. Hannah need not have been placed on a pedestal to be appreciated. She needed only to be known.

Then, toward the end of the nineteenth century, the modernist movement arose, led by, among others, Virginia Woolf, great-granddaughter of Claphamite James Stephen. The modernists defined themselves principally by their rejection of the values that most defined the Victorian age: duty, family, piety. More's reputation was irreparably tarnished when Augustine Birrell, a parliamentarian for North Bristol of the Liberal Party, proclaimed in a 1905 essay that he had planted his nineteen-volume set of her collected works in his garden.[5] He wrote unapologetically, "I shall leave them . . . buried in a cliff facing due north, with nothing between them and the Pole but leagues upon leagues of a windswept ocean."[6] Ten years earlier, he had written in a short biography of More that "the celebrated Mrs. Hannah More is one of the most detestable writers that ever held a pen. She flounders like a huge conger-eel in an ocean of dingy morality." She was, he announced, "a pompous failure," whose works consisted of "helping you to understand how sundry people who were old when you were young came to be the folk they were."[7] Birrell spent the remainder of his tirade questioning More's literary taste, her writing skill, and most of all, the authenticity of her religious faith, which he found insufficiently warm.

Then, with the publication of Lytton Strachey's critically acclaimed, iconoclastic *Eminent Victorians* in 1918, the reputation of the age as one of moral and cultural superiority came crashing down. The spell of reverence toward the era and its leading figures was broken. That "first Victorian," Hannah More, was among the casualties. Her age, along with her reputation, had finally passed.

Even so, today in pockets of her home country, her image and legacy are proclaimed with stained glass, marble busts, and plaques. Throughout the southwest region of England, schools, streets, and parks bear her name. The building in Cheddar where she opened her first Sunday school is now called Hannah More Cottage. People readily talk of her efforts. One who grew up in Wedmore, where she operated one of the Sunday schools, complains now about the "interesting stuff" that "interfering meddler snuffed out." A Bristol barrister praises More and her sisters for bringing the "self-improvement ethos" to the region. A neighbor of Cowslip Green speaks wryly of the "havoc" that More wreaked in London because she knew what happened in the slave trade in Bristol. Throughout the Mendip region, residents swap stories about Jacob and Mary More, recount William Turner's broken engagement with Hannah, describe the visits of Wilberforce to Cowslip Green, and talk about the house with a ceiling too low for a grandfather clock.

In most of the world today, however, More has now been largely forgotten—an unknown abolitionist, an obscure poet, and an outdated reformer. Yet she should be known. Somewhere between Birrell's hatred and Roberts's hagiography is a woman who was at once ordinary and remarkable. She was a woman with virtues and flaws, faith and fears, vision and blind spots. But she was also one whose unique gifts and fierce convictions transformed first her life and subsequently her world and ours.

> The woman who derives her principles from the Bible, and her amusements from intellectual sources, from the beauties of

nature, and from active employment and exercise, will not pant for beholders. She is no clamorous beggar for the extorted alms of admiration. She lives on her own stock. She possesses the truest independence. She does not wait for the opinion of the world, to know if she is right; nor for the applause of the world, to know if she is happy.[8]

ACKNOWLEDGMENTS

My first thanks are owed to Dr. George R. Levine who chaired my doctoral dissertation, which was the seed for this project. Years later, if it weren't for Eric Metaxas, whose encouragement and nudges set the wheels in motion, the book would have continued to languish in the proposal stage. Thank you, Eric, for supporting and contributing to this work in so many ways.

I am utterly indebted to Anne Stott for her incredible kindness and expertise, which she gave in assisting with my travels in England, reading the manuscript, and answering countless questions. Anne is one of the most gracious scholars I know. William Evans and M. J. Crossley-Evans were also generous with their rich knowledge of all things Hannah More. Thanks to each of you for making me feel at home in Hannah More's world.

The team at Thomas Nelson is incredible. Thank you to Joel Miller for believing so enthusiastically in the book from the start. Webster Younce and Katherine Rowley handled the manuscript with wisdom and skill and handled me (and my occasional moments of panic) with grace. I'm not sure I will ever want to write a book without them.

Thank you to Rebecca Harper, Cara Strickland, Tracey Finck, and Caryn Rivadeneira for reading the manuscript (or portions thereof) and making it better with such helpful feedback.

In serving as my research assistant, Julia Saavedra exceeded all expectations and requirements, and I am truly grateful for her.

It would not have been possible to write this book without the considerable and continued support of Liberty University, in particular, Dr. Ron Godwin, Dr. Ron Hawkins, Dr. Roger Schultz, and Dr. Matthew Towles. I am humbled and grateful for all you have done to allow me to devote myself to this work. In addition, the always efficient and thorough research assistance from Randy Miller and Matthew Grannell of Liberty University's Jerry Falwell Library was invaluable.

Thanks to my mother, Shirley Swallow, for helping with typing and to my father, Albert Swallow, for proofreading. Thank you to both of you for your continuous love and support in all I do.

And finally thank you to my beloved husband, Roy, for traipsing with me through the English countryside and through life. I couldn't have done any of this without you.

NOTES

PREFACE

1. *Online Etymology Dictionary*, s.v. "guinea," www.etymonline.com
   /index.php?term=guinea.
2. William Roberts, *Memoirs of the Life and Correspondence of Mrs.
   Hannah More*, 2 vols. (New York: Harper & Brothers, 1834), 1:354.
3. Madge Dresser, *Slavery Obscured: The Social History of the Slave
   Trade in Bristol* (Bristol: Redcliffe Press, 2007), 178.

CHAPTER 1: A BRIGHT IMAGINATION

1. Some material in this book draws upon my PhD dissertation,
   "Hannah More and the Evangelical Influence on the English Novel"
   (State University of New York at Buffalo, 1999).
2. William Roberts, *Memoirs of the Life and Correspondence of Mrs.
   Hannah More*, 2 vols. (New York: Harper & Brothers, 1834),
   1:18–19.
3. Ibid., 1:17.
4. Henry Thompson, *The Life of Hannah More, with Notices of Her
   Sisters* (London: Cadell, 1838), 6.
5. Mary Alden Hopkins, *Hannah More and Her Circle* (London:
   Longmans, 1947), 12.
6. Thompson, *The Life of Hannah More, with Notices of Her Sisters*, 8.

7. William Evans, personal correspondence, October 25, 2013.

8. Anne Stott, *Hannah More: The First Victorian* (Oxford: Oxford University Press, 2003), 5.

9. Hopkins, *Hannah More and Her Circle*, 10–11.

10. Ibid., 12.

11. Quoted in Thompson, *The Life of Hannah More, with Notices of Her Sisters*, 6.

12. Roberts, *Memoirs of the Life and Correspondence of Mrs. Hannah More*, 1:19.

13. Ibid., 1:15.

14. John Wesley, "The Way to the Kingdom," Sermon 7, June 6, 1742, reprinted in *Wesley Center Online*, http://wesley.nnu.edu/john -wesley/the-sermons-of-john-wesley-1872-edition/sermon-7-the -way-to-the-kingdom/.

15. Thompson, *The Life of Hannah More, with Notices of Her Sisters*, 5.

16. Ibid., 6.

17. Roberts, *Memoirs of the Life and Correspondence of Mrs. Hannah More*, 1:15.

18. What follows is drawn from an article by William Evans, "Hannah More's Parents," *Transactions of the Bristol and Gloucestershire Archaeological Society* 124 (2006), 113–30, and from a personal interview on July 2, 2013.

19. Evans, personal correspondence.

20. This marks the end of Evans's research and analysis.

21. Anon [John Gibson Lockhart], "Art. VI–Memoirs of the Life and Correspondence of Mrs. Hannah More," (1834), in J. T. Coleridge, ed., *Quarterly Review*, vol. 52 (London: John Murray), 416–41.

22. See, for example, Elizabeth Kowaleski-Wallace, *Their Fathers' Daughters: Hannah More, Maria Edgeworth, and Patriarchal Complicity* (New York: Oxford University Press, 1991).

23. Stott, *Hannah More*, 59–60.

24. Roberts, *Memoirs of the Life and Correspondence of Mrs. Hannah More*, 2:106.

25. Hannah More, *Collected Works*, 10 vols. (London: Harrison and Sons, 1853), 10:335–36.

26. Jeremy and Margaret Collingwood, *Hannah More* (Oxford: Lion Publishing, 1990), 11.

CHAPTER 2: A SCHOOL OF SISTERS

1. Quoted in Anne Stott, *Hannah More: The First Victorian* (Oxford: Oxford University Press, 2003), 9–10.

2. Jeremy and Margaret Collingwood, *Hannah More* (Oxford: Lion Publishing, 1990), 11, 134.

3. Susan Skedd, "Women Teachers and the Expansion of Girls' Schooling in England, c. 1760–1820," in *Gender in Eighteenth-Century England*, ed. Hannah Barker and Elaine Chalus (Essex: Addison Wesely Longman, 1997), 101–25.

4. Katherine Rogers, *Feminism in Eighteenth-Century England* (Urbana: University of Illinois Press, 1982), 27.

5. Jean-Jacques Rousseau, *Emile*, trans. and ed. Christopher Kelly and Allan Bloom (Lebanon, NH: University Press of New England), 540.

6. Quoted in Elizabeth Eger and Lucy Peltz, *Brilliant Women: 18th-Century Bluestockings* (New Haven: Yale University Press, 2008), 33.

7. Ibid., 96.

8. Edward H. Clarke, *Sex in Education; or, A Fair Chance for the Girls* (Boston: James R. Osgood and Company, 1873).

9. Nos. 32 and 63, http://archive.org/stream/cu31924073799029/cu31924073799029_djvu.txt.

10. Rosemary O'Day, ed., *Cassandra Brydges, First Duchess of Chando: Life and Letters* (Woodbridge, UK: Boydell and Brewer, 2007), 406.

11. Skedd, "Women Teachers and the Expansion of Girls' Schooling in England," 104–5.

12. Rogers, *Feminism in Eighteenth-Century England*, 19.

13. Collingwood, *Hannah More*, 12.

14. Rogers, *Feminism in Eighteenth-Century England*, 20.

15. Hannah More, *Collected Works*, 10 vols. (London: Harrison and Sons, 1853), 3:49–50.

16. Ibid., 3:188.

17. Ibid., 3:250.

18. Ibid., 6:320.

19. Ibid.

20. Ibid., 3:50.

21. Ibid., 3:318.

22. Ibid., 3:144.

23. Ibid., 3:141.

24. Ibid., 3:120.

25. Ibid., 3:124.

26. Ibid., 3:144.

27. Ibid., 3:192.

28. Ibid., 6:266.

29. Ibid.

30. Rogers, *Feminism in Eighteenth-Century England*, 17.

31. Ibid., 19.

32. Henry Thompson, *The Life of Hannah More, with Notices of Her Sisters* (London: Cadell, 1838), 13.

33. Stott, *Hannah More*, 10.

34. Skedd, "Women Teachers and the Expansion of Girls' Schooling in England," 113.

35. Stott, *Hannah More*, 10.

36. Ibid., 14–15.

37. "History of Theatre Royal in Bristol," *The Theatres Trust Database*, March 2013, http://www.theatrestrust.org.uk/resources/theatres /show/736-theatre-royal-bristol; comments on O'Toole and Lewis, "Peter O'Toole, legendary actor who trained in Bristol, has died aged 81," *Western Daily Press*, Dec. 15, 2013, http://www .westerndailypress.co.uk/Peter-O-Toole-legendary-actor-trained -Bristol/story-20324920-detail/story.html.

38. Collingwood, *Hannah More*, 17–18.

39. Mary Alden Hopkins, *Hannah More and Her Circle* (London: Longmans, 1947), 20–21.

40. Collingwood, *Hannah More*, 17.

41. Leslie Stephen, *Dictionary of National Biography*, vol. 38. (London: Smith, Elder, and Co., 1894), 416.

42. More, *Collected Works*, 3:159–60.

43. Collingwood, *Hannah More*, 17.

44. Hopkins, *Hannah More and Her Circle*, 15.

45. Thompson, *The Life of Hannah More, with Notices of Her Sisters*, 167.

46. William Evans, interview, July 2, 2013.

47. *The Oxford Encyclopedia of Economic History* (Oxford: Oxford University Press, 2003), 510.

48. Jamie Doward, "How Bristol's Gracious Mansions Mask the Shameful Past of Britain's Links to Slavery," *Guardian*, January 11, 2014.

49. James A. Rawley, *London, Metropolis of the Slave Trade* (Columbia: University of Missouri Press, 2003), 39.

50. Tim Lambert, "A Brief History of Bristol, England," http://www.localhistories.org/bristol.html.

51. Doward, "How Bristol's Gracious Mansions Mask the Shameful Past."

CHAPTER 3: THE ROAD TO SINGLEDOM

1. Virginia Woolf, *A Room of One's Own* (Orchard Park, NY: Broadview Press, 2001), 1.

2. Sir William Blackstone, "The Rights of Persons," *The Literary Encyclopedia*, http://www.litencyc.com/php/anthology.php?UID =141, emphasis in original.

3. Mary Alden Hopkins, *Hannah More and Her Circle* (London: Longmans, 1947), 32.

4. Ibid., 33.

5. Ibid.

6. Ibid.

7. Hannah More, *Collected Works*, 10 vols. (London: Harrison and Sons, 1853), 5:263.

8. Anne Stott, *Hannah More: The First Victorian* (Oxford: Oxford University Press, 2003), 18.

9. William Roberts, *Memoirs of the Life and Correspondence of Mrs. Hannah More*, 2 vols. (New York: Harper & Brothers, 1834), 1:29.

10. Jeremy and Margaret Collingwood, *Hannah More* (Oxford: Lion Publishing, 1990), 24.

11. Roberts, *Memoirs of the Life and Correspondence of Mrs. Hannah More*, 1:29.

12. Hopkins, *Hannah More and Her Circle*, 34.

13. Charlotte M. Yonge, *Hannah More* (London: W. H. Allen, 1888), 7.

14. Stott, *Hannah More*, 19.

15. Henry Thompson, *The Life of Hannah More, with Notices of Her Sisters* (London: Cadell, 1838), 22.

16. Quoted in ibid.

17. Thompson, *The Life of Hannah More, with Notices of Her Sisters*, 21.

18. Roberts, *Memoirs of the Life and Correspondence of Mrs. Hannah More*, 1:29.

19. Hopkins, *Hannah More and Her Circle*, 36.
20. Letter from Patty More to Ann Gwatkin, December 9, 1773 in the Gwatkin MSS collection, Courtesy of Lily Library, University of Indiana, Bloomington, Indiana.
21. Ibid.
22. See Nancy F. Cott. "Passionlessness: An Interpretation of Victorian Sexual Ideology," 1790-1850, *Signs: Journal of Women in Culture and Society* 4.2, 1978: 219-36.
23. It is worth noting, too, that neither did the two Austen sisters marry; only one of the three Brontë sisters did. Marriage seems not to have been compatible with the life of a woman writer during these years.
24. Hopkins, *Hannah More and Her Circle*, 37.
25. Roberts, *Memoirs of the Life and Correspondence of Mrs. Hannah More*, 1:29.
26. Thompson, *The Life of Hannah More, with Notices of Her Sisters*, 19.

CHAPTER 4: THE MAKING OF A FEMALE PEN

1. Anne Stott, *Hannah More: The First Victorian* (Oxford: Oxford University Press, 2003), 12.
2. Henry Thompson, *The Life of Hannah More, with Notices of Her Sisters* (London: Cadell, 1838), 11.
3. William Roberts, *Memoirs of the Life and Correspondence of Mrs. Hannah More*, 2 vols. (New York: Harper & Brothers, 1834), 1:19.
4. Mary Alden Hopkins, *Hannah More and Her Circle* (London: Longmans, 1947), 196.
5. Stott, *Hannah More*, 11.
6. Hopkins, *Hannah More and Her Circle*, 15.
7. Roberts, *Memoirs of the Life and Correspondence of Mrs. Hannah More*, 1:19.
8. Leslie Stephen, *The Dictionary of National Biography*, vol. 38 (London: Smith, Elder, and Co., 1894), 419.
9. Roberts, *Memoirs of the Life and Correspondence of Mrs. Hannah More*, 1:20.
10. Quoted in Martin J. Crossley-Evans, *Hannah More* (Bristol: Bristol Branch of the Historical Association, 1999), 14.
11. Virginia Woolf, *A Room of One's Own* (Orchard Park, NY: Broadview Press, 2001), 78.
12. Ibid.

13. Katherine Rogers, *Feminism in Eighteenth-Century England* (Urbana: University of Illinois Press, 1982), 21.

14. Quoted in Elizabeth Eger and Lucy Peltz, *Brilliant Women: 18th-Century Bluestockings* (New Haven: Yale University Press, 2008), 52–53.

15. Hannah More, *The Search After Happiness* (Boston: Manning and Loring, 1808), 16.

16. Hannah More, *Collected Works*, 10 vols. (London: Harrison and Sons, 1853), 3:194.

17. Roberts, *Memoirs of the Life and Correspondence of Mrs. Hannah More*, 1:20.

18. "When I came to you, I did not come with eloquence" (1 Cor. 2:1 NIV).

19. Augustine, *On Christian Teaching* (Oxford: Oxford University Press, 2008).

20. Thompson, *The Life of Hannah More, with Notices of Her Sisters*, 14.

21. Ibid., 15.

22. Ibid., 12.

23. Roberts, *Memoirs of the Life and Correspondence of Mrs. Hannah More*, 1:20; Ernest Campbell Mossner, *The Life of David Hume* (Oxford: Oxford University Press, 2001), 89.

24. Jeremy and Margaret Collingwood, *Hannah More* (Oxford: Lion Publishing, 1990), 21.

25. Susan. J. Skedd, *Oxford Dictionary of National Biography*, s.v. "More, Hannah (1745–1833)," Oxford University Press, 2004, http://www.oxforddnb.com/view/article/19179.

26. More, *Collected Works*, 6:226.

27. Thompson, *The Life of Hannah More, with Notices of Her Sisters*, 12.

28. More, *Collected Works*, 6:226.

29. Ibid., 6:238.

30. Stott, *Hannah More*, 21.

31. Ibid., 22.

32. Crossley-Evans, *Hannah More*, 3.

33. Roberts, *Memoirs of the Life and Correspondence of Mrs. Hannah More*, 1:27.

34. Collingwood, *Hannah More*, 19.

35. Quoted in ibid., 20.

CHAPTER 5: LONDON AT LAST

1. William Evans, personal correspondence, December 11, 2013.
2. Jeremy and Margaret Collingwood, *Hannah More* (Oxford: Lion Publishing, 1990), 16.
3. Ibid., 37.
4. William Roberts, *Memoirs of The Life and Correspondence of Mrs. Hannah More*, 2 vols. (New York: Harper & Brothers, 1834), 1:34.
5. Ibid., 1:35.
6. Ibid.
7. Ibid., 1:36.
8. Anne Stott, *Hannah More: The First Victorian* (Oxford: Oxford University Press, 2003), 23.
9. Ibid., 25.
10. Ibid.
11. Ibid., 25–26.
12. Ibid., 27.
13. Henry Thompson, *The Life of Hannah More, with Notices of Her Sisters* (London: Cadell, 1838), 25.
14. Ralph Griffiths, *The Monthly Review* reprint, vol. 50 (Charleston: Nabu Press, 2012), 243.
15. Collingwood, *Hannah More*, 37.
16. Thompson, *The Life of Hannah More, with Notices of Her Sisters*, 24.
17. Roberts, *Memoirs of the Life and Correspondence of Mrs. Hannah More*, 1:109.
18. Thompson, *The Life of Hannah More, with Notices of Her Sisters*, 24.
19. Roberts, *Memoirs of the Life and Correspondence of Mrs. Hannah More*, 1:37.
20. Ibid., 1:40.
21. Ibid., 1:38.
22. Collingwood, *Hannah More*, 34.
23. Mary Alden Hopkins, *Hannah More and Her Circle* (London: Longmans, 1947), 62.
24. Ibid.
25. Roberts, *Memoirs of the Life and Correspondence of Mrs. Hannah More*, 1:53.
26. Hopkins, *Hannah More and Her Circle*, 62.

27. Roberts, *Memoirs of the Life and Correspondence of Mrs. Hannah More*, 1:40.
28. Ibid., 1:36.
29. Ibid., 1:38.
30. Collingwood, *Hannah More*, 32.
31. Roberts, *Memoirs of the Life and Correspondence of Mrs. Hannah More*, 1:37–38.
32. Ibid., 1:40.
33. Ibid., 1:47.
34. Ibid., 1:50.
35. Ibid., 1:45.
36. Ibid., 1:46.
37. Ibid., 1:45.
38. James Boswell, *Life of Samuel Johnson, LL.D.*, ed. Wallace Brockway (Chicago: University of Chicago Press, 1952), 182.
39. Ibid.
40. Roberts, *Memoirs of the Life and Correspondence of Mrs. Hannah More*, 1:145.
41. Ibid., 1:41.
42. Ibid.
43. Ibid.
44. Ibid., 1:47.
45. Ibid., 1:54.
46. Collingwood, *Hannah More*, 35.
47. Boswell, *Life of Samuel Johnson*, 474.
48. Roberts, *Memoirs of the Life and Correspondence of Mrs. Hannah More*, 1:39.
49. Ibid., 1:82.
50. Ibid., 1:40.
51. Ibid., 1:146.
52. Stott, *Hannah More*, 41.
53. Martin J. Crossley-Evans, *Hannah More* (Bristol: Bristol Branch of the Historical Association, 1999), 4.
54. Boswell, *Life of Samuel Johnson*, 553.
55. Roberts, *Memoirs of the Life and Correspondence of Mrs. Hannah More*, 1:64.
56. Ibid., 1:38–39.
57. Ibid., 1:49.

58. Crossley-Evans, *Hannah More*, 4.

59. Hopkins, *Hannah More and Her Circle*, 63.

60. Roberts, *Memoirs of the Life and Correspondence of Mrs. Hannah More*, 1:48–49.

61. Ibid., 1:57–58.

62. Collingwood, *Hannah More*, 44.

63. Roberts, *Memoirs of the Life and Correspondence of Mrs. Hannah More*, 1:71.

64. Collingwood, *Hannah More*, 140.

65. Roberts, *Memoirs of the Life and Correspondence of Mrs. Hannah More*, 1:77.

66. Ibid., 1:78.

67. Collingwood, *Hannah More*, 48.

68. Crossley-Evans, *Hannah More*, 27; Stott, *Hannah More*, 50.

69. Crossley-Evans, *Hannah More*, 4.

70. Thompson, *The Life of Hannah More, with Notices of Her Sisters*, 31–32.

71. Phil Norfleet, "Mozart's Personal Library," *Mozart's The Magic Flute*, 2011, http://mozart2051.tripod.com/mozart_library.htm.; Crossley-Evans, *Hannah More*, 4.

72. Echo Irving, "A Brief Life of Hannah More," Wrington: All Saints' Church, 2007, 5.

73. Roberts, *Memoirs of the Life and Correspondence of Mrs. Hannah More*, 1:78.

74. Ibid., 1:80.

75. Ibid.

76. Marion Harland, *Hannah More* (New York: Knickerbocker Press, 1900), 51.

77. Roberts, *Memoirs of the Life and Correspondence of Mrs. Hannah More*, 1:72, emphasis in original.

78. Ibid., 1:90.

79. Ibid., 1:91.

80. Ibid., 1:94–95.

81. Ibid., 1:95.

82. Ibid., 1:97.

83. Thompson, *The Life of Hannah More, with Notices of Her Sisters*, 36.

84. Roberts, *Memoirs of the Life and Correspondence of Mrs. Hannah More*, 1:124. I am obliged to Anne Stott for pointing out that the Catholic writers More was in the habit of reading were French

Jansenists, a Calvinist strain of Catholicism with which More and other evangelicals found much in common. More preferred these writers over Methodist writers, in fact. The pope condemned Jansenism in 1713, so such writers fell outside the official recognition of the Roman Catholic Church.

85. Hannah More, *Collected Works*, 10 vols. (London: Harrison and Sons, 1853), 5:172.

86. Collingwood, *Hannah More*, 52.

87. Thompson, *The Life of Hannah More, with Notices of Her Sisters*, 37–38.

88. Stott, *Hannah More*, 45.

89. Roberts, *Memoirs of the Life and Correspondence of Mrs. Hannah More*, 1:98.

90. Stott, *Hannah More*, 46.

91. Ibid.

92. Roberts, *Memoirs of the Life and Correspondence of Mrs. Hannah More*, 1:61.

Chapter 6: Learned Ladies

1. William Roberts, *Memoirs of the Life and Correspondence of Mrs. Hannah More*, 2 vols. (New York: Harper & Brothers, 1834), 1:39, emphasis in original.

2. Ibid.

3. Norma Clarke, *Dr. Johnson's Women* (New York: Random House, 2011), 14–15.

4. Elizabeth Eger and Lucy Peltz, *Brilliant Women: 18th-Century Bluestockings* (New Haven: Yale University Press, 2008), 43.

5. Emily J. Climenson, *Elizabeth Montagu, The Queen of the Bluestockings, Her Life and Correspondence from 1720 to 1761* (London: John Murray, 1906), ix, 1, 111–114, 191.

6. Roberts, *Memoirs of the Life and Correspondence of Mrs. Hannah More*, 1:39.

7. James Boswell, *Life of Samuel Johnson, LL.D.*, ed. Wallace Brockway (Chicago: University of Chicago Press, 1952), 476–77.

8. Anne Stott, *Hannah More: The First Victorian* (Oxford: Oxford University Press, 2003), 51.

9. Jeremy and Margaret Collingwood, *Hannah More* (Oxford: Lion Publishing, 1990), 64.

10. Roberts, *Memoirs of the Life and Correspondence of Mrs. Hannah More*, 1:190.

11. Collingwood, *Hannah More*, 64.

12. Roberts, *Memoirs of the Life and Correspondence of Mrs. Hannah More*, 1:221, emphasis in original.

13. Eger and Peltz, *Brilliant Women*, 32.

14. Quoted in ibid., 74.

15. Quoted in ibid., 33.

16. Roberts, *Memoirs of the Life and Correspondence of Mrs. Hannah More*, 1:238.

17. Eger and Peltz, *Brilliant Women*, 24.

18. Hannah More, *Collected Works*, 10 vols. (London: Harrison and Sons, 1853), 5:313–27, emphasis in original. All the lines from the introduction and poem beginning here and continuing in the next few paragraphs are from this source.

19. Roberts, *Memoirs of the Life and Correspondence of Mrs. Hannah More*, 1:183.

20. Ibid.

21. Ibid.

22. Boswell, *Life of Samuel Johnson*, 477.

23. Mary Alden Hopkins, *Hannah More and Her Circle* (London: Longmans, 1947), 56.

24. Quoted in Eger and Peltz, *Brilliant Women*, 32–33.

25. Quoted in ibid., 32.

26. Hopkins, *Hannah More and Her Circle*, 79.

27. Roberts, *Memoirs of the Life and Correspondence of Mrs. Hannah More*, 1:82.

28. Ibid., 1:48.

29. Ernest Marshall Howse, *Saints in Politics: The "Clapham Sect" and the Growth of Freedom*, 2nd ed. (London: Ruskin House, 1960), 166.

30. Roberts, *Memoirs of the Life and Correspondence of Mrs. Hannah More*, 1:142.

31. Ibid., 2:330.

32. Ibid., 1:316, emphasis in original.

33. More, *Collected Works*, 3:69.

34. Ibid.

35. Roberts, *Memoirs of the Life and Correspondence of Mrs. Hannah More*, 1:168, emphasis in original.

36. Robert Hole, ed., *Selected Writings of Hannah More* (London: William Pickering, 1996), xvii.

37. Sylvia Myers, *The Bluestocking Circle: Women, Friendship, and the Life of the Mind in Eighteenth-Century England* (Oxford: Clarendon, 1990), 16.

38. John Wolffe, *The Expansion of Evangelicalism: The Age of Wilberforce, More, Chalmers and Finney* (Downers Grove: InterVarsity Press, 2007), 145–46.

39. Roberts, *Memoirs of the Life and Correspondence of Mrs. Hannah More*, 1:41.

40. David Hume, "Essays Moral, Political, and Literary," *Library of Economics and Liberty*, 1742, http://www.econlib.org/library/LFBooks /Hume/hmMPL40.html.

41. Eger and Peltz, *Brilliant Women*, 50.

42. Roberts, *Memoirs of the Life and Correspondence of Mrs. Hannah More*, 2:21–22.

43. Ibid., 2:266.

44. Ibid., 1:302.

45. Ibid., 1:201.

46. Eger and Peltz, *Brilliant Women*, 73.

47. Hopkins, *Hannah More and Her Circle*, 80.

48. Ibid., 81.

49. Quoted in Collingwood, *Hannah More*, 42.

50. Roberts, *Memoirs of the Life and Correspondence of Mrs. Hannah More*, 1:152.

51. Eger and Peltz, *Brilliant Women*, 17.

52. Ibid., 18.

53. Quoted in ibid., 130, emphasis in original.

54. Eger and Peltz, *Brilliant Women*, 18.

CHAPTER 7: ALL THAT GLISTENS IS NOT GOLD

1. Hannah More, *Collected Works*, 10 vols. (London: Harrison and Sons, 1853), 5:340.

2. W. S. Ross, *Gray's Odes: With Notes, and a Scheme of Grammatical Analysis* (Edinburgh: Ballantyne and Company, 1870), 33.

3. Ibid.

4. William Roberts, *Memoirs of the Life and Correspondence of Mrs. Hannah More*, 2 vols. (New York: Harper & Brothers, 1834), 2:54.

5. Ibid., 1:50.

6. Quoted in Marion Harland, *Hannah More* (New York: Knickerbocker Press, 1900), 75.

7. Roberts, *Memoirs of the Life and Correspondence of Mrs. Hannah More*, 1:113, emphasis in original.

8. Quoted in Henry Thompson, *The Life of Hannah More, with Notices of Her Sisters* (London: Cadell, 1838), 44.

9. Roberts, *Memoirs of the Life and Correspondence of Mrs. Hannah More*, 1:159.

10. More, *Collected Works*, 5:vii.

11. Ibid., 5:xiii.

12. Thompson, *The Life of Hannah More, with Notices of Her Sisters*, 70.

13. More, *Collected Works*, 5:340.

14. Samuel Johnson, *The Lives of the Most Eminent English Poets with Critical Observations on Their Works*, vol. 1 (Charlestown: Samuel Etheridge, 1810), 38.

15. Roberts, *Memoirs of the Life and Correspondence of Mrs. Hannah More*, 1:50.

16. Ibid., 1:49–50.

17. Mary Alden Hopkins, *Hannah More and Her Circle* (London: Longmans, 1947), 102.

18. Ibid.

19. Roberts, *Memoirs of the Life and Correspondence of Mrs. Hannah More*, 1:213–15.

20. Ibid., 1:45.

21. Ibid., 1:38.

22. Ibid., 1:46.

23. Ibid., 1:53, emphasis in original.

24. Ibid., 1:81.

25. Ibid., 1:53, 160.

26. Ibid., 1:41.

27. Ibid.

28. Ibid., 1:52.

29. Ibid., 1:70.

30. Jeremy and Margaret Collingwood, *Hannah More* (Oxford: Lion Publishing, 1990), 36.

31. Roberts, *Memoirs of the Life and Correspondence of Mrs. Hannah More*, 1:293.

32. James Boswell, *Life of Samuel Johnson, LL.D.*, ed. Wallace Brockway (Chicago: University of Chicago Press, 1952), 356.

33. Collingwood, *Hannah More*, 12.
34. Roberts, *Memoirs of the Life and Correspondence of Mrs. Hannah More*, 1:244.
35. Ibid., 1:290.
36. Ibid., 1:291.
37. Martin J. Crossley-Evans, *Hannah More* (Bristol: Bristol Branch of the Historical Association, 1999), 4–5, 27.

CHAPTER 8: FAITH TO SEE

1. William Roberts, *Memoirs of the Life and Correspondence of Mrs. Hannah More*, 2 vols. (New York: Harper & Brothers, 1834), 1:111.
2. John Newton, *Cardiphonia* (Chicago: Moody Press, 1950), 25.
3. Richard Cecil, *Memoirs of the Rev. John Newton*, 2nd ed. (London: J Hatchard, 1808), 80.
4. "Extracts from John Newton's Journal," *International Slavery Museum*, June 1754, http://www.liverpoolmuseums.org.uk/ism /slavery/middle_passage/john_newton.aspx.
5. Cecil, *Memoirs of the Rev. John Newton*, 133–134.
6. Roberts, *Memoirs of the Life and Correspondence of Mrs. Hannah More*, 1:138.
7. Noel Davidson, *How Sweet the Sound* (Greenville: Emerald House, 1997), 228.
8. Roberts, *Memoirs of the Life and Correspondence of Mrs. Hannah More*, 1:258.
9. Jonathan Aitken, *John Newton: From Disgrace to Amazing Grace* (Wheaton: Crossway, 2007), 284.
10. *The Oxford Encyclopedia of Economic History* (Oxford: Oxford University Press, 2003), 510.
11. Chuck Stetson, *Creating the Better Hour: Lessons from William Wilberforce* (Macon: Stroud & Hall, 2007), xii.
12. Ernest Marshall Howse, *Saints in Politics: The "Clapham Sect" and the Growth of Freedom*, 2nd ed. (London: Ruskin House, 1960), 28–29.
13. Quoted in ibid., 30.
14. Stetson, *Creating the Better Hour*, ix.
15. Quoted in Howse, *Saints in Politics*, 31.
16. Howse, *Saints in Politics*, 31.
17. Samuel Johnson, *The Idler*, no. 87, 286, quoted in Lionel Thomas Berguer, *The British Essayists* (London: T. and J. Allman Publishers, 1823).

18. Samuel Johnson, "Taxation No Tyranny," quoted in *The Works of Samuel Johnson*, vol. 14 (Troy, NY: Pafraets & Company, 1913), 93–144.

19. Quoted in Howse, *Saints in Politics*, 30–31.

20. Howse, *Saints in Politics*, 31–32.

21. Ibid., 35.

22. Howse, *Saints in Politics*, 31.

23. Ibid., 12–13.

24. Zachary Macaulay, *Life and Letters of Zachary Macaulay* (London: Edward Arnold, 1900), 8.

25. Ibid., 88.

26. Ibid., 89.

27. Howse, *Saints in Politics*, 13–14.

28. William Hague, *William Wilberforce: The Life of the Great Anti-Slave Trade Campaigner* (San Diego: Harcourt, 2008), 62.

29. Anne Stott, *Wilberforce: Family and Friends* (Oxford: Oxford University Press, 2012), 24–28.

30. John C. Colquhoun, *William Wilberforce: His Friends and His Times* (London: Longmans, Green, Reader, and Dyer, 1866), 100–1.

31. Ibid., 101–2.

32. Robert Isaac and Samuel Wilberforce, *The Life of William Wilberforce*, 5 vols. (London: John Murray, 1838), 1:110.

33. J. Wesley Bready, *England: Before and After Wesley* (London: Hodder and Stoughton Limited, 1938), 298–99.

34. Stephen Tomkins, *The Clapham Sect: How Wilberforce's Circle Transformed Britain* (Oxford: Lion Hudson, 2010), 42–43, 48.

35. Quoted in Howse, *Saints in Politics*, 12.

36. Mark A. Noll, *The Rise of Evangelicalism: The Age of Edwards, Whitefield and the Wesleys* (Downers Grove: InterVarsity Press, 2003), 238.

37. Roberts, *Memoirs of the Life and Correspondence of Mrs. Hannah More*, 1:147.

38. Ibid.

39. Ibid., 1:147–48.

40. M. G. Jones, *Hannah More* (Cambridge: Cambridge University Press, 1952), 90.

41. Quoted in ibid., 91.

42. Roberts, *Memoirs of the Life and Correspondence of Mrs. Hannah More*, 1:303.

43. Tomkins, *The Clapham Sect*, 64.
44. Colquhoun, *William Wilberforce*, 104.

CHAPTER 9: THE LABOR FOR LIBERTY

1. Anne Stott, *Hannah More: The First Victorian* (Oxford: Oxford University Press, 2003), 87.
2. Ibid.
3. Clare Midgley, *Women Against Slavery: The British Campaigns 1780–1870* (London: Routledge, 1992), 16.
4. M. G. Jones, *Hannah More* (Cambridge: Cambridge University Press, 1952), 82.
5. Thomas Clarkson, *History of the Rise, Progress, and Accomplishment of the Abolition of the African Slave-Trade by the British Parliament* (London: R. Taylor and Co., 1808), 267–75.
6. Jones, *Hannah More*, 81–82.
7. Robert Isaac and Samuel Wilberforce, *The Life of William Wilberforce* (London: John Murray, 1838), 1:149.
8. William Roberts, *Memoirs of the Life and Correspondence of Mrs. Hannah More*, 2 vols. (New York: Harper & Brothers, 1834), 1:286.
9. Ibid., 1:266.
10. Madge Dresser, *Slavery Obscured: The Social History of the Slave Trade in Bristol* (Bristol: Redcliffe Press, 2007), 147, 173.
11. Roberts, *Memoirs of the Life and Correspondence of Mrs. Hannah More*, 1:266.
12. Ibid., 1:323.
13. Ibid.
14. Ibid., 1:311, emphasis in original.
15. Ibid., emphasis in original.
16. Ibid., 1:309–10.
17. Percy Bysshe Shelley, *A Defence of Poetry,* Bartleby.com, http://www.bartleby.com/27/23.html.
18. Quoted in Ernest Marshall Howse, *Saints in Politics: The "Clapham Sect" and the Growth of Freedom*, 2nd ed. (London: Ruskin House, 1960), 33.
19. Roberts, *Memoirs of the Life and Correspondence of Mrs. Hannah More*, 1:274–75.
20. Hannah More, *Collected Works*, 10 vols. (London: Harrison and Sons, 1853), 2:268.

21. Roberts, *Memoirs of the Life and Correspondence of Mrs. Hannah More*, 1:309.
22. Dresser, *Slavery Obscured*, 177.
23. Roberts, *Memoirs of the Life and Correspondence of Mrs. Hannah More*, 1:347.
24. Ibid., 1:272.
25. "James Ramsay Argues Against the Slave Trade," *A North East Story: Scotland, Africa and Slavery in the Caribbean*, http://www.abdn.ac .uk/slavery/resource8a.htm.
26. Jones, *Hannah More*, 84.
27. Roberts, *Memoirs of the Life and Correspondence of Mrs. Hannah More*, 1:310.
28. Ibid.
29. Mary Mark Ockerbloom, ed., "Mary Darby Robinson (1758–1800)," *University of Pennsylvania Digital Library*, http://digital.library.upenn .edu/women/robinson/biography.html.
30. Dresser, *Slavery Obscured*, 165.
31. Quoted in ibid.
32. Dresser, *Slavery Obscured*, 164.
33. Quoted in ibid.
34. Midgley, *Women Against Slavery*, 35.
35. Stott, *Hannah More*, 322.
36. Jones, *Hannah More*, 84.
37. John Newton, *The Works of the Rev. John Newton*, vol. IV (New Haven: Nathan Whiting, 1824), 533.
38. Jones, *Hannah More*, 90.
39. Quoted in ibid.
40. "Anti-slavery medallion, by Josiah Wedgwood," *The British Museum*, 1787, https://www.britishmuseum.org/explore /highlights/highlight_objects/pe_mla/a/anti-slavery_medallion, _by_jos.aspx.
41. Robert Isaac and Samuel Wilberforce, *The Life of William Wilberforce* (London: John Murray, 1838), 4:112.
42. Shelley, *A Defence of Poetry*.
43. Roberts, *Memoirs of the Life and Correspondence of Mrs. Hannah More*, 1:282.

44. More, *Collected Works*, 5:341–53.

45. Roberts, *Memoirs of the Life and Correspondence of Mrs. Hannah More*, 1:284–85, emphasis in original.

46. Quoted in Jones, *Hannah More*, 90.

47. Martin J. Crossley-Evans, interview, July 5, 2013.

48. Jeremy and Margaret Collingwood, *Hannah More* (Oxford: Lion Publishing, 1990), 71.

49. Howse, *Saints in Politics*, 36.

50. John Pollock, "William Wilberforce," in *Creating the Better Hour: Lessons from William Wilberforce*, ed. Chuck Stetson (Macon: Stroud & Hall, 2007), 4.

51. "Sorrows of Yamba; or, the Negro Woman's Lamentation," London, 1797, http://www.brycchancarey.com/slavery/yamba.htm.

52. Roberts, *Memoirs of the Life and Correspondence of Mrs. Hannah More*, 2:345–46.

53. Jones, *Hannah More*, 83.

54. Dresser, *Slavery Obscured*, 141.

55. Quoted in Tom Morris, *If Aristotle Ran General Motors: The New Soul of Business* (New York: Henry Holt, 1997), 140.

56. Roberts, *Memoirs of the Life and Correspondence of Mrs. Hannah More*, 1:293.

57. Ibid., 1:327, emphasis in original.

58. Jones, *Hannah More*, 91.

59. Roberts, *Memoirs of the Life and Correspondence of Mrs. Hannah More*, 1:417, emphasis in original.

60. Ibid., 1:450.

61. Ibid., 2:320–21.

62. Ibid., 2:382.

63. Quoted in Stetson, *Creating the Better Hour*, 7.

64. Pollock quoted in Stetson, *Creating the Better Hour*, 7.

65. More, *Collected Works*, 2:252.

66. Stott, *Hannah More*, 336.

67. Isaac and Wilberforce, *The Life of William Wilberforce*, 5:264–65.

68. Midgley, *Women Against Slavery*, 9, 17, 23, 35.

69. Ibid., 16.

70. Ibid., 29–31.

71. Howse, *Saints in Politics*, 40–41.

72. Isaac and Wilberforce, *The Life of William Wilberforce*, 4:358.

73. Shelley, *A Defence of Poetry*.

CHAPTER 10: TEACHING THE NATION TO READ

1. Jeremy and Margaret Collingwood, *Hannah More* (Oxford: Lion Publishing, 1990), 56.

2. Quoted in Martha More, *Mendip Annals: Or, A Narrative of the Charitable Labours of Hannah and Martha More in Their Neighbourhood: Being the Journal of Martha More* (New York: Robert Carter & Brothers, 1859), 47.

3. Ibid., 13.

4. Ibid., 12–13, emphasis in original.

5. More, *Mendip Annals*, 64.

6. William Roberts, *Memoirs of the Life and Correspondence of Mrs. Hannah More*, 2 vols. (New York: Harper & Brothers, 1834), 1:397.

7. Ibid., emphasis in original.

8. More, *Mendip Annals*, 42.

9. Ibid., 62.

10. Ibid., 48.

11. Ibid., 167.

12. Collingwood, *Hannah More*, 79.

13. More, *Mendip Annals*, 22–23.

14. Ibid., 18.

15. Ibid., 19.

16. Ibid., 16.

17. Ibid., 29.

18. Ibid., 18, emphasis in original.

19. Ibid., 28.

20. Ibid., 67.

21. Ibid., 32.

22. Ibid., 84.

23. Ibid., 40.

24. Quoted in ibid., 31.

25. More, *Mendip Annals*, 14.

26. Ibid., 14.

27. Quoted in ibid., 16.

28. More, *Mendip Annals*, 14, 17.

29. Ibid., 14–15.
30. Echo Irving, "A Brief Life of Hannah More," Wrington: All Saints' Church, 2007, 8.
31. More, *Mendip Annals*, 15.
32. Ibid., 15–17.
33. Ibid., 17.
34. Ibid., 17–18.
35. Ibid., 60.
36. Ibid., 28.
37. Quoted in ibid., 51.
38. More, *Mendip Annals*, 18.
39. Ibid., 22.
40. Lillian Millard, "The Life of Hannah More," in *The Lives of John Locke 1632–1704 and Hannah More 1745–1833* (n.p.), 12.
41. Collingwood, *Hannah More*, 82.
42. More, *Mendip Annals*, 24.
43. Quoted in ibid., 52–53.
44. More, *Mendip Annals*, 30.
45. Quoted in ibid., 32, emphasis in original.
46. More, *Mendip Annals*, 58.
47. Ibid., 23, 203.
48. Ibid., 31.
49. Ibid., 28.
50. James A. Huie, *Records of Female Piety* (Edinburgh: Oliver and Boyd, 1841), 295–96.
51. Martin J. Crossley-Evans, *Hannah More* (Bristol: Bristol Branch of the Historical Association, 1999), 11.
52. More, *Mendip Annals*, 72–73.
53. Ibid., 79.
54. Ibid., 78.
55. Ibid., 70.
56. Crossley-Evans, *Hannah More*, 11.
57. Roberts, *Memoirs of the Life and Correspondence of Mrs. Hannah More*, 1:376.
58. More, *Mendip Annals*, 133.
59. Millard, "The Life of Hannah More," 13.
60. More, *Mendip Annals*, 24.
61. Ibid., 64.

62. Ibid., 65.

63. Ibid., 65–66.

64. Ibid., 66.

65. Collingwood, *Hannah More*, 81.

66. More, *Mendip Annals*, 64.

67. Ibid., 64.

68. Ibid., 64–65.

69. Ibid., 84, emphasis in original.

70. Ibid., 36–37.

71. Ibid., 52, 55.

72. Collingwood, *Hannah More*, 96.

73. M. G. Jones, *Hannah More* (Cambridge: Cambridge University Press, 1952), 172.

74. Quoted in Collingwood, *Hannah More*, 97.

75. Henry Thompson, *The Life of Hannah More, with Notices of Her Sisters* (London: Cadell, 1838), 193.

76. Quoted in ibid., 199.

77. Roberts, *Memoirs of the Life and Correspondence of Mrs. Hannah More*, 2:111.

78. Ibid., 2:56.

79. Ibid., 2:117–18.

80. Roberts, *Memoirs of the Life and Correspondence of Mrs. Hannah More*, 2:237.

81. Jones, *Hannah More*, 15.

82. Collingwood, *Hannah More*, 135.

83. Hannah More, *Collected Works*, 10 vols. (London: Harrison and Sons, 1853), 3:160.

84. More, *Mendip Annals*, 6.

85. Ibid., 67.

86. Ibid., 70–71.

87. Quoted in Ernest Marshall Howse, *Saints in Politics: The "Clapham Sect" and the Growth of Freedom*, 2nd ed. (London: Ruskin House, 1960), 96.

88. Quoted in Ivanka Kovacevic, *Fact into Fiction: English Literature and the Industrial Scene 1750–1850* (Leicester: Leicester University Press, 1975), 47.

89. Leslie Stephen, *Dictionary of National Biography*, vol. 38 (London: Smith, Elder, and Co., 1894), 419.

90. Roberts, *Memoirs of the Life and Correspondence of Mrs. Hannah More*, 2:360.

91. Ibid., 2:330.
92. More, *Mendip Annals*, 6.
93. Howse, *Saints in Politics*, 8.
94. Clare MacDonald Shaw, "Introduction," in *Tales for the Common People: and Other Cheap Repository Tracts* (Nottingham: Trent Editions, 2002), xi.
95. Mary Alden Hopkins, *Hannah More and Her Circle* (London: Longmans, 1947), 2.
96. Roberts, *Memoirs of the Life and Correspondence of Mrs. Hannah More*, 1:477.
97. Jones, *Hannah More*, 148.
98. Roberts, *Memoirs of the Life and Correspondence of Mrs. Hannah More*, 2:340.
99. Crossley-Evans, *Hannah More*, 11.
100. Irving, "A Brief Life of Hannah More," 10.
101. Stephen Tomkins, *The Clapham Sect: How Wilberforce's Circle Transformed Britain* (Oxford: Lion Hudson, 2010), 54.
102. Thompson, *The Life of Hannah More, with Notices of Her Sisters*, 2–3.
103. Quoted in Collingwood, *Hannah More*, 147.
104. Collingwood, *Hannah More*, 8.

CHAPTER 11: AN AMPLE TABLE

1. "Holy Trinity Clapham: Connecting People with God," 2014, http://holytrinityclapham.org/welcome/history/.
2. Anne Stott, personal correspondence, December 16, 2013.
3. Stephen Tomkins, *The Clapham Sect: How Wilberforce's Circle Transformed Britain* (Oxford: Lion Hudson, 2010), 112.
4. "Holy Trinity Clapham," http://holytrinityclapham.org/welcome/history/.
5. Tomkins, *The Clapham Sect*, 113.
6. From *Songs by the Way*, ed. William Croswell Doane (New York: D. Appleton, 1860), http://anglicanhistory.org/usa/gwdoane/songs1860/090.html.
7. John Wolffe, *The Expansion of Evangelicalism: The Age of Wilberforce, More, Chalmers and Finney* (Downers Grove: InterVarsity Press, 2007), 12.
8. Ernest Marshall Howse, *Saints in Politics: The "Clapham Sect" and the Growth of Freedom*, 2nd ed. (London: Ruskin House, 1960), 166.

9. D. W. Bebbington, *Evangelicalism in Modern Britain: A History from 1730 to the 1980s* (London: Unwin Hyman, 1989).

10. Tomkins, *The Clapham Sect*, 11.

11. Ibid., 12.

12. Howse, *Saints in Politics*, 26.

13. Ibid.

14. John Pollock, "William Wilberforce," in *Creating the Better Hour: Lessons from William Wilberforce*, ed. Chuck Stetson (Macon: Stroud & Hall, 2007), 11.

15. Martha More, *Mendip Annals: Or, A Narrative of the Charitable Labours of Hannah and Martha More in Their Neighbourhood: Being the Journal of Martha More* (New York: Robert Carter & Brothers, 1859), 205.

16. William Roberts, *Memoirs of the Life and Correspondence of Mrs. Hannah More*, 2 vols. (New York: Harper & Brothers, 1834), 1:461.

17. Walpole, letter to More, February 13, 1795, emphasis in original, http://images.library.yale.edu/walpoleimages/hwcorrespondence/31/456.pdf.

18. From a letter to the Countess of Upper Ossory, August 16, 1776, cited in *Bartlett's Familiar Quotations*, 16th ed. (Boston: Little, Brown and Company, 1992), 324.

19. Roberts, *Memoirs of the Life and Correspondence of Mrs. Hannah More*, 2:478.

20. Henry Thompson, *The Life of Hannah More, with Notices of Her Sisters* (London: Cadell, 1838), 159–61.

21. Anne Stott, *Hannah More: The First Victorian* (Oxford: Oxford University Press, 2003), 199.

22. Thompson, *The Life of Hannah More, with Notices of Her Sisters*, 161–62.

23. Roberts, *Memoirs of the Life and Correspondence of Mrs. Hannah More*, 2:442–43.

24. Hannah More, *Collected Works*, 10 vols. (London: Harrison and Sons, 1853), 2:329.

25. Ibid., 2:289.

26. Quoted in M. G. Jones, *Hannah More* (Cambridge: Cambridge University Press, 1952), 94.

27. Quoted in ibid., 99.

28. Jones, *Hannah More*, 96.

29. Howse, *Saints in Politics*, 172.

30. Anne Stott, personal correspondence, December 16, 2013.

31. Wolffe, *The Expansion of Evangelicalism*, 13.

32. Roberts, *Memoirs of the Life and Correspondence of Mrs. Hannah More*, 2:292.

33. J. Wesley Bready, *England: Before and After Wesley* (London: Hodder and Stoughton Limited, 1938), 304.

34. Howse, *Saints in Politics*, 135–36.

35. Jones, *Hannah More*, 82.

36. Howse, *Saints in Politics*, 172.

37. Noel Davidson, *How Sweet the Sound* (Greenville: Emerald House, 1997), 198.

38. Pollock, "William Wilberforce," in *Creating the Better Hour*, 11.

39. Ibid.

40. Leslie Stephen, *The Dictionary of National Biography*, vol. 38 (London: Smith, Elder, and Co., 1894), 417.

41. Howse, *Saints in Politics*, 100.

42. Doreen N. Rosman, *Evangelicals and Culture* (London: Croom Helm, 1984), 303.

43. *The Christian Observer*, vol. 33, 1833, 660.

44. Quoted in Stott, *Hannah More*, 254.

45. Howse, *Saints in Politics*, 107.

46. Ibid., 123.

47. John C. Colquhoun, *William Wilberforce: His Friends and His Times* (London: Longmans, Green, Reader, and Dyer, 1866), 110.

48. Kevin Belmonte, *William Wilberforce* (Grand Rapids: Zondervan, 2007), 126.

49. More, *Mendip Annals*, 167.

50. Tomkins, *The Clapham Sect*, 53–54.

51. Howse, *Saints in Politics*, 97.

52. Quoted in ibid., 99.

53. Stott, personal correspondence, December 30, 2013.

54. See Tomkins, *The Clapham Sect*.

55. Stott, *Hannah More*, 295–96.

56. Quoted in Howse, *Saints in Politics*, 66.

57. Clifford Hill, "Wilberforce and the Clapham Circle," in *Creating the Better Hour: Lessons from William Wilberforce*, ed. Chuck Stetson (Macon: Stroud & Hall, 2007), 28.

58. "A Brief History of CMS," *CMS: Sharing History Changing*

Lives, 2014, www.cms-uk.org/Whoweare/AboutCMS/History /tabid/181/language/en-US/Default.aspx.

59. Lawrence Taylor and R.G. Thorne, "Henry Thornton (1760–1815), of Battersea Rise, Clapham Common, Surr.," *The History of Parliament: British Political, Social, and Local History,* http://www.historyofparliamentonline. org/volume/1790-1820/member/thornton-henry-1760-1815.

60. Howse, *Saints in Politics*, 126.

61. Kevin Belmonte and Chuck Stetson, "A Man of Character," in *Creating the Better Hour: Lessons from William Wilberforce,* ed. Chuck Stetson (Macon: Stroud & Hall, 2007), 37.

62. Stott, *Hannah More*, 197–98.

63. See, for example, Mark A. Noll, *The Rise of Evangelicalism: The Age of Edwards, Whitefield and the Wesleys* (Downers Grove: InterVarsity Press, 2003), 253–55.

64. See Anne Stott, *Wilberforce: Family and Friends* (Oxford: Oxford University Press, 2012), 146–47.

65. "Cotton Factories Bill," February 19, 1818, *Hansard*, UK Parliament, http://hansard.millbanksystems.com/commons/1818/feb/19/cotton -factories-bill.

66. I am indebted to Anne Stott's insight and analysis in contextualizing the work of Wilberforce and the Clapham Sect on the issue of labor reform.

67. Herbert Schlossberg, *The Silent Revolution and the Making of Victorian England* (Columbus: Ohio State University Press, 2000).

68. Bready, *England: Before and After Wesley*, 304.

69. Stott, *Hannah More*.

CHAPTER 12: BURDENED FOR THE BEASTS

1. Hannah More, *Collected Works*, 10 vols. (London: Harrison and Sons, 1853), vol. 5.

2. Robert Burton, *The Anatomy of Melancholy*, vol. 3 (New York: A. C. Armstrong & Son, 1880), 290.

3. Emma Major, *Madam Britannia: Women, Church, and Nation 1712–1812* (Oxford: Oxford University Press, 2011), 74.

4. William Cowper, *The Task,* book III, in *The Works of William Cowper,* ed. John S. Memes, vol. 3 (Edinburgh: Fraser & Co., 1835), 217.

5. Quoted in Anne Stott, *Hannah More: The First Victorian* (Oxford: Oxford University Press, 2003), 87.

6. Soame Jenyns, *Disquisitions on Several Subjects* (London: Charles Baldwyn, 1822), 23–26.

7. Robert W. Malcolmson, *Popular Recreations in English Society 1700–1850* (Cambridge: Cambridge University Press, 1973), 45.

8. Ibid., 46.

9. Ibid., 119.

10. *Memoirs of the Literary and Philosophical Society of Manchester* (London: R. Bickerstaff, 1805), 195–96.

11. Malcolmson, *Popular Recreations in English Society*, 46.

12. James Macaulay, *Essay on Cruelty to Animals* (Edinburgh: John Johnstone, 1839), 124, https://archive.org/details /essayoncrueltyt00macagoog.

13. Malcolmson, *Popular Recreations in English Society*, 47.

14. Ibid., 49.

15. Quoted in ibid., 50.

16. Macaulay, *Essay on Cruelty to Animals*, 124.

17. Malcolmson, *Popular Recreations in English Society*, 48.

18. Quoted in ibid.

19. Malcolmson, *Popular Recreations in English Society*, 48.

20. Quoted in ibid.

21. Malcolmson, *Popular Recreations in English Society*, 119–21.

22. Ibid., 124.

23. Quoted in ibid., 135.

24. Quoted in ibid., 136–37.

25. Quoted in ibid., 137.

26. Malcolmson, *Popular Recreations in English Society*, 127.

27. Quoted in ibid., 137.

28. Quoted in ibid.

29. Quoted in ibid.

30. Malcolmson, *Popular Recreations in English Society*, 125.

31. John Wesley, "General Observations and Reflections," chapter 6, section 9, in *Compendium of Natural Philosophy, Being a Survey of the Wisdom of God in the Creation,* http://wesley.nnu.edu/john -wesley/a-compendium-of-natural-philosophy/chapter-6-general -observations-and-reflections/.

32. Malcolmson, *Popular Recreations in English Society*, 119.

33. Cowper, *The Task*, book III, 222.

34. Cowper, *The Task*, book VI, 295.

35. William Wilberforce, *A Practical View of the Prevailing Religious System of Professed Christians*, 123, http://www.gutenberg.org /files/25709/25709-h/25709-h.htm.

36. Robert Isaac and Samuel Wilberforce, *The Life of William Wilberforce* (London: John Murray, 1838), 2:366.

37. Chuck Stetson, ed., *Creating the Better Hour: Lessons from William Wilberforce* (Macon: Stroud & Hall, 2007), 13.

38. Tobias Menely, "Acts of Sympathy: Abolitionist Poetry and Transatlantic Identification," in *Affect and Abolition in the Anglo-Atlantic, 1770–1830*, ed. Stephen Ahern (London: Ashgate Press, 2013), 48.

39. Ibid., 47–48.

40. More, *Collected Works*, 6:53.

41. Ibid., 2:181–207.

42. Ibid., 2:85–98.

43. Tobias Menely, "Zoophilpsychosis: Why Animals Are What's Wrong with Sentimentality," *Symploke*, vol. 15, no. 1–2 (Dec. 2007): 254.

44. Ibid., 250.

45. Ibid., 255.

46. Ernest Marshall Howse, *Saints in Politics: The "Clapham Sect" and the Growth of Freedom*, 2nd ed. (London: Ruskin House, 1960), 122.

47. Malcolmson, *Popular Recreations in English Society*, 124.

48. Ibid., 172.

49. Ibid., 129.

50. E. M. Forster, "Mrs. Hannah More," *The New Republic*, December 16, 1925, 106

CHAPTER 13: REFORM, NOT REVOLUTION

1. William Roberts, *Memoirs of the Life and Correspondence of Mrs. Hannah More*, 2 vols. (New York: Harper & Brothers, 1834), 1:419, emphasis in original.

2. Ibid., 1:349.

3. Hannah More, *Collected Works*, 10 vols. (London: Harrison and Sons, 1853), 2:280.

4. Jeremy and Margaret Collingwood, *Hannah More* (Oxford: Lion Publishing, 1990), 61.

5. Roberts, *Memoirs of the Life and Correspondence of Mrs. Hannah More*, 1:273.

6. Ibid., 1:250.

7. Ibid., 2:323.

8. Ibid., 1:301, emphasis in original.

9. Ibid., 1:288.

10. Anne Stott, *Hannah More: The First Victorian* (Oxford: Oxford University Press, 2003), 97.

11. Helen Cross Knight, *A New Memoir of Hannah More, or, Life in Hall and Cottage* (New York: M.W. Dodd, 1851), 111.

12. Roberts, *Memoirs of the Life and Correspondence of Mrs. Hannah More*, 1:273.

13. Ibid., 1:274, emphasis in original.

14. Stott, *Hannah More*, 97.

15. Ibid., 98.

16. Roberts, *Memoirs of the Life and Correspondence of Mrs. Hannah More*, 1:288.

17. More, *Collected Works*, 2:322.

18. Ibid., 2:265, emphasis in original.

19. Ibid., 2:255.

20. Ibid., 2:250.

21. Ibid., 2:263.

22. Ibid., 2:264.

23. Ibid., 2:272.

24. Ibid., 2:275.

25. Henry Thompson, *The Life of Hannah More, with Notices of Her Sisters* (London: Cadell, 1838), 81.

26. Ibid., 127, emphasis in original.

27. Roberts, *Memoirs of the Life and Correspondence of Mrs. Hannah More*, 1:351, emphasis in original.

28. Ibid., 1:361–62.

29. More, *Collected Works*, 2:289.

30. Ibid., 2:292.

31. Ibid., 2:300.

32. Ibid., 2:305.

33. Ibid., 2:329.

34. Ibid., 2:371.

35. Roberts, *Memoirs of the Life and Correspondence of Mrs. Hannah More*, 1:374.

36. Leslie Stephen, *Dictionary of National Biography*, vol. 38 (London: Smith, Elder, and Co., 1894), 419.

37. Quoted in Stott, *Hannah More*, 146.

38. Stott, *Hannah More*, 139.

39. Roberts, *Memoirs of the Life and Correspondence of Mrs. Hannah More*, 1:413.

40. More, *Collected Works*, 2:222, emphasis in original.

41. Stott, *Hannah More*, 145.

42. More, *Collected Works*, 2:381, emphasis in original.

43. Ibid., 2:384.

44. Roberts, *Memoirs of the Life and Correspondence of Mrs. Hannah More*, 1:421.

45. Ibid., emphasis in original.

46. More, *Collected Works*, 2:385.

47. Ibid., 2:397.

48. Ibid., 2:408.

49. Thompson, *The Life of Hannah More, with Notices of Her Sisters*, 141.

50. Ibid., 146–47.

51. Roberts, *Memoirs of the Life and Correspondence of Mrs. Hannah More*, 1:427.

52. Stott, *Hannah More*, 215.

53. More, *Collected Works*, 3:12, emphasis in original.

54. Ibid., 3:48.

55. Ibid.

56. Anne Mellor, *Mothers of the Nation: Women's Political Writing in England, 1780–1830* (Bloomington: Indiana University Press, 2000), 21.

57. More, *Collected Works*, 3:63–64.

58. Hannah More, *Strictures on the modern system of female education, with a View of the Principles and Conduct Prevalent among Women of Rank and Fortune* (London: Cadell, 1799), 49–51.

59. More, *Collected Works*, 3:188.

60. More, *Strictures*, 194.

61. Ibid., 187.

62. More, *Collected Works*, 3:188.

63. Ibid., 3:167.

64. Ibid., 3:168.

65. Ibid., 3:170.

66. Thompson, *The Life of Hannah More, with Notices of Her Sisters*, 186.

67. Roberts, *Memoirs of the Life and Correspondence of Mrs. Hannah More*, 2:82.

68. Stott, *Hannah More*, 260.

69. Roberts, *Memoirs of the Life and Correspondence of Mrs. Hannah More*, 2:39.

70. Stott, *Hannah More*, 262.

71. Roberts, *Memoirs of the Life and Correspondence of Mrs. Hannah More*, 2:131.

72. Stott, *Hannah More*, 266.

73. Ibid., 263.

74. Roberts, *Memoirs of the Life and Correspondence of Mrs. Hannah More*, 2:432.

CHAPTER 14: AN IMAGINATION THAT MOVED THE WORLD

1. Quoted in Anne Stott, *Hannah More: The First Victorian* (Oxford: Oxford University Press, 2003), 170.

2. Preface to a collection of the tracts later bound in a two-volume set, *Stories for Persons in the Middle Ranks and Tales for the Common People. The Miscellaneous Works of Hannah More*, vol. 1 (London: Thomas Tegg, 1840), 130.

3. Clare MacDonald Shaw, "Introduction," in *Tales for the Common People: and Other Cheap Repository Tracts* (Nottingham: Trent Editions, 2002), xx.

4. Horace, *The Art of Poetry in Classical Literary Criticism*, Trans. T. S. Dorsch, and Penelope Murray (New York: Penguin Books, 2000), 108.

5. Ibid., xxiii.

6. Ibid., xxv.

7. Ibid., xvii.

8. Ibid., xxi.

9. Olivia Smith, *The Politics of Language 1791–1819* (Oxford: Clarendon Press, 1984), 95.

10. Stott, *Hannah More*, 176.

11. Quoted in Stephen Tomkins, *The Clapham Sect: How Wilberforce's Circle Transformed Britain* (Oxford: Lion Hudson, 2010), 143.

12. M. G. Jones, *Hannah More* (Cambridge: Cambridge University Press, 1952), 147.

13. Tomkins, *The Clapham Sect*, 143.

14. Martin J. Crossley-Evans, *Hannah More* (Bristol: Bristol Branch of the Historical Association, 1999), 14.

15. Jeremy and Margaret Collingwood, *Hannah More* (Oxford: Lion Publishing, 1990), 117.

16. Hannah More, *Collected Works*, 10 vols. (London: Harrison and Sons, 1853), 1:vii.

17. Stott, *Hannah More*, 174.

18. Shaw, "Introduction," in *Tales for the Common People*, xvii.

19. Hannah More, "Cottage Cook" in *Cheap Repository Tracts: Entertaining, Moral and Religious* (London: F. C. & J. Rivington, 1810), 304.

20. Shaw, "Introduction," in *Tales for the Common People*, xix.

21. The remainder of this chapter is drawn from my book *Coelebs in Search of a Wife: A New Review and Analysis* (Lewiston, NY: Edwin Mellen Press, 2003).

22. Samuel Johnson, "The Rambler," No. 4, 1750, http://www.english.upenn.edu/~mgamer/Etexts/johnson.rambler.html.

23. William Roberts, *Memoirs of the Life and Correspondence of Mrs. Hannah More*, 2 vols. (New York: Harper & Brothers, 1834), 1:101.

24. Robert Isaac and Samuel Wilberforce, *The Life of William Wilberforce* (London: John Murray, 1838), 3:67–68.

25. More, *Collected Works*, 3:126.

26. Crossley-Evans, *Hannah More*, 17.

27. More, *Collected Works*, 3:28.

28. Stott, *Hannah More*, 33.

29. Ibid., 272.

30. Roberts, *Memoirs of the Life and Correspondence of Mrs. Hannah More*, 2:168.

31. Stott, *Hannah More*, 274.

32. Ibid., 277.

33. Roberts, *Memoirs of the Life and Correspondence of Mrs. Hannah More*, 2:147, 168.

34. Ibid., 2:264.

35. Crossley-Evans, *Hannah More*, 19; Stott, *Hannah More*, 281.

36. Leslie Stephen, *Dictionary of National Biography*, vol. 38 (London: Smith, Elder, and Co., 1894), 418.

37. Robin Reed Davis, "Anglican Evangelicalism and the Feminine Literary Tradition" (PhD diss., Duke University, 1982), 71.

38. Robert Alan Colby, *Fiction with a Purpose: Major and Minor Nineteenth-Century Novels* (Bloomington: Indiana University Press, 1952), 80.

39. Stephen, *Dictionary of National Biography*, 418.

40. Stott, *Hannah More*, 281.

41. One suspects that use of the name Coelebs in the title was the publisher's decision, not the author's.

42. Elizabeth Eger and Lucy Peltz, *Brilliant Women: 18th-Century Bluestockings* (New Haven: Yale University Press, 2008), 28–29.

43. Hannah More, *Coelebs in Search of a Wife* (Bristol: Thoemmes Press, 1995), 13.

Chapter 15: We Shall Be Equal

1. Quoted in Anne Stott, *Hannah More: The First Victorian* (Oxford: Oxford University Press, 2003), 254.

2. Stott, *Hannah More*, 254.

3. Basil Cottle, "The Life (1770–1853), Writings, and Literary Relations of Joseph Cottle of Bristol" (PhD diss., University of Bristol, 1958), 242.

4. Leslie Stephen, *Dictionary of National Biography*, vol. 38 (London: Smith, Elder, and Co., 1894), 416.

5. William Roberts, *Memoirs of the Life and Correspondence of Mrs. Hannah More*, 2 vols. (New York: Harper & Brothers, 1834), 2:373.

6. Ibid., 1:398, emphasis in original.

7. Ibid.

8. Ibid., 1:468–69.

9. Ibid., 2:110.

10. Ibid., 2:111.

11. Ibid., 2:247.

12. Clare MacDonald Shaw, "Introduction" in *Tales for the Common People: and Other Cheap Repository Tracts* (Nottingham: Trent Editions, 2002), xii.

13. Roberts, *Memoirs of the Life and Correspondence of Mrs. Hannah More*, 2:421.

14. Henry Thompson, *The Life of Hannah More, with Notices of Her Sisters* (London: Cadell, 1838), 306–7.

15. Roberts, *Memoirs of the Life and Correspondence of Mrs. Hannah More*, 2:289.

16. Stott, *Hannah More*, 283.

17. Roberts, *Memoirs of the Life and Correspondence of Mrs. Hannah More*, 2:215–16.

18. Jeremy and Margaret Collingwood, *Hannah More* (Oxford: Lion Publishing, 1990), 137.

19. Charlotte M. Yonge, *Hannah More* (London: W. H. Allen, 1888), 186.

20. Robert Isaac and Samuel Wilberforce, *The Life of William Wilberforce* (London: John Murray, 1838), 4:148.

21. Stott, *Hannah More*, 304.

22. Martin J. Crossley-Evans, interview, July 5, 2013.

23. Martin J. Crossley-Evans, *Hannah More* (Bristol: Bristol Branch of the Historical Association, 1999), 17.

24. Stott, *Hannah More*, 304–5.

25. Ibid., 290–91.

26. Quoted in Stott, *Hannah More*, 291.

27. Stott, *Hannah More*, 294–95, 326.

28. Roberts, *Memoirs of the Life and Correspondence of Mrs. Hannah More*, 2:238.

29. Ibid., 2:410–12.

30. Ibid., 2:263.

31. Ibid., 2:220.

32. Stott, *Hannah More*, 325.

33. Roberts, *Memoirs of the Life and Correspondence of Mrs. Hannah More*, 2:482.

34. Ibid., 2:483.

35. S. J. Skedd, *Oxford Dictionary of National Biography*, s.v. "Hannah More," http://www.oxforddnb.com/view/printable/19179.

36. Stott, *Hannah More*, 317.

37. Ibid., 284.

38. Ibid., 250.

39. Roberts, *Memoirs of the Life and Correspondence of Mrs. Hannah More*, 2:321–22.

40. Stott, *Hannah More*, 322.

41. Madge Dresser, *Slavery Obscured: The Social History of the Slave Trade in Bristol* (Bristol: Redcliffe Press, 2007), 204–5.

42. Quoted in ibid., 205.

43. Stott, *Hannah More*, 302.

44. Roberts, *Memoirs of the Life and Correspondence of Mrs. Hannah More*, 2:214.

45. Stott, *Hannah More*, 314.

46. Quoted in ibid., 315.

47. Roberts, *Memoirs of the Life and Correspondence of Mrs. Hannah More*, 2:369.

48. Ibid., 2:367.

49. Quoted in Crossley-Evans, *Hannah More*, 25.

50. Joseph Cottle, "Hannah More in Reminiscences of Samuel Taylor Coleridge and Robert Southey," 1847, http://spenserians.cath.vt.edu /CommentRecord.php?action=GET&cmmtid=12825.; Basil Cottle, "The Life (1770–1853), Writings, and Literary Relations of Joseph Cottle of Bristol" (Thesis A292, University of Bristol, 1958), 175.

51. Henry Hunt, *Memoirs of Henry Hunt*, vol. 3 (London: T. Dolby, 1820), in Dodsley's *Collection of Poems,* vol. 2 (n.p., 1748), 111, http://archive.org/stream/memoirsofhenryhu08463gut/8hnt310.txt.

52. Ibid., emphasis in original.

53. Roberts, *Memoirs of the Life and Correspondence of Mrs. Hannah More*, 2:118.

54. Hannah More, *Collected Works*, 10 vols. (London: Harrison and Sons, 1853), 9:13.

55. Roberts, *Memoirs of the Life and Correspondence of Mrs. Hannah More*, 2:402.

56. Ibid., 2:398.

57. Stott, *Hannah More*, 307.

58. Crossley-Evans, *Hannah More*, 20.

59. Roberts, *Memoirs of the Life and Correspondence of Mrs. Hannah More*, 2:441.

60. Ibid., 2:428.

61. Cottle, "The Life (1770–1853), Writings, and Literary Relations of Joseph Cottle of Bristol," 241.

62. Stephen, *Dictionary of National Biography*, 419.

63. Jones, *Hannah More*, 221.

64. English Poetry 1579-1830: Spenser and the Tradition, "Hannah More," Thomas Babington Macaulay to Napier, 15 June 1837; Life and Letters, ed. Trevelyan; in Moulton, Library of Literary Criticism (1901-05) 5:191, http://spenserians.cath.vt.edu/CommentRecord.php?action=GET&cmmtid=3565.

65. John C. Colquhoun, *William Wilberforce: His Friends and His Times* (London: Longmans, Green, Reader, and Dyer, 1866), 130.

66. Stott, *Hannah More*, 331.
67. Roberts, *Memoirs of the Life and Correspondence of Mrs. Hannah More*, 2:215.
68. Ibid., 2:456.
69. Ibid., 2:451.
70. Ibid., 2:453.
71. Ibid., 2:447–50.
72. Ibid., 2:458–59.
73. Ibid., 2:459.
74. Collingwood, *Hannah More*, 145–46.

EPILOGUE
1. Anne Stott, *Hannah More: The First Victorian* (Oxford: Oxford University Press, 2003), vii.
2. Ibid., 313.
3. Ibid., 336.
4. Catharine Maria Sedgwick, *The Linwoods; or, 'Sixty years since' in America: Volume 2* (New York: Harper & Brothers, 1835) 39.
5. Birrell was also an antisuffragist whose greatest fame resulted from an injury to his knee that occurred during his attempt to escape a group of suffragists who surrounded him after an encounter on the street. See Alice Stone Blackwell, *Militant Methods* (New York: National American Woman Suffrage Association, 1912), 13.
6. Augustine Birrell, "Hannah More Once More," *In the Name of the Bodleian and Other Essays* (New York: Charles Scribner's Sons, 1905), 80, http://www.gutenberg.org/files/12244/12244-h/12244-h.htm#2H_4_16.
7. Augustine Birrell, *Essays About Men, Women and Books* (London: Elliot Stock, 1894), 71–72.
8. Hannah More, Collected Works, 10 vols. (London: Harrison and Sons, 1853) 6:363.

ABOUT THE AUTHOR

KAREN SWALLOW PRIOR IS A PROFESSOR OF ENGLISH AT LIBERTY University. She is the author of *Booked: Literature in the Soul of Me* and contributes to *Christianity Today*, the *Atlantic*, and *Relevant* magazine, among other publications. She is also a research fellow with the Ethics and Religious Liberty Commission of the Southern Baptist Convention. She lives in Amherst, Virginia.

INDEX

Index

U

universities, 17
upper classes, responsibility of, 202–203

V

Veigel, Eva Maria. *See* Garrick, Eva Maria Veigel
Venn, Henry, 166
Venn, John, 164, 166, 225
Vesey, Elizabeth, 78, 83
Village Politics Addressed to all the Mechanics . . . (More), 209–210, 242
villages, poverty in, 142–145
A Vindication of the Rights of Woman (Wollstonecraft), 212–213
virtue, 87–88

W

Walpole, Horace, xvi, 83, 135, 210
   The Castle of Otranto, 228
   and Gray, 93–94
   More's friendship with, 35, 167–170
   More's letter to, 103, 122, 134
   on More's Thoughts, 204
   wealth of H. More, beneficiaries, 251
Wedgwood, Josiah, 128
Wesley, Charles, 6, 163
Wesley, John, 5–6, 109–110, 113, 136, 163, 203
   Compendium of Natural Philosophy, . . . , 193
West Indian sugar, boycott of, 126

Weston-super-Mare, 35
Whitefield, George, 6, 163
wigs, 100–101
Wilberforce, William, xiii, 111–116, 128, 135, 137–138, 164–165
   bill for abolition of slave trade, 123–124
   at Cowslip Green, 139–141
   death, 136
   faith of, 112
   financial backing for schools, 148
   financing for Cheap Repository Tracts, 222
   meeting with Middletons, 119
   meeting with More, 115, 119
   meeting with Newton, 113
   optimism of, 122
   Parliament, and labor workers, 181–182
   A Practical View of the Prevailing Religious System of Professed Christians in the Higher and Middle Classes . . . , 165, 175, 194
   and proclamation in favor of improved morals, 174
   speech in Parliament, 131
   visit with More, 249
   warning from Wesley, 136
Wilde, Oscar, The Importance of Being Earnest, 202
Windsor Terrace (Clifton), 248

Wollstonecraft, Mary, A Vindication of the Rights of Woman, 212–213
Wollstonecrafts, school, 25
women
   English society recognition of talent, 84–85
   as inferior, 80
   rights of, 212
   role in abolition movement, 136–137
   Rousseau on duties of, 18
   as writers, 42, 43
women's education
   girls and, 17–24
   in mid-18th century, 2–3
   More on, 85–86, 215–216
   opposition to, 18–19
Woolf, Virginia, 42, 252
   A Room of One's Own, 31, 40
Worcester, bishop of, 226
writing
   More's love of, 39
   opposition to teaching poor, 159, 178–179
   as profession for women, 40–41

Y

Yearsley, Ann, 78–79
   Poems on Several Occasions, 79
Yonge, Charlotte, 35

Z

Zara, Garrick role in, 54
Zong massacre of 1781, 110